PROTECTIONISM AND THE
EUROPEAN COMMUNITY

PROTECTIONISM AND THE EUROPEAN COMMUNITY
IMPORT RELIEF MEASURES TAKEN BY
THE EUROPEAN ECONOMIC
COMMUNITY AND THE MEMBER
STATES, AND THE LEGAL REMEDIES
AVAILABLE TO PRIVATE PARTIES

E.L.M. Völker (Editor)
Europa Instituut,
University of Amsterdam

J.H.J. Bourgeois
Commission of the European Community,
Brussels

M.C.E.J. Bronckers
Member of the Bar of Rotterdam

C.W.A. Timmermans
Professor of Law,
University of Groningen

R.J.P.M. van Dartel
Ministry of Economic Affairs,
The Hague

J. Steenbergen
Member of the Bar of Brussels,
School of Law,
University of Leuven

Second Edition

KLUWER LAW AND TAXATION PUBLISHERS
DEVENTER · ANTWERP · LONDON · FRANKFURT · BOSTON · NEW YORK

Distribution in the USA and Canada
Kluwer Law and Taxation Publishers
101 Philip Drive
Norwell, MA 02061
USA

Library of Congress Cataloging-in-Publication Data

Protectionism and the European community.

    Edited by E.L.M. Völker.
    1. Import quotas——European Economic Community countries. 2. General Agreement on Tariffs and Trade (Organization) I. Bourgeois, J.M.J.
II. Völker, E.L.M. (Edmond L.M.)
KJE6792.P76 1987   343.4'0877   87–17020
ISBN 90-6544-313-4   344.03877

D /1987/2664/76

ISBN 90 6544 313 4

© 1987 Kluwer Law and Taxation Publishers, Deventer, The Netherlands

All rights reserved. No part of this publication may be reproduced, stored in a retrieval system or transmitted in any form or by any means, mechanical, photocopying, recording or otherwise, without prior written permission of the publishers.

PREFACE
to the first edition

At the beginning of 1981 the Europa Instituut established a Working Group on the law of international economic relations. The Group has a twofold purpose. In the first place it analyses and discusses rules of national and international public law in the field of international economic relations. Secondly, the Group examines the process which leads to the formulation of these rules. The Group consists of fifteen members, occupied in the Dutch, Belgian, and Community administration, private practice, the judicature and universities respectively.

One very important problem, which figures on the agenda of almost every meeting of the Working Group, is that of increasing protectionism. As a consequence of the economic crisis, the European Communities and the Member-States have to deal with an ever increasing number of requests for protective measures. Although these measures are officially qualified as dangerous and inappropriate for solving the crisis, Member-States and Communities nevertheless cannot abstain from this kind of action completely. Both of them will, however, have to respect the relevant international rules and to care for the legality of the measures which ultimately might be adopted.

The Europa Instituut highly appreciates that a number of members of the Working Group was prepared to elaborate parts of this problem in separate studies. The first two contributions deal with the common commercial policy of the EEC as such. The following three studies cover more specific topics, while the book ends with a view on future policy in respect of non-tariff barriers in GATT. Although the book could not cover the whole field – and in this respect, too, a certain *selectivity* had to be adopted – it is hoped that it will make a useful contribution to the debate on a problem which every day becomes more important and may have considerable consequences for the future.

The general set-up of the book has been cared for by Drs. E.L.M. Völker, senior lecturer at the Europa Instituut and secretary of the Working Group. He was assisted in the final editing of the contributions by Miss Annelies Kramers, student assistant.

On behalf of the Europa Instituut,

R.H. Lauwaars
Director.

PREFACE
to the second edition

The second edition is a completely revised, and, for a large part, rewritten, version of the first edition, with the exception of the original Chapter Six. Assistance in the final editing was provided by Hubert van Vliet, student assistant of the Europa Instituut. Most cases and legal acts referred to, as well as the text of the GATT Agreement may be found in: Völker and Steenbergen (eds.) *Leading Cases and Materials on the External Relations Law of the E.C.*, Kluwer Law and Taxation Publishers, Deventer 1985.

On behalf of the Europa Instituut,

R.H. Lauwaars,
Director.

SUMMARY OF CONTENTS

PREFACE by R.H. Lauwaars, Professor of Law, Director of the Europa Instituut, Department of Law, University of Amsterdam.

CHAPTER ONE

The Common Commercial Policy – Scope and Nature of the Powers

by Jacques H.J. Bourgeois, Head of the Trade Policy Instruments Division, Commission of the European Communities; Associate Professor of Law at the College of Europe (Bruges).

CHAPTER TWO

The Major Instruments of the Common Commercial Policy of the EEC

by E.L.M. Völker, Senior Lecturer, Europa Instituut, Department of Law, University of Amsterdam.

CHAPTER THREE

A Legal Analysis of Protectionist Measures affecting Japanese Imports into the European Community – Revisited

by Marco C.E.J. Bronckers, Member of the Bar of Rotterdam.

CHAPTER FOUR

The EEC's Commercial Policy concerning Textiles

by R.J.P.M. van Dartel, Ministry of Economic Affairs, The Hague.

CHAPTER FIVE

Community Commercial Policy on Textiles: A Legal Imbroglio

by C.W.A. Timmermans, Professor of Law, State University of Groningen, The Netherlands.

CHAPTER SIX

Trade Regulation since the Tokyo Round

by J. Steenbergen, Member of the Bar of Brussels; Associated Senior Lecturer at the School of Law, University of Leuven, Belgium.

TABLE OF CONTENTS

CHAPTER ONE

THE COMMON COMMERCIAL POLICY – SCOPE AND NATURE OF THE POWERS

By Jacques H.J. Bourgeois

Introduction	1
I. Some background elements	2
II. Scope of the powers	3
III. Nature of the powers	7
IV. The powers applied	8
V. The Common Commercial Policy as it stands; some comments	11
A. Coverage	11
B. Instruments	13
C. Procedures	14

CHAPTER TWO

THE MAJOR INSTRUMENTS OF THE COMMON COMMERCIAL POLICY OF THE EEC

By E.L.M. Völker

Introduction	17
I. The GATT System	18
A. Tariffs	19
B. The elimination of quantitative restrictions	19
C. The elimination of other non-tariff barriers in the GATT Agreement	20
D. The most favoured-nation treatment clause (MFN-clause)	21
E. Amendments and supplements	22
II. The major Community instruments in the field of tariffs and quantitative restrictions on imports	23
A. The Common Customs Tariff (CCT)	23
1. Regulation 950/68 on the Common Customs Tariff	23
2. Preferential customs treatment accorded by the EEC under bi-lateral agreements	26
3. The valuation of goods for customs purposes	28
4. Determination of the origin of goods for customs purposes	31
B. Quantitative restrictions	34

III. Safeguard measures 37
    A. General 37
    B. The imposition of quantitative restrictions or the establishment of surveillance in the trade with non-state trading countries 39
        1. Basic provisions 39
        2. Further provisions regarding surveillance and protective measures 42
    C. Comparison between Regulation 288/82 and Regulation 1765/82 regarding the application of safeguard measures 43
    D. Regulation No. 2641/84 on the strengthening of the common commercial policy with regard in particular to protection against illicit commercial practices 44
    E. Common rules on exports 50
    F. Administering quantitative restrictions 53
Conclusion 53

CHAPTER THREE

A LEGAL ANALYSIS OF PROTECTIONIST MEASURES AFFECTING JAPANESE IMPORTS INTO THE EUROPEAN COMMUNITY – REVISITED

By Marco C.E.J. Bronckers

Introduction 57
I. The development of trade relations between the European Community and Japan within GATT 58
    A. Background 59
    B. Reliance on and abandonment of GATT Article XXXV in trade relations between EEC Member States and Japan; bilateral agreements of Member States with Japan 60
    C. The replacement of the EEC Member States by the Community within GATT 63
II. The paradox in trade relations with Japan: Community powers, national measures 64
    A. Community powers but no policy on trade relations with Japan 65
        1. The scope of Article 113 of the EEC Treaty 65
        2. The lack of an all-embracing Community trade agreement with Japan; bilateral agreements of the Member States 67
        3. The 1983 export restraint arrangement between Japan and the EEC; the Commission's authority to negotiate VERs ... 69

B. National restrictions on Japanese imports 72
  1. National restrictions on *direct* imports of Japanese products: Regulation (EEC) no 288/82 73
     (a) The 'negative list' 73
     (b) Interim safeguard measures 74
     (c) Public policy exceptions 74
     (d) Italian 'experimental list' 75
     (e) Measures having equivalent effect; Poitiers 75
     Illustration: national restrictions on imports of Japanese passenger cars 76
     (a) Italy's country-specific quota 77
     (b) Spanish and Portuguese global quotas 77
     (c) Measures introduced by France having an effect equivalent to import restrictions 78
     (d) Export-restraint arrangements between British and Japanese car industries; antitrust and government action 79
     Final remark 83
  2. Intra-Community restrictions maintained by Member States on *indirect* imports of Japanese products: Article 115 of the EEC Treaty 83
  3. Origin Rules and National Import Restrictions 85
C. Ways in which the Commission can forge common positions in EEC trade policy *vis-à-vis* Japan 88
III. Compatibility with the GATT of restrictions on imports from Japan 90
A. Some GATT basics 90
B. Review of certain typical restrictions on Japanese imports 93
  1. Country-specific quotas 93
  2. Voluntary export restraints 96
     (a) The law as it stands 96
     (b) Proposals for reform 99
  3. Modifications of tariff concessions 102
IV. Status and supervision of GATT principles in the Community's legal order 105
A. Some findings 105
B. Some comments 107
  1. Awkward results 107
  2. Creating domestic law effect of GATT principles 109
V. Community action against Japanese trade restrictions in GATT ... 111
A. The 1982 GATT dispute between the EEC and Japan 112
  1. The procedure of Article XXIII GATT 113
  2. The concept of 'nullification or impairment' 114
     The panel reports regarding Uruguay's complaint under Article XXIII GATT 115

3. Evaluating the EEC complaint against Japan 117
B. Outlook for new trade negotiations between the EEC and Japan in GATT 119

CHAPTER FOUR

THE EEC'S COMMERCIAL POLICY CONCERNING TEXTILES

By R.J.P.M. van Dartel

I. Introduction 121
II. The policy regarding countries party to the MFA 122
  A. The drafting of the Multifibre Arrangement within the framework of GATT 122
    1. History 122
    2. The Multifibre Arrangement and the first and second extension 123
    3. The third extension of the MFA 129
  B. The application of the MFA by the EEC 134
    1. The objectives of the EEC in the bilateral negotiations ... 135
      a. Quantitative objectives 135
      b. The text of the bilateral agreements 136
    2. The progress in the bilateral negotiations 138
    3. The internal application of the MFA 139
III. The policy regarding a number of preferential countries 140
  A. The Mediterranean countries 140
    1. The legal form of these arrangements 140
    2. The present arrangements 141
    3. The internal application of the preferential arrangements 142
  B. The countries falling under the Lomé Convention 142
IV. The autonomous textiles policy 143
  A. Relationship with a number of state-trading countries 143
  B. Taiwan 144
V. The policy regarding the industrialised countries 144
VI. The policy regarding the new EEC member states 145
VII. The policy for outward processing traffic (OPT) 146
  A. General 146
  B. The contents of the OPT Regulation 147
    1. Territorial scope 147
    2. Recourse to the Regulation 148
    3. The management system for outward processing traffic ... 149

VIII. The application of the safeguard clause of Article 115 of the
    EEC Treaty 149
    A. The contents of Article 115 150
    B. The implementing decision 150
    C. Intra-Community surveillance 151
       1. Economic difficulties 151
       2. The authorisation from the Commission 151
       3. The granting of the licence 152
    D. Further reaching protective measures 152
    E. The *Tezi* Case 153
IX. Conclusion 155
X. Annexes 156

CHAPTER FIVE

COMMUNITY COMMERCIAL POLICY ON TEXTILES: A LEGAL IMBROGLIO

By C.W.A. Timmermans

Introduction 159
I. Legal questions relating to Article 113 of the EEC Treaty 160
   A. Division of powers between EEC and Member States 160
   B. National subquota or quota limited to one or more Member
      States: compatible with Article 113 of the EEC Treaty? 165
II. The application of Article 115 of the EEC Treaty on textiles 169
    A. General 169
    B. Application of Article 115 of the EEC Treaty in practice 171
    C. Scope of Article 115 of the EEC Treaty 171
       1. MFA regime of Regulation No. 3589/82 171
       2. Preferential régimes 177
       3. Autonomous régimes 178
    D. The new procedure for applying Article 115 of the EEC
       Treaty (Decision 80/47) 179
III. Judicial Protection 181

CHAPTER SIX

TRADE REGULATION SINCE THE TOKYO ROUND

By J. Steenbergen

I. Issues on which no agreement was reached in the Tokyo Round   185

II. The implementation in the EC and the application of the Agreements of the Tokyo Round 187
   A. Agreement on technical barriers to trade 187
      1. Implementation 187
      2. Application 191
   B. The Agreement on government procurement 192
      1. Implementation 192
      2. Application 193
   C. The subsidies and countervailing duties Code 194
      1. Implementation 194
      2. Application 196
   D. The new anti-dumping Code 197
      1. Implementation 197
      2. Application 197
   E. The Agreement on customs valuation 200
      1. Implementation 200
      2. Application 200
III. Community trade law beyond the scope of the Tokyo Round Agreements 200
IV. Legal remedies and settlement of disputes 202
   A. The Tokyo Round 202
   B. Application 204
V. Conclusions on an agenda for further negotiations 209
   A. The Uruguay Round 210
   B. Key issues on the Uruguay Round agenda 211
      1. US–EC trade relations 211
      2. North–South trade 212
      3. Factual background 214
   C. Some selected issues 215
      1. Agriculture 215
      2. Subsidies 216
         a. Subsidies to competitive industries 217
         b. Aid to infant industries or specific regions 217
         c. Aid to ailing industries 218
      3. Technical standards 218
      4. Government procurement 219
      5. Services 219
   D. Conclusions 220

TABLES 225

I. Cases 225
II. Opinions 226

III. EEC Treaty	226
Articles	226
Regulations	227
Decisions	227
Directives	228
IV. International Agreements	228
V. GATT Articles	229

INDEX ... 231

CHAPTER ONE

THE COMMON COMMERCIAL POLICY – SCOPE AND NATURE OF THE POWERS

By Jacques H.J. Bourgeois*

INTRODUCTION

1. The present contribution is one piece of the puzzle which the Europa Instituut of the University of Amsterdam has put together.

It focuses on the scope and nature of the powers conferred on the European Economic Community. For brevity's sake the commercial policy in the European Coal and Steel Community had to be left out[1] as well as the specific provisions on external relations of the Treaty establishing the European Atomic Energy Community. The term 'Community' without any qualification refers in this paper to the European Economic Community.

Part I deals with some background elements that help to explain the content of the Community policy and the manner in which the Community exercises its powers. The legal framework in which the Community uses its commercial policy instruments, particularly the General Agreement on Tariffs and Trade, will be examined by Völker, in Chapter Two.

Part II examines the scope of the commercial policy powers *ratione materiae*.

Part III analyses the nature of these powers and more precisely how they relate to the Member States' powers.

Part IV explores how the exclusive nature of the Community powers and Community commercial policy can be reconciled with the day to day needs and the attitudes of some third countries.

* Head of the Trade Policy Instruments Division, Commission of the European Communities; associate professor of law at the College of Europe (Bruges). The views expressed are presented in a personal capacity.
  1. This subject would require another paper. Suffice it to say that Article 71 ECSC stating that 'the powers of the Governments of Member States in matters of commercial policy shall not be affected by this Treaty, save as otherwise provided therein' has lost its *raison d'être* as a result of the establishment of the EEC. The practice followed by the Council and the Member States is rather untidy. See *e.g.* Steenbergen, 'De Tokyo Ronde', 12 *SEW* (1980) 752–773, 763–764; for a reply see Bourgeois, 'The Tokyo Round Agreements on Technical Barriers and on Government Procurement in international and EEC Perspective', 19 *CMLRev.* (1982) 5–33 at 22–23; Ehlermann, 'The Scope of Article 113 of the EEC Treaty' in *Mélanges P. H. Teitgen* (Paris, 1984).

In a final part (V) and by way of conclusion some outstanding issues and some suggestions as to the way they could be resolved are treated.

I. SOME BACKGROUND ELEMENTS

2. By establishing a 'customs union', as distinct from a 'free trade area', the EEC Treaty had to provide for a common customs tariff. By taking the further step of establishing a 'common market', a concept used in a series of Treaty provisions without being defined but clearly designed to cover the free movement of goods, persons, services and capital, it had to provide for a common commercial policy, at least for the exchange of goods as part and parcel of the common market. Without it such common market would not function properly as, according to Articles 9 and 10, a product originating in a third country which is in free circulation in Member States benefits from the rules on free circulation within the common market.

The implications are obvious. The further the common market develops towards a market operating under conditions of a national market for products originating in the Community, the greater is the required degree of uniformity of the rules applying to products originating in third countries imported into the common market. If *e.g.* technical standards are harmonised in the Community, their divergent application by Member States to products originating in third countries would partly defeat one of the purposes of such harmonisation: intra-community controls would still be necessary for third country products and even the entry of Community products into the territory of another Member State, or their use or sale on that territory, would still be subject to certain formalities, such as proof of origin.

3. A second important element is undoubtedly the considerable degree to which industrialised economies have become interdependent over the last two decades. The fact that interest rates and more generally macro-economic policies of governments have become regular topics of summit meetings of industrialised countries is a well publicised illustration of a phenomenon with many aspects and wide implications which led an observer to note already in 1973 that virtually all sectors of virtually all economies now rely heavily on external transactions.[2]

4. A third element, which underlines the specific importance of the interdependency for the Community, is the relatively high degree, in global terms, to which the Community is dependent on the world economy. First, the Community relies mainly on third countries for its supply of a series of important raw materials (*e.g.* aluminium: 61%; nickel 100%; tin 87%; iron-ore

---

2. Bergsten in Bergsten (ed.), *The Future of the International Economic Order: an Agenda for Research* (Lexington, Mass., 1973), at 4.

79%; manganese 100%; antimony 95%; chromium, cobalt, titanium, asbestos 100%).[3]

Second, international trade is more important for the Community economy than for other countries. Excluding intra-Community trade, the Community, in 1984, represents approximately one-fifth of world trade (21.9% of world imports, 20.9% of world exports), it has a weight on world trade exceeding that of Japan (8.8% of world imports, 11.5% of world exports) and of the US (21.1% of world imports, 14.8% of world exports).[4]

In 1984 Community exports and imports, excluding intra Community trade of goods, excluding services, are both at a level which represents approximately 12.6%, respectively 12%, of the GDP in the Community, whereas the figures in percentage of GDP but *including* services are 16.3%, respectively 12% for Japan and 7.4%, respectively 10.8% for the USA.[5]

5. A fourth element, linked to the third element, relates to the interests of industry and labour in the Community with respect to external trade. These interests vary of course considerably from industry to industry, and it is one of the Government's tasks to promote equitable trade-offs between the conflicting interests of the various sectors of the economy with respect to external trade. In the Community this task is all the more complex and difficult. Not only are there conflicts of interests between the various sectors of the economy, but the weight of external trade in the economy varies considerably from Member State to Member State, *e.g.* for exports from 66.7% of the GDP in Belgium/Luxemburg to 12.3% in Greece. In addition, in the absence of a common general economic policy and of a common industrial policy, the Community does not have the usual instruments on which governments rely to make the necessary trade-offs socially and politically acceptable.

II. SCOPE OF THE POWERS

6. The EEC Treaty is rather poorly drafted with respect to commercial policy.

To the extent that the Treaty itself qualifies the common commercial policy as an integral part of the 'common market' (Article 3 b), logically it ought to have organised the section on the common commercial policy accordingly; it should have defined the common commercial policy as the external face of the 'common market' encompassing exchange of goods and services, movement of workers and of capital, and establishment of non-EEC individuals and companies. Article 113, which is the basic Treaty provision conferring powers

---

3. Hager and Noelke, *Community – Third World; the challenge of interdependence*, 2nd ed. at 56; Commission of the European Communities, Documentation Bulletin, Series A, Brussels 1980.

4. Eurostat, *Structural Data EUR 12* (June–July 1985) more detailed figures and comments appear in Steenbergen, De Clerq and Foqué, *Change and adjustment: external relations and industrial policy of the E.C.* (Deventer, 1983), and in Chapter Five under V.

5. Commission of the European Communities, *The European Economy* (No. 26, November 1985) tables 26, 28, 29 and 30.

to the Community with respect to commercial policy, does not define what is meant by commercial policy. It only gives examples: tariff amendments, measures of liberalisation, export policy, protective measures including measures to be taken in case of dumping or subsidies.

The Commission has always taken the view that Article 113 is not limited to the exchange of goods (and connected payments) but that it covers also the exchange of services (and connected payments). There are a certain number of provisions in bilateral agreements concluded on the basis of Article 113 which deal with services.[6]

The Commission has however never taken the position that Article 113 of the EEC Treaty extends to free circulation of persons, freedom of establishment and free circulation of capital arguing that these transactions are not the object of 'trade'.[7]

There are some inconsistencies in the international trade aspects of areas which are covered by common sectoral policies (agriculture and transport). Agreements on agricultural products are concluded on the basis of Article 113, while agreements on transport are concluded on the basis of Article 75 of the EEC Treaty, although transport is a type of service.

7. It is not surprising that differing views developed not only on the proper relationship between Article 113 of the EEC Treaty on the common commercial policy and the other Treaty provisions which confer external powers on the Community, but also and more importantly on the scope of the commercial policy powers of the Community under Article 113. (The ensuing brief analysis examines the issue of the scope of these powers irrespective of the way in which they are exercised, *i.e.*, by entering into international agreements or by autonomous measures.)

8. On this last point the differing views held by the Council and the Commission have been clearly set out in the *International Rubber Agreement* opinion which the Court of Justice rendered pursuant to Article 228 of the EEC Treaty.[8]

The reasons behind this difference of views are twofold. First, as will be explained (*infra* III), the Community's powers under Article 113 are exclusive: Member States are no longer entitled to take on their own any measure in the field covered by Article 113. Second, Member States, and particularly the

---

6. In the agreements with Mexico (of 15 July 1975, OJ 1975, L247); Brazil (of 19 Dec. 1973, OJ 1974, L102); Argentina (of 8 Dec. 1971, OJ 1971, L249) and Uruguay (of 2 April 1973, OJ 1973, L333), the Parties grant each other mfn treatment on taxes on regulations concerning payment in respect of, and regulations affecting the use of services; the agreement with China (of 3 April 1978, OJ 1978, L123) provides that '. . . the provision of services between the two contracting parties shall be exported at market-related prices and rates'.

7. To a certain extent the gap between Art. 113 thus interpreted and the need to manage the external face of the 'common market' has been filled by the Court of Justice. In its Opinion 1/76 it affirmed that 'the power to bind the Community *vis-à-vis* third countries nevertheless flows by implication from the provisions of the Treaty creating the internal power and in so far as the participation of the Community in the international agreement is (. . .) necessary for the attainment of one of the objectives of the Community' (Opinion 1/76 of 26 April 1977, (1977) ECR 741, para. 4).

8. Opinion 1/78 of 4 October 1979, (1979) ECR, 2871.

'larger' ones, are anxious to keep their own powers as much as possible and are reluctant to relinquish them to the Community because they fear that the Community would be unable to act or that the Community policy would be wrong, and because they want to preserve their external identity.

According to the Council – the Council's view is not necessarily shared by all Member States – a commercial policy measure is any measure that aims at influencing the volume or flow (pattern) of trade. At first glance this interpretation appears convincing: other Treaty provisions on common policies (Articles 43 and 75) are generally interpreted in this way and the interpretation is teleological, a method which the Court has used time and again persuasively.

This interpretation has, however, two main drawbacks. First, for the purposes of autonomous Community commercial policy measures it has results that are hardly satisfying where applied to measures that are inherent in the conduct of any commercial policy: *e.g.*, customs formalities and rules of origin would under the Council's interpretation probably not be covered by Article 113, since it would more than often be difficult to affirm that they aim at influencing the volume or pattern of trade. Second, it contains a subjective element that carries with it the risk of abuse, allowing reluctant Member States to claim that, in their view, because of its purpose, a measure either is beyond the EEC Treaty or could only be taken under another EEC Treaty provision requiring unanimity.

In the Commission's interpretation a measure of commercial policy must be assessed primarily by reference to its specific character as an instrument regulating international trade. When it put forward this interpretation the Commission was mainly concerned by the necessity to avert the dangers lurking in the Council's views on the scope of Article 113 of the EEC Treaty. The Commission's interpretation is not entirely satisfying either, in that the 'instrument' continues to be too broad.

9. In its Opinion on the *International Rubber Agreement* the Court clarified important points: the Community may develop a commercial policy aimed at regulation of the world market; 'repercussions on certain sectors of economic policy such as the supply of raw materials to the Community or price policy' do not constitute a reason for excluding such objectives from the common commercial policy; in order to determine whether a subject matter falls under Article 113 regard should be had to the 'essential objective'.

However, although the Court did clarify certain points, the Commission's attempt to settle its underlying broader dispute with the Council failed. Both Council and Commission are relying on the *International Rubber Agreement* Opinion to defend their unchanged views. A renewed attempt to have the dispute resolved judicially was made by the Commission in challenging the Council's refusal to rely on Article 113 for the purpose of implementing the Community's Generalized Sytem of Preferences.[9]

9. Judgment of the Court in Case 45/86, *Commission* v. *Council*, of 26 March 1987, (not yet published).

10. The better interpretation of Article 113 lies probably in a combination of both views.[10]

All measures which regulate openly and specifically trade with third countries should always be considered as part of the common commercial policy; they are *per se* measures of commercial policy unless the Treaty provides for an exception. Other measures should be considered as part of such policy by a sort of 'rule of reason' *viz.* when their *dominant purpose* is to influence the volume or flow of trade.

11. In this construction the following measures would be *per se* commercial policy measures:

(a) measures expressly mentioned in Articles 113 and 112 of the EEC Treaty (tariffs, quotas, protective measures in case of dumping and subsidies, export credits);

(b) measures ancillary to measures under (a) (*e.g.* customs regulations, procedures for import and export licences);

(c) all other formally discriminating measures which are not expressly mentioned and not ancillary in character (*e.g.* taxes, and measures of equivalent effect to quantitative restrictions which discriminate openly between intra-Community trade and trade with third countries, such as *e.g.* origin markings for non EEC-products).

Exceptions from the *per se* rule result *inter alia* from
– Article 28 of the EEC Treaty for tariffs;[11]
– Article 27 of the EEC Treaty for regulations on customs matters;
– Article 43 of the EEC Treaty for quotas, taxes and measures of equivalent effect on agricultural products;
– Article 224 of the EEC Treaty for national measures in case of international tensions.

12. It is obvious that certain measures, even though they do not regulate openly and specifically trade with third countries, can nonetheless have an important impact on international commerce. The Tokyo Round Agreements on subsidies, government procurement and technical barriers to trade[12] illustrate the need to exceed modern trade policy to measures which apply to imports, exports and the internal market alike. The criterion of the impact on international trade of measures that do not regulate openly and specifically such trade would be too broad and hardly practicable. It appears more appropriate to rely on their dominant purpose.

---

10. *Cf.* Ehlermann, *loc. cit. supra* n. 1. The following developments of this interpretation are based on Ehlermann's analysis.

11. The Council seems to have accepted to follow the approach proposed by the Commission in two fairly recent instances. Two sets of amendments of customs duties designed to give added protection to the Community consumer electronics industry rely on Art. 113 and not, as in the past, on Art. 28. (Council Reg. (EEC) No. 3506/83 (OJ 1983, L351/1) mainly for digital audio disk players; and Council Reg. (EEC) No. 3679/85 (OJ 1985, L351/2) mainly for video-recorders.)

12. For further comments see Bourgeois, *loc. cit.* n. 1.

To ascertain whether the dominant purpose is to influence the flow of trade, the following guidelines may be helpful. The dominant purpose should be established in an objective and incontestable way; it should be deduced
- from the agreement (purpose, structure, instruments, effects)
- from the framework in which the agreement is reached (*e.g.* is it part of a wider package deal or is it negotiated within an international organisation whose aim is to promote trade?).

13. Although this construction would need some further elaboration, it could go a long way towards solving the difference of views between the Commission and the Council (or at least some Member States) and eliminating the present uncertainties.

III. NATURE OF THE POWERS

14. The Community power with respect to commercial policy is said to be 'exclusive': Member States may no longer on their own enter into international agreements or take autonomous measures in this field.

This was made clear by the Court of Justice in its Opinion on the *Understanding on a Local Cost Standard*.[13]

After having referred to the specific point of the necessary uniformity of credit conditions, which were the subject-matter of the *Understanding* on which its opinion was sought, the Court based the Community's exclusive power on the following more general grounds:
- the common commercial policy is conceived in the Treaty 'in the context of the operation of the common market, for the defence of common interests of the Community'; any claim of concurrent power on the part of Member States entails the risk of 'compromising the effective defence' of these interests;
- acknowledging such concurrent power 'would amount to recognising that, in relations with third countries, Member States may adopt positions which differ from those which the Community intends to adopt, and would thereby distort the institutional framework, call into question the mutual trust within the Community and prevent the latter from fulfilling its tasks in the defence of the common interest';
- 'the provisions of Articles 113 and 114 concerning the conditions under which, according to the Treaty, agreements on commercial policy must be concluded show clearly that the exercise of concurrent powers by the Member States and the Community in this matter is impossible'.

---

13. Opinion 1/75, given by the Court pursuant to Article 228 of the EEC Treaty, 11 November 1975, (1975) ECR, 1355.

The exclusive nature of the Community's commercial policy power was confirmed by the *Donckerwolcke* judgment.[14]

15. For a subject-matter such as commercial policy this type of division of powers between the Community and the Member States makes more sense than a system of concurrent powers or even parallel powers. In the internal Community sphere – as illustrated by the case law on the common agricultural policy – the existence of Member States' concurrent or even parallel powers creates less difficulties: if the use of such powers gives rise to conflicts of substance with Community measures, such conflicts can be solved. In the external sphere, and commercial policy is external policy, the risks deriving from concurrent Member States' powers are much greater since such conflicts of substance are much more difficult to solve: third countries' interests are involved and judicial resolution of these conflicts is practically non-existent.

16. It should, however, be pointed out that in its *International Rubber Agreement* Opinion[15] the Court found that, at the time it rendered its Opinion, no decision had been taken on who would assume the financial burden of the operation of the buffer-stock to be set up by the Agreement. While qualifying this Agreement as a commercial policy matter, the Court considered that, in the event the Community would not assume this financial burden and the Member States would do so, Member States would have to participate in the Agreement alongside the Community.

Whatever the theoretical justifications for this departure from the exclusiveness of Community power with respect to commercial policy may be,[16] some Member States took advantage of this possibility and are now claiming the right to participate alongside the Community in commodity agreements on the ground that they contribute to even purely administrative expenses of such agreements.

IV. THE POWERS APPLIED

17. The Community's commercial policy was not and could not be fully established by the end of the transitional period of the EEC Treaty (31 December 1969). In order to bridge the gap between the progressive establishment of such policy and the exclusiveness of the Community's power

14. Case 41/76, 15 Dec. 1976, (1976) ECR, 1921 *et seq.*, in which the Court stated that 'as full responsibility in the matter of commercial policy was transferred to the Community by means of Article 113, para. 1, measures of commercial policy of a *national* character are *only* permissible after the end of the transitional period by virtue of specific authorization by the Community' (para. 32) (emphasis added).
15. *Supra*, n. 8.
16. See *e.g.* Steenbergen, 'La notion de politique commerciale commune après l'avis 1/78 de la Cour de Justice,' (1980) *Cahiers de droit européen* 54; Pescatore's contribution to the discussion in: Timmermans and Völker (eds.), *Division of Powers between the European Communities and their Member States in the field of external Relations* (Deventer, 1981), 69–75, at 70–71; Bourgeois, 'Some Comments on the Practice', *ibid.*, 97–110, n. 28.

as of 1 January 1970, the Community has developed a practice of authorising Member States to keep national commercial policy measures. This technique, which the Court found acceptable,[17] has been mainly used in those cases where the policy or economic interests of the Member States are too divergent to establish uniform Community rules, e.g. with respect to trade with Japan,[18] and in instances where, for political or economic reasons, third countries, especially State-trading countries, are unwilling to enter into trade agreements with the EEC.

18. As far as *autonomous* measures are concerned, this technique of 'specific authorization' of national commercial policy measures is used in the basic regulations setting up common import régimes, presently Regulation (EEC) No 288/82[19] and Regulation 3420/83,[20] with respect to the few imports (products and origin), for which the basic principle of these common import régimes, i.e. the absence of quantitative restrictions, could not be achieved: these imports are too sensitive in some Member States, and other Member States do not want to accept a Community-wide restrictive policy.

Article 1, para. 2, of Regulation 288/82 refers to national import restrictions which may be maintained, and Article 20 subjects changes by Member States to such national import restrictions to a Community procedure. Similarly, Regulation No. 3420/83 on (national) import arrangements in respect of State-trading countries, subjects, save for minor changes, any amendment to the national import arrangements, which are laid down every year by a Council Decision, to a Community procedure.[21]

As a rule, no national commercial policy measures may therefore be maintained unless so authorised and no existing national commercial policy measures may be modified unless in accordance with the Community procedures set out in these Regulations.

19. This authorisation of national commercial policy measures should be distinguished from certain flexibilities where these Regulations provide for protective measures with respect to imports of products which fall under the common import régime: i.e. regional protective measures[22] and triggering of

17. In *Donckerwolcke*, *supra* note 14, where the Court used the term 'specific authorization', confirmed, with respect to export controls, by its judgment of 18 February 1986, *Bulk Oil* v *Sun International*, Case 174/84 (not yet published).
18. See contribution by Bronckers, Chapter Three.
19. Council Reg. (EEC) No. 288/82, on common rules for imports (OJ 1982, L35/1) as amended by Council Reg. (EEC) No. 1243/86 (OJ 1986, L113 /1). The Commission publishes regularly an updated annex to that Regulation listing the products still subject to national quantitative restrictions (*e.g.* OJ 1986, C213/1).
The parallel Regulation for imports from State-trading countries (Reg. (EEC) No. 1765/82 (OJ 1982, L195/1), as amended by Council Reg. (EEC) No. 1243/86 (OJ 1986, L113/1)) deals only with products under a common regime. See further the contribution by Völker, Chapter Two.
20. Council Regulation 3420/83 on import arrangements with respect to State-trading countries (OJ 1983, L346/6).
21. There are, however, a number of differences between Reg. 288/82 and Reg. 3420/83 with respect to the way in which they implement the technique of specific authorisation of national measures. See the contribution by Völker, Chapter Two.
22. Protective measures may be taken against imports of products under the common régime effected in a region of the EEC, in fact in one or more Member States (Art. 15(3) of Reg. 288/82,

protective action by a Member State, in a narrowly defined set of instances.[23]

20. The same Regulations provide that they do not preclude the adoption or application by Member States of prohibitions etc. on grounds of public morality, public policy or public security; the protection of health and life of humans, animals or plants, the protection of national treasures possessing artistic, historic or archaeological value, or the protection of industrial and commercial property.

Whether this provision is declaratory or whether it is to be interpreted as a specific authorisation of national commercial policy measures is an open question. The answer depends partly on how one defines the scope of commercial policy (see *supra* II).[24] It is interesting to note that most trade agreements concluded by the Community itself under Article 113 contain the same sort of provision.

In the wake of the Chernobyl nuclear power plant accident, the Council suspended and subsequently imposed minimum radiation protection norms for imports of foodstuffs. The Council, however, deleted the explicit reference to Art. 113 contained in the Commissions proposal.[25]

21. As far as *agreements* are concerned, the technique of 'specific authorization' is also used to authorise Member States to extend or renew tacitly trade agreements entered into before the end of the transitional period

---

Art. 11(3) of Reg. 1765/82). The interesting question to which such regional protective measures give rise is whether they open up the possibility for the Commission to authorise under Art. 115 of the EEC Treaty EEC measures in intracommunity trade against *indirect* imports of the same products in the Member State concerned (see the contribution by Timmermans). I would see this as a last resort measure when the normal measure, *i.e.* the taking by the Commission of a Community-wide safeguard measure, would have been repealed by the Council.

In its judgment of 5 March 1986, *Tezi B.V.* v. *Commission* (Case 59/84) (not yet published), the Court upheld the validity of a Commission decision under Art. 115 of the EEC Treaty authorizing intra-Community restrictions designed to prevent circumvention of a national sub-quota of a Community quota for certain textile products. Adv. gen. VerLoren van Themaat submitted conclusions to the contrary. For a critical comment, see note by Timmermans in 11 *SEW* 1986, 756–766.

23. Member States may take interim protective measures; such measures are to be notified immediately to the Commission; if the Commission decides not to introduce any measure or adopts another measure, the member State concerned may refer the Commission Decision to the Council; in that case the national measure continues to operate until the entry into force of a Council Decision and for maximum one month. (Art. 17 of Reg. 288/82, Art. 13 of Reg. 1765/82.) Even though the national measure is limited in time, this procedure does not appear to be consistent with the institutional set-up of the Treaty in that it allows a national measure to take precedence over a Community measure and that the administration of a safeguard clause, which ought to be left to the Commission, is in effect shared between the Member State and the Council. This 'national triggering' procedure did not get a new lease of life in 1984 and was allowed to lapse. It continues to apply in only two limited sets of circumstances: either when a Member State applies a safeguard clause of one of its remaining bilateral agreements, or, with respect to products that still are under national quantitative restrictions in a given Member State, for the benefit of other Member States where the imports of these products are free (Art. 17, para. 5 of Reg. (EEC) No. 288/82).

24. To illustrate the point, measures against imports of whale products were proposed by the Commission under Article 113 of the EEC Treaty, but they were adopted by the Council under Article 235 of the EEC Treaty, who accepted the view put forward by some Member States that the environmental protection purpose was decisive, not the nature of the measure taken (see Reg. (EEC) No. 348/81, OJ 1981, L39/1).

(31 December 1969), as well as the trade clauses of existing treaties of commerce, friendship and navigation.[26] The extension or tacit renewal of trade agreements with State-trading countries has not been authorised beyond 31 December 1974, but the trade clauses of the existing treaties of commerce, friendship and navigation with these countries are still authorised. The decisions authorising such extensions or renewals limit in their preamble this authorisation to 'maintenance of the relations based on Agreements, pending their replacement by Community Agreements' and state that they do 'not affect the obligations on Member States to avoid and where appropriate, eliminate any incompatibility between the Agreements in question and the provisions of Community Law'. More recent decisions make clear in their operative part that such agreements may be extended or tacitly renewed 'for those areas not covered by agreements between the Community and the third countries concerned' and 'in so far as their provisions are not contrary to existing common policies.'[27]

V. THE COMMON COMMERCIAL POLICY AS IT STANDS; SOME COMMENTS

22. Quite apart from the fact that no policy can ever be said to be final, there is some unfinished business in the common commercial policy. The ensuing observations are limited to import policy.

A. COVERAGE

23. In the first place as far as the *coverage* is concerned, the process whereby the Community takes over the responsibility from the Member States is not terminated. The import régime for a series of *products* imported from certain third countries that are particularly sensitive for some Member States, remains in substance national and thus divergent (see IV).

The drawbacks of this situation are illustrated by Bronckers' case study on trade with Japan. The consequences of the absence of a common import régime for the operation of the intracommunity market area are analysed by Timmermans.

24. Apart from a few clauses in agreements (*supra* II), no action has been

---

25. Council Reg. (EEC) No. 1388/86 (OJ 1986, L127/1); Council Reg. (EEC) No. 1707/86 (OJ 1986, L146/88).
26. Council Decision (EEC) No. 69/494 of 16 December 1969, OJ 1969, L326/39, which lays down the principle and the procedure. Council Decisions authorise from time to time the extension or the tacit renewal of such agreements up to dates specified in each case.
27. Council Decision (EEC) No. 82/502 of 12 July 1982, OJ 1982, L230/33.

taken so far by the Community to regulate the exchange of *services* with third countries. They represent an increasing importance in international trade and are usually estimated at roughly 30% of international trade for the OECD. They cover a broad range from so-called complementary services (such as shipping, insurance, engineering), to services embodied in goods (*e.g.* films) and substitute services (*e.g.* franchising and leasing).

At the GATT Ministerial meeting of September 1986 at Punta del Este it was agreed to launch negotiations on trade in services as part of the new round of multilateral trade negotiations. This will help the Community to face up to its own responsibility in this area.

25. As mentioned earlier (*supra* IV) national trade *agreements* which were entered into by Member States with third countries before 1 January 1970 are kept in operation (except those with State-trading countries). It is true that their extension or renewal is authorised by the Community for limited periods and on certain conditions.

Nevertheless the very fact that Member States keep these separate contractual relations with third countries is likely to create ambiguities and uncertainties for third countries[28] and may hamper the Community in the conduct of its commercial policy.[29] Common sense requires to permit Member States to conclude *cooperation agreements* with third countries as long as the Community does not itself make use of this instrument, taking for granted that Member States do not take advantage of cooperation agreements to conduct a commercial policy of their own. Repercussions of such national agreements on the common commercial policy are unavoidable: *e.g.* a Member State that succeeds in obtaining from a third country an order for a plant in the framework of such cooperation agreement, is likely to press for an improvement of the Community import régime for products exported by that third country to the Community or oppose the uniformisation of the import régime where those products are still under a national import régime. The present procedure whereby the negotiating and the administration of those cooperation agreements by the Member States is monitored by the Community[30] ought certainly to be improved at least by imposing on the Member States the obligation to communicate to the Commission information on specific operations resulting from cooperation agreements in order to improve the

---

28. In his contribution to the discussion in Timmermans and Völker, *op. cit.* n. 16, at 124, F. Jacobs stated that 'the Council has itself caused no little confusion' in doing so.

29. If *e.g.* the Community were contemplating a measure which would be inconsistent with an obligation entered into by a Member State *vis-à-vis* a third country under such agreement, the Member State would probably have to negotiate an amendment to such agreement or alternatively the Community would have to postpone the measure until the date at which such agreement comes up for renewal or extension. Even if the Community is itself not bound by such agreement, it has the duty not to impede the performance of the obligations by the Member State which stem from an agreement which was extended or renewed pursuant to a Community authorisation (*Cf.* Case 812/79, *Attorney General v. Burgoa*, 14 Oct. 1980, (1980) ECR 2787, para. 9).

30. Council Decision (EEC) No. 74/393 of 22 July 1974 (OJ 1974, L208/23).

coordination of the Member States' cooperation activities and to conduct a Community cooperation policy.[31]

B. INSTRUMENTS

26. In the second place as far as the *instruments* of import policy are concerned, the Community ought to diversify and to complement the array of measures of which it can at present dispose.

Import duties, surveillance, anti-dumping and countervailing duties, and quantitative restrictions imposed as protective measures may not always be appropriate or even possible. To further the common commercial policy interests, other actions and measures may be necessary. Legislation should be adopted under Article 113, *e.g.* to protect the commercial policy interests against boycott and against other actions by third countries,[32] or to act against trade in counterfeit goods.[33]

27. There is, however, a more fundamental defect. With a few minor exceptions, the Community has so far not adopted a two-tier import adjustment policy. When, either because of their prices or of their quantities and/or penetration ratios, imports call for adjustment action by the Community, the only type of import relief that the Community can give, under the legislation as it stands, is one aimed at monitoring or controlling imports. This practically exclusive action on imports appears inappropriate both economically, because of the Community's relatively high degree of dependency on external markets for its supply as well as for its sales, and legally, because of its multilateral and bilateral obligations restraining the use of protective action. Import relief in the form of assistance to Community industry to help it to cushion the impact of third-country competition and to adapt to it ought to become a possible alternative solution.[34]

---

31. Parliamentary Question 939/79 by Mr. Martinet (OJ 1980, C156/11); See also Weissenberg, *Die Kompetenz der Europäischen Wirtschaftsgemeinschaft zum Abschluss von Handels- und Kooperationsabkommen gemäss Artikel 113 EWG-Vertrag* (Berlin, 1978); Sasse, 'Kooperationsabkommen und EWG Handelspolitik, Parallelität oder Konflikt' (1975) *Europa-Archiv* 695–706.

32. When in June 1982 the US Government prohibited the Community to use US technology for the construction of the Siberian gas pipeline, the need to have such legislation became apparent. The Community made a formal 'démarche' to the US State Department and submitted comments to the US Department of Commerce, but countermeasures have so far been announced or taken only by some Member States, and not by the Community. On 16 November, 1982 these 'export controls' were removed by the US Government. The EEC should nonetheless have appropriate legislation on the books.

33. Against the latter practice the Council has enacted Reg. No. 3842/86 'laying down measures to prohibit the release for free circulation of counterfeit goods', OJ 1986 L357.

34. These views are also advocated with respect to US trade policy, see *e.g.* Lawrence and Litan, *Saving Free Trade. A Pragmatic Approach* (Washington D.C., 1986).

C. PROCEDURES

28. The first improvement relates to the decision-making process. In the light of the analysis of the scope of the commercial policy powers (*supra* II) the Community has all the required powers to carry out whatever commercial policy is necessary. The problem does not lie in the extent of these powers but rather in the way their exercise is organised.

For protective measures, anti-dumping and countervailing duty the Community has already devised fast-track procedures in which the investigation of the terms and conditions of such action and interim action (anti-dumping and countervailing duty) or provisional action subject to confirmation by the Council (protective measures) are entrusted to the Commission.

For other measures, however, so far no such procedures have been established and the Council has reserved for itself the possibility to act under Article 113 EEC on a proposal from the Commission. Although comparisons between legal systems are always somewhat hazardous exercises, it is at least noteworthy that the USA has availed itself of the means to act speedily in defence of its commercial policy interests. By a series of statutes, the US Congress, which generally has jealously guarded its special prerogative over international commerce, delegated certain powers which it originally holds under the Constitution, to the President, albeit with various devices to exercise a form of control over the use of these delegations.[35]

The Community might well draw some inspiration from this technique, if it wants to speed up the implementation of commercial policy action and increase its efficacy. Such actions could be delegated to the Commission under appropriate procedural safeguards.

The Council did, however, adopt in the Regulation establishing the so-called 'New Trade Policy Instrument',[36] a procedure that goes some way in that direction, in that the decision to start international dispute settlement with respect to illicit commercial practices within the meaning of that Regulation is left to the Commission.

29. The second and third improvements of a procedural nature relate to the position of the *private individual*.

30. The second improvement concerns the right of appeal against Community acts. Part of what appears to some as a 'deficit in legal protection'[37]

---

35. For more details see Jackson, John H., 'United States–EEC Trade Relations: Constitutional Problems of Economic Interdependence', 16 *CMLR.Rev.* (1979), 453–478.

36. Council Reg. (EEC) No. 2641/84, (OJ 1984, L252/1). For comments: Bourgeois and Laurent, 'Le nouvel instrument de politique commerciale: un pas en avant vers l'élimination des obstacles aux échanges internationaux', 21 *R.T.D.E.* 41–63 (1985); Steenbergen, 'The New Commercial Policy Instrument', 22 *CMLRev.* 421–439 (1985) and the contribution by Völker in Chapter Two.

37. Geelhoed, 'De kwaliteit van het gemeenschapsrecht', *Rechtsbescherming in de Europese Gemeenschappen*, (19) *Europese Monografieën* (Deventer, 1975), 129–158 at 147. Some criticism has also been levied against the Commission's administrative procedures, *see e.g.* Van Bael, 'Ten Years of EEC Anti-dumping Enforcement', 13 *JWTL* (1979), 395.

results from the judicial system of the EEC Treaty itself as it stands. The common commercial policy is established and managed by the Community Institutions; assuming that the technical hurdle of the limitations of the right of appeal, as laid down in Article 173 EEC, can be overcome, which may be difficult where the act in question is of a general nature, one wonders whether reviewing the Commission's administrative action with respect to protective measures, anti-dumping and countervailing duties, at least as a court of first and last instance, is a type of task for which the Court was created.

At any rate, in view of the present workload of the Court, granting jurisdiction over such cases to Chambers is only a palliative. The better solution would probably lie in the establishment of a lower tribunal acting as a court of first instance to which these appeals and other similar cases could be entrusted. The so-called European Act offers this possibility as it provides that 'a court with jurisdiction to hear and determine as first instance . . . certain classes of action or proceeding brought by natural or legal persons' may be attached to the Court of Justice.[38]

The solution to rely on national courts would not be adequate without additional and major changes viz. to let the Commission appear as defendant before such courts and to allow such courts to pass upon the legality of the Community's action without having to request a preliminary ruling under Article 177 EEC by the Court of Justice. The latter change would, institutionally and from the point of view of legal certainty, be highly questionable.

31. The third procedural improvement concerns the possibility for the private individual to petition the Commission to act. At present a private individual may under Article 175 complain to the Court that an Institution of the Community has failed to address to him any act other than a recommendation or an opinion. However, as the Court made clear in several cases,[39] a private party may not institute an action for default of a Community Institution to adopt a regulation or a directive. Since measures to be taken in the commercial policy field will take the form of an act of general nature, private individuals do not as a rule have effective legal means to prompt the Community to act. However, some possibilities do exist.

A practice has developed whereby private individuals lodge formal complaints with the Commission. The Commission has set up the necessary internal machinery to process such complaints, but the purpose of this machinery is less to give the complainant a fair hearing – there is in fact no hearing – than to use such complaints as additional means to carry out the Commission's task of watching over the application of Community law by the Member States.

For an analysis with respect to trade policy measures, see Temple-Lang, 'Judicial Review of Trade Safeguard Measures in the European Community' in 1985 *Annual Proceedings of the Fordham Corporate Law Institute* (New York, 1986) 643–693; see also Bronckers, ter Kuile en Steenbergen, 'Ondernemingen en handelspolitieke instrumenten', 10 *SEW* 1985, 599–673.

38. Single European Act, Art. 11, Commission of the EC, *Bulletin of the EC 1986, Suppl. 2*.
39. Lastly: Case 246/81, *Lord Bethel* v. *Commission*, 1982 ECR, 2277.

Moreover, the new import régime as laid down in Regulation 288/82 has set up an investigation procedure, which, as a rule, has to be followed by the Commission before it takes a surveillance or protective measure. In the course of this investigation the Commission may hear the interested natural and legal persons. Such persons have a right to be heard where they have applied in writing within the period laid down in the notice announcing the investigation, provided they show 'that they are actually likely to be affected by the outcome of the investigations and that there are special reasons for them to be heard'.[40]

In addition, private individuals may lodge complaints with the Commission if they consider themselves injured or threatened by dumped or subsidised imports, and provided they represent at least a major proportion of the Community production of the 'like product'.[41]

Finally, under the 'New Trade Policy Instrument' private individuals, representing at least a major proportion of the Community production or of the Community consumption of the like product may also lodge a complaint with the Commission if they consider themselves injured or threatened by illicit commercial practices with respect to trade in a given product.[42]

There are standing requirements limiting these rights[43] and the right to complain does not entail the right to have measures taken (anti-dumping and countervailing regulation, 'new trade policy instrument') or even the right to have an investigation opened ('new trade policy instrument'). However, the creation of a formalised petition, with a presentation of views and the conduct of hearings, not only channels and publicises the pressures on the Community to take action against unfair or illegal practices of third countries, they also encourage private individuals who are affected by such practices to make their views directly known there where commercial policy measures are taken.

40. Reg. 288/82, Art. 6; Reg. 1765/82, Art. 6. *Cf.* contribution by Völker, Chapter Two.
41. Art. 5 of Council Reg. (EEC) No. 2176/84, on protection against dumped or subsidized imports from countries not members of the European Economic Community (OJ 1984, L201/1).
42. Art. 2 (4) of Council Reg. (EEC) No. 2641/84, *supra*, n. 36.
43. For a critique of these limitations see Bronckers, 'Private Response to Foreign Trade Practices: United States and EEC Complaint Procedures', 6 *J. INT'L L. & BUS.* 201 (1985).

CHAPTER TWO

THE MAJOR INSTRUMENTS OF THE COMMON COMMERCIAL POLICY OF THE EEC

By E.L.M. Völker[*]

INTRODUCTION

This introduction seeks to give an overview of the instruments employed by the Community in regulating its commercial relations with its trading partners. A few observations should, however, be made first:

1. The term *instrument* will have different connotations depending on whether it is used in an economic context or in a legal one. Examples of economic instruments of commercial policy are customs tariffs on imports or exports, and quantitative restrictions. Obviously, the question as to the legal form used for the application of the economic instrument is a different one. On the international level one can think in terms of international treaties (conventional instruments) or autonomous measures applied without the formal consent of the trading partners affected. Internally recourse may be had to regulations, directives or decisions within the meaning of Article 189 of the EEC Treaty. The question as to which legal instrument to use will depend, as far as the international level is concerned, on the obligations which the Community has contracted with regard to the relations involved, if any. On the internal level the legal form used will depend on whether the measure is of general application or not (*e.g.* the institution or suspension of a general customs duty on the importation of a particular product[1] versus the awarding of a quota to one Member State for the importation of a particular product.[2]

2. When considering measures regulating the Community's commercial relations with its trading partners, we will be principally concerned with

---

[*] Senior Lecturer, Europa Instituut, University of Amsterdam.
[1] *E.g.* Reg. 1533/81 (OJ 1981, L155) temporarily suspending the autonomous Common Customs Tariff duties on certain industrial products.
[2] *E.g.* Dec. 81/149 (OJ 1981, L72/13) changing the import arrangements established by Dec. 80/1278 and applied in the United Kingdom in respect of imports of certain iron and steel products originating in the Soviet Union and the German Democratic Republic.

measures designed to influence the volume of trade in a particular product rather than measures concerned, for example, with quality control. Measures of the latter type are not (or at least ought not to be) designed to influence the quantity of trade but merely its quality, *e.g.* for health or safety reasons.

3. The content of the CCP is to a large extent explained by the international obligations which the Member States had already contracted in the field of trade prior to 1958. A predominant part of their multilateral obligations in this field were laid down in the General Agreement on Tariffs and Trade,[3] whereas their bi-lateral obligations were set out in the various trade agreements and treaties of friendship navigation and commerce. The GATT predates the EEC Treaty by some ten years. An outline of the former is given first since an understanding of the GATT obligations is essential background for an understanding of the Community's commercial policy.

I. THE GATT SYSTEM[4]

The basic idea behind the General Agreement on Tariffs and Trade is the creation and promotion of a system of fair international trade, freed to the largest extent possible from national governmental interventions. Moreover, if there has to be national intervention a strong preference is shown for tariffs (at the lowest level possible) over quantitative restrictions and other non-tariff barriers.[5]

The way in which the GATT Agreement sets out to achieve this aim is largely fourfold:

– an elaborate machinery for obtaining tariff concessions via multilateral trade negotiations and a system of registration of the concessions thus achieved, the so-called *tariff bindings*;

– the general elimination of quantitative restrictions and a number of other important non-tariff barriers;

– the Most-Favoured-Nation treatment obligation for all GATT parties;

---

3. *General Agreement on Tariffs and Trade*, Basic Instruments and Selected Documents, Volume VI. (GATT Secretariat, Geneva 1969).
4. See particularly: Jackson, *World Trade and the Law of GATT* (Indianapolis, 1969), and by the same author, *Legal Problems of International Economic Relations. Cases Materials and Texts on the National and International Regulation of Transnational Economic Relations* (St. Paul, 1979) on which Section I is largely based. Furthermore, Dam, *The GATT Law and International Economic Organization* (Chicago, 1970), Hudec, *The GATT Legal System and World Trade Diplomacy* (New York, 1975) and McGovern, *International Trade Regulation. GATT the United States and the European Community*, 2nd Edition (Exeter, 1986).
5. Some authors put more emphasis on the aspect of predictability of conditions of international trade particularly with regard to safeguarding the gains from international trade, *e.g.* Tumlir, 'GATT rules and Community Law' in Hilf, *et al.* (Eds.) *The European Community and GATT* (Deventer, 1986).

– a presumption of fair trade underpinned by procedures for the imposition of anti-dumping or countervailing duties.

The system also consists of exceptions to the above obligations, conflict settlement, safeguard and other procedures, and a number of agreements either amending or supplementing GATT articles, or specifying exceptions. With the exception of the various procedures, these subjects will be discussed briefly later in this contribution. The exceptions to the above obligations, however, will not be discussed separately but are treated with the subject to which they relate.

A. TARIFFS

One could argue that when tariffs are the single general means by which, under the GATT Agreement, Member States are allowed to regulate trade, many other obligations contained in the Agreement are aimed at ensuring that the protection by tariffs is not eroded (by the exporting state) or supplemented (by the tariff imposing state).

To obtain a progressive lowering of the overall level of tariff protection applied by the GATT contracting Parties, the GATT Agreement provides a procedure in the form of international tariff negotiating rounds. By this procedure tariff reductions should be achieved leading to an equitable package of trade advantages for all parties involved. Each party should receive, in exchange for the reduction in import tariffs which he is offering, an equivalent advantage through reductions by his major trading partners of their tariffs levied on his exports. The maximum tariff per product to which a contracting party has bound itself is called that country's *binding*, its bindings together form a party's *schedule*. The schedules form an integral part of the GATT Agreement. These general rounds of tariff negotiations are mentioned in Article XXVIII *bis*.

B. THE ELIMINATION OF QUANTITATIVE RESTRICTIONS

Subject to a number of listed exceptions the GATT Agreement prohibits quantitative restrictions on trade.[6] Apart from the usual sovereignty reserves, these exceptions relate to agricultural and fisheries products, the need to safeguard a country's foreign exchange reserves and its balance of payments and the more general possibility to avoid serious injury to domestic producers, included in Article XIX. The application of such exceptions is subject to a

---

6. Article XI, para. 1.

number of conditions, such as non-discriminatory application (for all exceptions[7]), the application of internal production limitations (for agricultural quotas), the avoidance of unnecessary damage to the interests of other parties to the Agreement (for the safeguarding of balance of payments) or prior consultation (all exceptions, the sovereignty reserves excluded). In the event that the use of quantitative restrictions is undesirable or when its non-discriminatory application proves difficult, resort is often had instead to certain forms of control applied by the exporting country rather than the importing one. Although formally prohibited under the GATT Agreement[8] and undermining the GATT system,[9] complaints are not likely as both parties involved have reached (an often informal) agreement on the matter.

C. THE ELIMINATION OF OTHER NON-TARIFF BARRIERS IN THE GATT AGREEMENT

A number of particular practices are prohibited by the Agreement. The national treatment obligation[10] requires the GATT parties to accord treatment to imports from GATT countries no less favourable than the treatment accorded to national products. This includes application of internal taxes or other internal charges or laws, regulations and requirements which affect the various stages between importer and consumer or user. This provision forms one 'half' of the non-discrimination requirement, *i.e.* in relation to national products, the other half being the MFN obligation contained in Article I (see below). The provision in the GATT Agreement dealing with anti-dumping measures and countervailing duties[11] submits the imposition of anti-dumping and countervailing duties to certain requirements, such as establishing actual or potential material injury to local producers, in an attempt to avoid measures in cases where dumping or subsidisation is not actually detrimental to producers of the import receiving state. Article VII contains the requirement that if the value of imports (or exports) forms the basis of the application of duties or charges or other restrictions on importation (or exportation) the value used should be formed by the price at which such merchandise is sold in the

---

7. For a different opinion see Bronckers, 'The non-discriminatory application of Article XIX GATT: Tradition or Fiction?' LIEI 1981/2, 35–76, also included in *Selected Safeguard Measures in Multilateral Trade Negotiations* (The Hague, 1985) by the same author, Koulen, 'The non-discriminatory interpretation of GATT Article XIX(1). A reply.' *LIEI* 1983/2, 87–113, and Bronckers, 'Reconsidering the non-discriminatory principle as applied to GATT safeguard measures. A rejoinder.' *LIEI* 1983/2, 113–135.
8. Art. I, III, XIII–XV, and XVII. See the Leutwiler Report, '*Trade Policies for a Better Future, Proposals for Action*' (Geneva, 1985) and Petersmann, 'The EEC as a GATT Member – Legal Conflicts Between GATT Law and European Community Law' in Hilf, *et al., op. cit.* n. 5.
9. Patterson, 'The European Community as a threat to the system' in Cline (Ed.) *Trade Policy in the 1980's* (Washington D.C. 1982) p. 223.
10. Art. III.
11. Art. VI.

ordinary course of trade under conditions of full competition. In this way artificially increased product values resulting in equally increased customs duties are prohibited.

Further possible restrictions on imports and exports pertaining to customs requirements are covered by other articles of the Agreement. These include fees and formalities[12] requirements on marks of origin[13] and publication and administration of trade regulations.[14] Article XVII concerns state trading enterprises and stipulates an obligation to act in a non-discriminatory manner where imports and exports by these entities are concerned. However for government procurement only fair and equitable treatment of the products of the other GATT parties is required, the national treatment obligation is therefore not applicable to this category.[15]

D. THE MOST-FAVOURED-NATION TREATMENT CLAUSE (MFN-CLAUSE)

The obligation contained in Article I(1) of the GATT Agreement entails that any advantage granted by a GATT member with regard to a product coming from or going to *any other country* is to be accorded to the like product coming from or going to any (other) GATT contracting party. Quite a number of observations can and have been made regarding MFN-treatment in general and about the MFN-clause of the General Agreement in particular. We will limit ourselves here to one; the question of the object of the clause. The clause is restricted to trade advantages accorded to a product originating in (or destined for) any other country. Thus the advantages covered are, first, those regarding products or goods and, second, those provided in the trade with *any* trading partner, including non-GATT members. The trade advantages so covered are to be granted to all (other) GATT parties.

As already mentioned, the MFN-clause forms one part of the general non-discrimination obligation, the other major part of which is formed by the national treatment rule of Article III. However, the Agreement also contains some further specific obligations relating to non-discrimination, which are included in articles dealing with other subjects. The most important are Article XVII(1) regarding commercial activities of State enterprises and the requirement of non discriminatory administration of quantitative restrictions of Article XIII(1).

There are also a number of important exceptions to the MFN-rule, not all of which are of the same character. First, there are the sovereignty reserve exceptions in Articles XX and XXI. Secondly, the general 'waiver' provision of

12. Art. VIII.
13. Art. IX.
14. Art. X.
15. Art. III(8)a.

Article XXV(5) and the nullification and impairment clause of Article XXIII by which the party whose benefit under the Agreement is nullified or impaired may be authorized to suspend the application of concessions in return. Thirdly, there is the exception contained in Article XXIV, very important for the EEC and Euratom, relating to the formation of free trade areas and customs unions. The formation of a customs union entails *inter alia* that duties and other restrictive trading regulations are eliminated between the countries forming such union. The strict application of the MFN obligation would eliminate the possibility of GATT parties taking part in such an undertaking.

E. AMENDMENTS AND SUPPLEMENTS

The GATT Agreement is amended and 'supplemented' by a number of further agreements, which mostly take the form of amendments to the tariff schedules of the parties. The agreements which amend the GATT text or its appendices have been accepted by all the contracting parties and thus bind all GATT members. One exception to this is part IV of the Agreement (covering trade and development) which has not yet been accepted by all contracting parties.

An example of an important supplementary agreement, negotiated within the framework of the GATT, is the Arrangement on International Trade in Textiles, better known as Multifibre Arrangement (MFA),[16] of December 1973 (meanwhile three times extended). The agreement itself contains exceptions to rules in the GATT Agreement in that it provides for the possibility of selective import restrictions, *i.e.* import restrictions which discriminate against a particular contracting party. Article XIX does not provide for such exception. Nor does the GATT provide for voluntary export restraint arrangements also found in the MFA.

Other examples of agreements concluded within the framework of the GATT are those reached at the end of the last round of multilateral trade negotiations, the so-called Multilateral Trade Negotiation (MTN) or Tokyo Round, held between 1973 and 1979. The negotiations resulted not only in agreements on lower tariffs, but also in agreements on various other subjects which supplement the General Agreement. The latter are the so called MTN or Tokyo Round *codes*, on *e.g.* anti dumping (Article VI) and customs valuation (Article VII) and other subjects. In addition, further agreements were concluded dealing with particular products, such as meat or dairy products.[17] However, as only a limited number of Contracting Parties are signatories to the codes their status in GATT law and the resulting obligations between the signatories and the remaining Contracting Parties pose complicated legal

---

16. See the contribution by van Dartel, Chapter Four.
17. For further discussion see the contribution by Steenbergen, Chapter Six.

questions. The Community has signed all codes as have the United States and Japan.[18]

The Community tradepolicy instruments in the field of tariffs and quantitative restrictions as well as the necessary implementing legislation will be discussed below (Section II, A–B), as will be the use of safeguard clauses (Section III). It should be recalled, however, that the Community can always act *ad hoc* on the basis of Article 113 of the EEC Treaty to take action not otherwise permitted under the instruments at present available. See the discussion by Bourgeois on this subject in Chapter One. Whether the MFN requirement is always adhered to by the Community when conducting its trade policy is discussed as the question arises in relation to each instrument. No separate treatment is accorded to the notions of conventional or autonomous instruments as such, as both are discussed in the framework of tariffs, quotas, safeguard clauses, etc. as applicable.

II. THE MAJOR COMMUNITY INSTRUMENTS IN THE FIELD OF TARIFFS AND QUANTITATIVE RESTRICTIONS ON IMPORTS

A. THE COMMON CUSTOMS TARIFF (CCT)[19]

1. REGULATION NO. 950/68 ON THE COMMON CUSTOMS TARIFF[20]

The CCT is the single most important instrument of the commercial policy of the Community. The system used is that of a basic regulation (No. 950/68) containing four short articles and an Annex. The latter contains the actual duties as well as the nomenclature (classification of goods). A new list of duties including amendments is published annually by substituting the Annex for a new one. Regulation 950/68 is based on Articles 28 and 111 of the EEC Treaty, confirming the view that Article 28, laying down the competence of the Council to amend Community customs duties, includes the power to lay down the tariff as a whole. By also basing the basic tariff Regulation on Article 111 the necessary link with the Chapter in the Treaty on the Common Commercial Policy is established.

---

18. For the application and constitutional effects of the Tokyo Round agreements see: Jackson, Louis, Masushita, *Implementing the Tokyo Round. National Constitutions, and International Economic Rules* (Ann Arbour, 1984).

19. For some early literature on the EEC and the ECSC tariff and customs legislation see: Amphoux, 'Customs legislation in the EEC' (1972) JWTL 133–184; Van der Burg, 'The Customs Tariff and the Customs Legislation of the European Communities' (1978) *CMLRev.* 184–204. Of a more recent date is: Vaulont, *The Customs Union of the European Economic Community* (Brussels, 1985) and Lasok and Cairns, *The Customs Law of the European Economic Community* (Deventer, 1983).

20. OJ 1968, L172.

Article 1 of the Regulation establishes that the tariff system included in the Annex is the Common Customs Tariff mentioned in Article 9 of the EEC Treaty, thus laying down that no goods fall outside it; this is confirmed by a provision in the Annex to the effect that a good not falling within any heading of the Tariff shall be classified under the heading appropriate to the goods to which it is most akin. The Regulation, however, does formally not apply to Coal and Steel products, although the nomenclature contains headings on these products. These headings are included for the sake of clarity only.[21] The Regulation is not applicable to coal and steel products as the ECSC Treaty contains a separate, less Community oriented, regime regarding customs duties in Article 72.[22]

The question of whether charges of equivalent effect, imposed by Member States on imports from third countries, are subject to the same regime as similar charges on products in free circulation and, if they are not, to what rules charges of this kind are subjected was answered by the Court at a fairly early stage in the *Indiamex* Case.[23] There the Court held that the incompatibility with Community law of charges of the kind mentioned should be considered individually in relation to their potentially distorting effects, and that the coming into force of Regulation No. 950/68 only prohibits the imposition of new charges of equivalent effect or increases in already existing ones. The Annex to Regulation No. 950/68, as replaced most recently by Regulation No. 3618/86,[24] consists of two parts; the first part contains the so-called Preliminary Provisions and the second contains the actual tariffs as grouped in the Schedule of Customs Duties. The schedule is divided into 21 sections (*e.g.* live animals, animal products, mineral products, textiles and textile articles, machinery and mechanical appliances, electrical equipment and parts thereof) which make up 99 chapters in total. All chapters consist of four columns, formed by: the heading numbers, the product descriptions, the autonomous duties and the conventional duties, respectively. The classification of the goods for customs purposes shall be determined by the terms of the headings or sub-headings, the relevant Section or Chapter notes, if any, and according to the Preliminary Provisions (as long as not required otherwise by the headings or notes).

The basis of the structure of the CCT is formed by the Brussels Convention on Customs Nomenclature of 15 December 1950 to which all Member States are a party.[25]

21. Last para. of the preamble of the last Regulation amending Reg. No. 950/68 *i.e.* Reg. No. 3618/86 (OJ 1986, L345).
22. Article 72 ECSC should be read in conjunction with Article 232 EEC which stipulates that the EEC Treaty shall not affect the ECSC Treaty provisions '. . . in particular as regards the rights and obligations of the Member States . . .'.
23. Joined Cases 37+38/73, *Diamantarbeiders* v. *Indiamex* (1973) ECR 1609 *et seq.*, paras. 14–20. See also Case 70/77, *Simmenthal* v. *Ammistrazione* (1978) ECR 1453, with annotations by Usher (1978) *Eur. L. Rev.* 412–416 and Barents (1979) SEW 263 *ff.*
24. See n. 21.
25. Usher, 'Uniform External Protection – EEC Customs Legislation before the Court of Justice' (1982) *CMLRev.* 389–412, at 391.

Meanwhile a new system for the classification of goods and other trade related purposes has been arrived at in 1983 within the framework of the Customs Cooperation Council (CCC), after thirteen years of study and negotiation. It will enter into force after seventeen ratifications have been received, *i.e.* 1 January 1988.

As mentioned above the CCT contains two sets of duties: the autonomous (column 3) and the conventional or bound duties (column 4). The former, computed from the duties applied in the four customs territories originally forming the Community, are the basis for tariff negotiations, of which the latter then result. The negotiations which produced the greater majority of the present rates of duty were the multilateral Kennedy[26] and Tokyo[27] rounds of trade negotiations held within the GATT. Although the results of the negotiations are only binding in the relations with GATT trading partners or with countries with whom the Community has concluded agreements containing a most favoured nation clause, the present conventional duties are applied to trade with *all* third countries. This situation will remain 'until such time as a common trade policy enters into force in this respect', *i.e.* with respect to the trade with the remaining countries, identifiable mainly as the group of *state trading countries*[28] with the exception of China, Roumania and Yugoslavia with whom the Community has concluded separate agreements.[29]

The last multilateral trade negotiations round (*i.e.* the Tokyo Round) was, unlike previous rounds, not conducted on the basis of separate tariff concessions per product but on the basis of a general tariff reduction formula applied in principle to all tariffs.

Tariffs have, generally speaking, diminished in importance as a major trade barrier as a result of the reductions achieved in the past trade negotiation rounds. The tariffs thus achieved are legally bound in GATT, which may make customs tariffs a rather inflexible trade policy instrument. Maybe partly as a result of these factors, the past ten years or so have shown a virtual explosion in the use of non-tariff barriers for the purpose of trade protection. The variety in these measures as well as the fact that they tend in practice to escape international control form an argument for greater reliance on tariffs as a trade protection instrument if protective measures are required. The transparency of

---

26. For a detailed account of the Kennedy Round negotiations (1963–1967), see: Preeg, *Traders and diplomats. Analysis of the Kennedy Round of negotiations under the General Agreement on Tariffs and Trade* (Washington, 1970).
27. See: Jackson, 'The Birth of the GATT–MTN System: A Constitutional Appraisal', 12 *Law & Pol. Int'l Buss.* 21(1980) and Steenbergen, 'De Tokyo-Ronde' (1980) *SEW* 752–773 and his contribution in Chapter Six.
28. For a description of the relations with eastern bloc countries see: Seeler, *Report on relations between the European Community and the Council for Mutual Economic Assistance (CMEA) and the Eastern European members states of the CMEA* of 19 December 1986, European Parliament Document A 2–187/86 and further Wellenstein, 'The Relationship of the European Communities with Eastern Europe', in O'Keeffe and Schermers (Eds.), *Essays in European Law and Integration* (Deventer, 1982) and Völker, 'Importing from East-bloc countries: common rules and remedies for the parties concerned', *LIEI* 1985/1, 99 at 100 *ff.*
29. China, OJ 1985, L250, Roumania, OJ 1980, L352, Yugoslavia OJ 1983, L41.

tariffs enhances the possibility for international control and reduction by negotiation in an economically more favourable period.[30]

Not included in the yearly amended annex of Regulation 950/68 are autonomous custom duty *suspensions* on goods originating in certain countries, such as the Community General Scheme of Preferences (GSP).[31] Also those instances where *preferential* customs treatment is accorded in pursuance of agreements concluded by the Community are not taken up as in the case of the association and cooperation agreements with the Mediterranean countries and the Lomé Convention (see further below). Furthermore it appears from the preamble that *temporary* tariff amendments (those laid down on the basis of Article 28 of the EEC Treaty) are also not included, although all groups of exceptions form an integral part of the CCT.

2. PREFERENTIAL CUSTOMS TREATMENT ACCORDED BY THE EEC UNDER BI-LATERAL AGREEMENTS

The various association, cooperation and preferential trade agreements which the Community has concluded with the ACP, Mediterranean and EFTA countries include elements, in particular as regards customs treatment, which cannot as such be reconciled with the GATT MFN obligation unless one of the exceptions to the MFN treatment can be invoked. *In casu* this would have to be either the waiver provision of Article XXV or Article XXIV, paras 4–10, concerning the formation of customs unions and free trade areas. As no waiver has been obtained with regard to the present agreements or group(s) of agreements there remains the possibility of using Article XXIV. The main criteria to be satisfied for the application of this Article in regard to customs unions and free trade areas are:

– that the common duties resulting from the formation of the customs union and applicable to the trade of the constituent territories with third countries, are substantially the same in each constituent territory of the union, and are not higher or more restrictive than the general incidence of the duties existing in the same constituent territories prior to the formation of the union;

– that the customs union or free trade area covers 'substantially all the trade'

---

30. See in this respect also Steenbergen,' Ondernemingen en handelspolitieke instrumenten' 1985 *SEW* p. 624 *et seq.* at 635.
31. Reg. No. 3924/86 applying generalized tariff preferences for 1987 in respect of certain industrial products originating in developing countries. (OJ 1986, L373/1)
Reg. No. 3925/86 applying generalized tariff preferences for 1987 to textile products originating in developing countries. (OJ 1986, L373/68)
Reg. No. 3926/86 applying generalized preferences in respect of certain agricultural products originating in developing countries. (OJ 1986, L373/126)
Dec. No. 86/638 (ECSC) applying for 1987 the generalized tariff preferences for certain steel products originating in developing countries. (OJ 1986, L373/162)

concerned between the parties to such customs union or free trade area and that it reaches its final form within a reasonable length of time.

The Association Agreement with Turkey (1963) sets out to create a customs union between the Community and Turkey.[32] The agreement provides for free movement of goods between the parties by a prohibition of customs duties and quantitative restrictions and all other charges and measures with equivalent effect.[33] Most Turkish industrial and agricultural products are now enjoying free access to the Community market; the reverse is however not the case. There is a fixed date foreseen as to when the customs union is to be attained.

The Association Agreements with Malta (1970)[34] and Cyprus (1972)[35] also foresee the final adoption of the CCT by these two associated countries as well as the elimination of restrictions on the trade between these parties and the Community. Although a certain time schedule was agreed upon, this could not be adhered to.

Under all three association agreements Community products are awarded mfn treatment by the Community's association partners.

The following (groups of) Community agreements provide for the setting up of free trade areas rather than customs unions.

The third Lomé Convention[36] provides, in the field of trade, for duty-free access of ACP products into the Community market[37] and for the abolition of quantitative restrictions and measures of equivalent effect.[38] Remaining agricultural levies are of a preferential type,[39] while for various products like bananas, rum and sugar special arrangements are included.[40] Community products are to receive mfn treatment in return.[41] The arrangements provided for in the field of trade have been fully implemented in the meantime. The Cooperation Agreements concluded by the Community with the Arab countries of the Mediterranean and Yugoslavia provide for duty free access to the Community and the removal of charges of equivalent effect for most industrial products. The same applies for quantitative restrictions and measures with equivalent effect. Agricultural products receive a certain amount of preferential duty treatment varying to a certain extent from agreement to agreement.[42] As for Community products mfn treatment is

32. OJ 1977, L361, Art. 2(2).
33. Art. 10(2).
34. JO 1971, L61.
35. OJ 1973, L133.
36. OJ 1986, L86. See further: Huber, 'From Lomé II to Lomé III: Improvements and New Features in the Third ACP-EEC Convention Signed on 8 December 1984' *LIEI* 1985/1, 1–26 and Simmonds, 'The Third Lomé Convention' 1985 *CMLRev.* 389–420.
37. Art. 130(1).
38. Art. 131(1).
39. Art. 130(2)a, sub(ii).
40. Protocols 4, 5 and 7 resp.
41. Art. 136(2)a.
42. *E.g.* Cooperation Agreement between the EEC and the Kingdom of Morocco (OJ 1978, L264), Art. 9(1) and part 'B. Agricultural products', respectively.

foreseen.[43] In all cases the possibility that the Community partners may reintroduce trade restrictions if necessary for development purposes is provided for.[44]

With each EFTA member country an agreement has been concluded establishing a free trade area. The arrangements involve mutual dismantling of tariffs and quantitative restrictions and charges and measures with equivalent effect. The products covered are industrial products and processed agricultural products. Agricultural products *per se* are excluded (except for fisheries products in the agreement with Iceland.

Given the strict requirements which Article XXIV, paras 4–10 GATT imposes on the establishment of customs unions and free trade areas it can be argued that it is doubtful, to say the least, whether the various Community agreements providing for preferential treatment of the products of one or both parties involved are in conformity with GATT obligations of the Community. It concerns either the obligation that 'substantially all the trade' is to be covered by the agreement in question as in the case of the EFTA agreements, or the requirement, in the case of a customs union like the one's with Turkey, Malta and Cyprus, that substantially similar customs duties are to be applied by the parties to the agreement. Also the condition that the final stage is to be achieved 'within a reasonable length of time'[45] has posed problems in the latter cases.

As appears from the above discussion of the CCT there are two essential elements without which customs duties cannot be imposed on an imported good; a definition of the value of a product and rules to estalish its origin. The relevant Community rules will be discussed here because of their close relation to the tariff legislation. When it is stated that valuation and origin are two essential elements, this does not mean of course that no further legislation is necessary to apply tariffs in practice such as to define the customs area, the definition of importation etc. These rules, however, pertain more to the area of *customs* law a discussion of which falls outside the scope of this contribution.[46]

3. THE VALUATION OF GOODS FOR CUSTOMS PURPOSES[47]

The rules governing the valuation of goods for customs purposes were originally laid down at about the same time as the first publication of the

43. *Ibid.* Art. 27(1).
44. *Ibid.* Art. 28(2).
45. See also Huber, 'The practice of GATT in examining regional arrangements under Article XXIV', *(1981) J. Comm. Mark. Studies*, 281–298, and on activities of the International Law Commission in this respect, Ustor, 'The MFN Customs Union Exception', (1981) JWTL, 377–387.
46. See Amphoux and Van den Burg, *loc. cit.* n. 19, and Terra, 'Introduction to Customs Law', *LIEI* 1981/2, 77–107.
47. See Van Raan, 'The Valuation of Goods for Customs Purposes' (1981) *Intertax*, 126–133 and also De Pachter en Van Raan, *The Valuation of Goods for Customs Purposes* (Deventer, 1981).

Common Customs Tariff, *i.e.* in Regulation No. 803/68 of 28 June 1968.[48] Article 235 of the EEC Treaty was chosen as the legal basis of this Regulation because Article 27 of the EEC Treaty, although concerned with customs legislation, does not empower the institutions of the EEC to issue binding provisions. Binding Community acts are essential to ensure the uniform application of the CCT in order to achieve a uniform level of protection throughout the Community and to prevent distortion of competition. The new Regulation No. 1224/80,[49] replacing Regulation No. 803/68, is based on Article 113 of the EEC Treaty, according to which the Common Commercial Policy shall be based on uniform principles. Whilst Article 113 does not expressly refer to matters of tariff law it is arguable that the scope of Article 113 does in fact include tariff related matters such as valuation rules. The advantage is that unlike Article 27 Article 113 does provide for binding Community rules.

The valuation principle of Regulation No. 803/68 was that the value of imported goods for customs purposes was the 'normal price'. This is the price a good fetches in the open market between a buyer and seller independent of each other. The contents of the Regulation followed the Customs Cooperation Council Valuation Convention of 1950. As all Member States are Contracting Parties to the GATT as well as to the Convention, the CCC based valuation principle of the hypothetical sale should conform with Article VII of the GATT dealing with customs valuation. Article VII defines the customs value to be the *actual value*,[50] *i.e.* the price at which such or like merchandise is sold or offered for sale in the ordinary course of trade under fully competitive conditions, at a time and place determined by the legislation of the country of importation.

According to the Notes and Supplementary Provisions on Article VII(2) GATT, the 'actual value' may be represented by the invoice price plus non-included charges and abnormal discounts. To this it is added that the wording of para. 2 permits that the value be determined uniformly either (1) on the basis of a particular exporter's price of the imported merchandise, or (2) on the basis of the general price level of like merchandise. The latter possibility may have provided the basis for the Community Regulation.

The series of agreements reached at the end of the Tokyo Round of multilateral trade negotiations includes an agreement on the implementation of Article VII of the GATT.[51] The implementation of this Agreement is effected by the new Community regulation on valuation, Regulation No. 1224/80. The GATT basis of this regulation forms the second reason for it being based on Article 113 of the EEC Treaty. The Agreement consists of a preamble containing general introductory commentary and of the actual text, of which Part I contains the substantive provisions and Part III exceptions thereto in

48. JO 1968, L148.
49. OJ 1980, L134.
50. Art. VII(2)b, GATT.
51. Agreement on implementation of Article VII of the GATT, GATT Doc MTN/E/6 (Annex II) and OJ 1980, L71.

favour of developing countries. The Regulation follows Part I of the agreement closely, albeit that occasionally a different order of the provisions is used and that certain parts of the Interpretive Notes are included in the text thereof. The Agreement and thus also the Regulation[52] forego the hypothetical sales price of the CCC Convention in favour of the invoice or 'transaction value'. This is the price actually paid or payable for the goods when sold for export to the customs territory of the Community ('to the country of importation'), adjusted in accordance with the terms of Article 8. Thus the obvious suspicion aroused by intercompany sales and pricing, which at the time decided the options made available by Article VII GATT and the Note pertaining thereto in favour of the hypothetical sales price, no longer prevents the more literal and logical interpretation of the GATT Article from prevailing.

Acceptance of the *transaction value* for valuation purposes is, according to Article 3, subject to a number of conditions. First, on there being no restrictions as to the disposition of the goods by the buyer (with some exceptions). Second, that no part of the sales proceeds will accrue to the buyer. And, last but not least, that buyer and seller are not related or, if they are, that this does not influence the sales price.

The Articles 4 to 7 inclusive of the Regulation contain further methods for determining the customs value. The methods of valuation, including the transaction price are set out in sequential order of application; the transaction price is to be used whenever the stipulated conditions, as outlined above, are satisfied. Where the customs value cannot be determined on the basis of the transaction value, it is to be determined by proceeding sequentially through the succeeding Articles under which the value can be determined. Article 8 para. 2 leaves the choice to the contracting parties to base the value of imported goods on either the FOB value or on the CIF value. Article 8 of the Regulation, which reads the same as Article 8 of the Agreement, stipulates that costs, insurance and freight charges should be added to the price actually paid to arrive at the proper customs value, thus basing itself on the CIF value. Title II of the Regulation establishes the Community Committee on customs valuation. The rules regarding further implementation of the Agreement and the Regulation will be laid down by the Commission, after having obtained a concurring opinion by the Committee. If no such opinion is obtained the Commission proposal is referred to the Council for decision. If such decision is not reached within three months the Commission proposal will be implemented[53] (a so-called regulatory Committee procedure).

---

52. Art. 3.
53. For case-law by the Court of Justice on these subjects in relation to the older Regulations see Usher *op. cit.* n. 25 at 398.

4. DETERMINATION OF THE ORIGIN OF GOODS FOR CUSTOMS PURPOSES

If customs tariffs and trade policy measures would be uniformly applied to all imported goods rules for determining the origin of goods for customs purposes would not be required. As, however, extensive systems of *e.g.* preferential tariff treatment, depending on the origin of goods, exist in the Community, as we have seen above, it is necessary to enact common rules for the determination of the origin of goods imported into the Community.[54] However, one then encounters the difficulty that as the manufacture of products is increasingly carried out by undertakings located in more than one country, one must determine which of the countries involved represents the country of origin. The necessary common definition is contained in Regulation No. 802/68,[55] the last piece of tariff legislation of particular general significance dating from the time of the enactment of the Common Customs Tariff (mid-1968). Noticeable about this Regulation is that – in contrast to the previous Regulations regarding the CCT and common valuation rules – no mention is made either in the preamble or in the provisions of international obligations of the Community or the Member States in relation to the subject of the Regulation. This reflects the situation that there were and are no international conventions in force in this field binding on the Community and also that no material definition was provided in the GATT or other more general agreements concerning trade.

The legal basis for the act is found in various Articles of the EEC Treaty. These are Articles 111 and 113, because of the obvious link with commercial policy and the application of the CTT, and Article 155 because of the powers delegated to the Commission for further implementation of the Regulation. Furthermore Article 227 because of the provisions in the Regulation regarding products taken from the sea or (beneath) the seabed located outside the territorial waters and finally Article 235 because, as was discussed above, no specific powers to legislate in the sphere of customs law in general or rules of origin in particular are provided for in the Treaty.

Article 1 enumerates the particular purposes of the act: the uniform application of all measures adopted in relation to the importation and exportation of goods by the Community or the Member States, including the CCT and quantitative restrictions, and furthermore the preparation and issue of certificates of origin. The reference to measures by the Member States refers to exclusion from Community treatment of certain goods of particular non-Community origin on the basis of a Commission authorization under Article 115 of the EEC Treaty or to the application of national import controls

---

54. For an extensive treatment of the Community system of origin rules see Forrester, 'EEC Customs Law: Rules of Origin and Preferential Duty Treatment' (1980) *Eur. L. Rev.*, 167–187 and 257–286.
55. JO 1968, L148.

or import controls on a 'regional basis' authorized by the Council under *e.g.* Regulation No. 288/82.[56]

Articles 4 and 5 contain the elements of the common definition of origin. Article 4(1) as regards the goods 'wholly obtained or produced' in one country which, not surprisingly are considered to originate in that country, and Article 5 as regards products in the production of which two or more countries are involved. To determine the origin in the latter case a product: 'shall be regarded as originating in the country in which the last substantial process or operation that is economically justified was performed, having been carried out in an undertaking equipped for the purpose, and resulting in the manufacture of a new product or representing an important stage of manufacture'.[57]

The underlying aim is to establish a reasonable connection between a particular product and the economy of a particular country to the exclusion of all other countries in order to decide on the regime to be applied to that particular good.[58] This aim is expressed by the succeeding article laying down that origin shall in no case be provided on the basis of Article 5 where it is established that the sole object of the process or work was to circumvent the provisions applicable to goods from specific countries. In terms of the tariff nomenclature the last manufacturing stage should normally result in a so-called 'tariff jump' *i.e.* the not yet finished and the finished product should fall under different headings of the CCT.

The various elements of the definition contain criteria to be applied in a cumulative manner. It has been pointed out that to require this is rather odd, *i.e.* it is unlikely that a substantial operation on a product would be carried out if it were not economically justifiable, or did not constitute an important manufacturing stage.[59] The explanation offered is that the definition of origin for Community purposes is derived from the various origin rules of the, at the time six, Member States.

The common origin rules do not apply to petroleum products listed in Annex I which includes crude oil and most derivatives. The origin rules as regards these products were to be defined later. At present, almost twenty years later, the Community has not yet been able to accomplish this task. Article 2 contains exemptions from the Regulation for special rules on origin concerning trade of the Community or Member States with third countries to whom they are bound by agreements which derogate from the GATT MFN obligation *i.e.* because of the trade preferences contained therein. At the time this concerned the association agreements with Greece and Turkey.[60,61] As the system of origin rules developed over time it appeared that the definition of Regulation

---

56. Reg. No. 288/82 on common rules for imports, OJ, 1982 L35, Art. 15(3)a. See further the Contribution by Timmermans, Chapter Five.
57. Art. 7(2).
58. Forrester, *loc. cit.*, n. 54 at 173.
59. *Ibid.*, at 174.
60. JO 1963, L293 (Greece).
61. JO 1964, L3687 (Turkey).

No. 802/68 was applied only to establish the origin of imports not receiving preferential treatment. All later special trade regimes awarding Community preferences of whatever sort, whether autonomous (*e.g.* the General Scheme of Preferences: GSP) or bi-lateral (*e.g.* preferential trade agreements), contain separate more stringent, sets of rules of origin.[62]

Separate rules of origin were also enacted with regard to particular products or categories of products (*e.g.* textiles).

The origin rules regarding special trade regimes are often contained in a protocol of the treaty establishing such special regime (*e.g.* Norway,[63] Jordan,[64] Cyprus[65]), and are implemented via separate Community Regulations.

The rules regarding particular products or categories of products are enacted by Commission Regulations on the basis of Regulation No. 802/68, Article 14. This Article provides for a Regulatory Committee procedure involving the *Committee on Origin* established under Article 12, the procedure of which is identical to that of the Valuation Committee of Regulation No. 1224/80, discussed under the last sub-heading. Article 10 of the Regulation is concerned with certificates certifying Community origin *e.g.* for export purposes.

Community origin excludes national origin unless the 'needs of the export trade' require national origin to be certified. The latter is not possible in the case of origin being acquired on the basis of the 'last substantial process' (Article 5) if this process was carried out in more than one Member State. In such a case only Community origin may be certified. This is the logical result of the stipulation that for the purpose of the application of Articles 4–7 the Member States are considered a single territory (Article 8) as is required by Article XXIV,8(a) of the GATT.

The basic provisions of the Regulations establishing the origin of textile products and the preferential trade regimes are in essence the same as the definition of the basic Community Regulation as both normally will require a tariff heading for the product to be classified different from the headings covering the various products utilized in the manufacture of the end product. The exceptions to the general rule of these Regulations are contained in list A; in addition to the change of tariff heading special conditions have to be fulfilled in order to arrive at a 'last substantial process' qualifying to confer origin (*e.g.* the manufacture of incomplete outer and under garments qualifies only if the weaving of the material used has taken place in the same country). It is these extra conditions which are responsible for the restrictive character of the separate origin Regulations.

List B contains working and processing operations which do not result in a

---

62. See Pomfret, 'Protectionism and preferences in the EEC's Mediterranean policy', (1982) *The World Today*, 51–60, and McQueen, 'Lomé and the Protective Effect of Rules of Origin', 1982 JWTL, 119–132, at 124 *et seq.*
63. OJ 1973, L171/45.
64. OJ 1978, L268/24.
65. OJ 1977, L339/19.

different tariff heading of the resulting product but which do confer origin all the same. Not surprisingly list A contains many more headings than list B.

B. QUANTITATIVE RESTRICTIONS

'No prohibitions or restrictions other than duties, taxes or other charges . . . shall be instituted or maintained by any Contracting Party on the importation of any product of the territory of any other Contracting Party . . .' according to Article XI(1) of the GATT.[66]

Article 1(2) of Council Regulation No. 288/82 on common rules for imports states accordingly: 'Importation into the Community of the products referred to in paragraph 1 shall be free, and therefore not subject to any quantitative restriction'. This is, however, without prejudice to:

– measures which may be taken under Title V (*i.e.* safeguard measures allowed under Article XIX GATT);

– measures maintained under Title VI;

– quantitative restrictions for the products listed in Annex I and maintained in the Member States indicated opposite these products in that Annex.

The Regulation according to Article 1(1) is applicable to all imports from third countries to which the EEC Treaty applies, with the exception of:

– textile products subject to specific common import rules (*e.g.* the Multi Fibre Arrangement and the bilateral agreements between the EEC and a number of the textile producing countries; see further the contributions by Van Dartel and Timmermans);

– the products originating in State-trading countries;[67]

– the products originating in China[68] and Cuba.

There is no distinction as regards imports from GATT or non-GATT members.

The exception in Article 1(2) regarding Title V measures refers to the implementation in Community law of Article XIX(1)a GATT. This clause authorizes a Contracting Party in case 'any product is being imported into the

---

66. For a general discussion see Merciai, 'Safeguard Measures in GATT' *(1981) JWTL* 41–66, Bronckers *loc. cit.* n. 7, and Van Bael and Bellis, *International Trade Law and Practice of the European Community; EEC Anti-Dumping and other Trade Protection Laws* (Bicester, UK, 1985).

67. Listed in Reg. No. 1765/82 'on the common rules for imports from State trading countries' OJ 1982, L195, as amended by Reg. No. 1243/86 OJ 1986, L113 and Reg. No. 3420/83 'on import arrangements for products originating in State-trading countries, not liberalized at Community level' OJ 1983, L346/6. For discussion see: Völker *op. cit.* n. 28.

68. Reg. No. 1766/82 'on common rules for imports from the People's Republic of China' OJ 1982, L195/21.

territory of that Contracting Party in such increased quantities and under such conditions as to cause or threaten serious injury to domestic producers in that territory of like or directly competitive products' to remedy such situation by taking safeguard measures against the importation of those like or directly competitive products (*e.g.* quantitative restrictions). Article XIX thus forms an exception to *inter alia* Article XI GATT; Title V forms the equivalent exception to Article 1(2) of the Regulation (see further below). The Community has so far availed itself of this possibility only on a limited number of occasions and then mainly to lay down safeguard measures applicable to imports not into the Community as a whole but to imports from third countries into certain Member States only.[69] Such measures are foreseen under the Regulation on the basis of Article 15(3)a, second sentence. Whether safeguard measures on a regional or national basis are in conformity with the conditions which GATT imposes on the customs union exception on which the Community is based is at least doubtful. Article XXIV 8(a)ii and 5(c), strictly interpreted, do not seem to provide the necessary room in this respect. The measures maintained under Title VI[70] and referred to in Article 1(2) are various including the sovereignty exceptions regarding public policy etc. Whether the fact that Title VI measures are referred to in Article 1(2) as being *maintained* would mean that in none of the categories covered new measures can be introduced is unlikely given the categories concerned.

Also excluded from the basic rule of free importation into the Community are quantitative restrictions (q.r.'s) still maintained on a national basis *i.e.* by the Member States. The products 'not yet liberalized at Community level', *i.e.* for which national q.r.'s are still in force in certain Member States, are listed in Annex I to the Regulation. The reason for the existence of national quotas, as distinct from Community safeguard measures applied on a regional basis as discussed above, in the field where the Community has an exclusive competence is, as the Court acknowledged in the *Donckerwolcke* Case,[71] the fact that the Common Commercial Policy is not yet completed. In this way each Member State is permitted to keep certain interests protected by national q.r.'s despite the legal obligation that the CCP be based on uniform principles (Article 113 of the EEC Treaty) and that it is to cover all goods (Article 9). The legal construction used is that of a specific authorization by the Community allowing for such national measure, as stipulated in the *Donckerwolcke* Case.[72] A number of these restrictions must be considered as contravening Article XI(1) GATT, the majority are however maintained in trade with non-GATT members. As such, however, essentially transitional q.r.'s on a national basis still maintained almost twenty years after the imposition of the Common

---

69. *E.g.* Reg. No. 3528/82, OJ 1982, L369/27 'introducing protective measures in respect of imports into France and the United Kingdom of tableware and other articles of a kind . . .' and Reg. No. 1087/84, OJ 1984, L106/31 'introducing protective measures in respect of certain electronic piezo-electric quartz watches with digital display' (only applicable to France).
70. As amended by Reg. No. 1243/86, OJ 1986, L113.
71. Case 41/76, *Donckerwolcke* v. *Procureur* (1976) ECR, 1921 *et seq.*, at 1934.
72. *Id.*, para. 32.

Customs Tariff, are to be considered as contravening the requirements of Article XXIV(5)c and (8)a of GATT and basic characteristics of the Common Market as was indicated above. As already mentioned, the trade relations concerning imports between the Community and State-trading countries are subject to a separate regime. The relevant Regulations are 1765/82 'on common rules for imports from State-trading countries'[73] and 1766/82 'on common rules for imports from the People's Republic of China'.[74] The former is applicable to trade with: Bulgaria, Hungary, Poland, Roumania, Czechoslovakia, the German Democratic Republic, the USSR, Vietnam, North Korea and Mongolia. Not listed are Cuba,[75] Albania[76] and Yugoslavia.[77]

For the implementation of the safeguard clauses contained in the preferential trade agreements of the Community with third countries sometimes separate procedures are foreseen which are largely similar to the main Regulation 'on common rules for imports',[78] sometimes reference to the main Regulation was deemed sufficient.[79] These separate procedures were provided for in Regulation No. 288/82 and Regulation No. 1765/82 in Articles 21(1) and 16(1) respectively, as amended.

The main rule of Regulations No. 1765+66/82 states that the products covered by the Annex are not subject to quantitative restrictions on import (Article 1). The Annex forms the so-called common liberalization list of products in the trade with the State-trading countries. The q.r.'s still maintained by the Member States in trade with State-trading countries are listed in Annex III of the separate Regulation No. 3420/83.[80]

The treatment of the two groups of remaining *national* quotas contained in the Annexes to Regulations No. 288/82 and 3420/83 differs in various respects. Article 3(1) of Regulation No. 3420/83 charges the Council with laying down, before 1 December of each year, the import quotas to be opened by the Member States for the following year.

Regulation No. 288/82 does not have a similar provision. The reason may be that, as already noted, part of the national quotas in this group are not GATT

---

73. *Op. cit.* n. 67.
74. *Op. cit.* n. 68. For a general background see Kapur, *China and the EEC: the New Connection* (Dordrecht, 1986).
75. Cuba is also expressly excluded from Reg. No. 288/82 and no separate provisions exist for dealing with imports from that country, although Cuba is listed in the list of beneficiary countries of the Community's GSP system. At present there are no Commission authorizations in force under Article 115 of the EEC Treaty excluding products from Cuba from free circulation within the Community.
76. With regard to imports from Albania a number of Article 115 authorisations have been granted by the Commission and Albania has not been expressly excluded from the application of Reg. No. 288/82.
77. The Regulation laying down the procedure for the application of the safeguard clause in the Co-operation Agreement with Yugoslavia declares the predecessor to Reg. No. 288/82 applicable for that purpose; Reg. No. 1661/80, OJ 1980, L164.
78. *E.g.* Turkey Reg. 1842/71, OJ 1971, L192/14, and Austria Reg. 2837/72, OJ 1972, L300/94.
79. *E.g.* Yugoslavia *op. cit.* nt. 77.
80. OJ 1983, L346.

consistent. The comparable task in this respect is the Commission's duty to publish at regular intervals updated versions of Annex I. A similar difference is also noticeable in the procedures applicable for amending national quotas. In the case of amendments of national quotas applied in the trade with State-trading countries, the Commission is charged with adoption and application of the national proposals for amendments, unless the Commission itself proposes the adoption of a measure to the Council on the basis of Article 113 of the EEC Treaty (*i.e.* a Community quota).[81] In urgent cases national amendments are possible until such time as the Council or the Commission acts.[82] Under Regulation No. 288/82 Member States are still competent to amend their quotas where the Commission or any of the other Member States do not object. If they do object, the Council can lay down a measure on the basis of Article 113 of the EEC Treaty, *e.g.* a Community quota.[83] (For the complicated decision making procedure foreseen in Regulation 3420/83 for the amendment of national quotas, see Annex I to this chapter. For a comparison to the equivalent procedure in Regulation 288/82 see Annex II). The scope of the Regulations laying down the common rules for imports, and in fact of the common import regime as such, is restricted to measures of commercial policy[84] and the measures foreseen in Title VI *i.e.* particularly the sovereignty exceptions regarding public policy etc. Thus not covered are measures with equivalent effect to quantitative restrictions. The Treaty articles dealing with the CCP do not contain a prohibition on measures with equivalent effect similar to Article 30 of the EEC Treaty.[85]

The imposition of quantitative restrictions will be discussed below.

III. SAFEGUARD MEASURES

A. GENERAL

The Community trade policy instruments in the field of imports can be divided into measures directed at the price of imports or at the volume thereof. Also a combination of the two is possible. The measure imposed in cases of dumping or subsidies is a duty levied at importation of the dumped or subsidized goods or an arrangement regarding their minimum price at import. For the imposition of such duty or measure it is required that the dumped or subsidized

---

81. Article 9.
82. Art. 10.
83. Art. 20(1–3). In urgent cases quotas can be increased when economic requirements call for additional imports; Art. 20(4) as amended.
84. For a discussion of the content of this notion see the contribution by Bourgeois, Chapter One.
85. Case 51/75 *EMI Records* (1976) ECR 811, paras 14–20 and Case 225/78 *Bouhelier* (second) (1979) ECR 3151, para. 6.

imports cause material injury to an established Community industry[86] and that the balance of the Community interests involved call for Community intervention.[87] The levy or measure is applied to offset the artificially enhanced or 'unfair' competitive position of the product sold at a dumped or subsidized price; such price is considered neutralized by the price-increasing effect of the levy or measure. The compensatory action is to be applied in a discriminatory manner, *i.e.* directed on the goods sold on the unacceptable condition; goods not sold at such condition from other exporters are not to be affected.

The same, *i.e.* obligatory discriminatory application, applies to trade policy measures taken under Regulation No. 2641/84 'on . . . protection against illicit commercial practices',[88] 'in order to remove the injury resulting therefrom'.[89] Where the basis of the measures involved is formed by illicit commercial behaviour 'attributable to third countries',[90] such measures can be directed against such practice and the practising state only. This Regulation is further discussed in section D below.

Safeguard measures, when applied under the general import regimes, are to prevent imports of a particular product from causing substantial injury to Community producers of like or directly competing products if the interests of the Community so require. The injury should be caused by the product concerned being imported in greatly increased quantities and/or by the terms and conditions on which it is imported.

In all cases (anti-dumping, subsidisation and safeguards) injury to Community producers of like or directly competing products is required as a condition for the imposition of a protective measure. In the case of dumping and subsidies it is by definition the (sub-normal) price that is to distinguish the product causing the injury. The duty or measure is directed at that product, the amount of it is based on the difference between its normal value and the price for export to the Community. A quantitative restriction is imposed on the import of a product for the reason that the quantity and/or the terms and conditions of importation are injurious. The action therefore covers all imports and is not to be applied selectively. In principle it does not rectify any term or condition on which imports are made; in themselves these are not unacceptable in the ordinary course of trade.

---

86. Art. 2 of Reg. 2176/84 'on protection against dumped or subsidized imports from countries not members of the European Economic Community' OJ 1984, L201.

87. *Id.*, Art. 12.

88. Reg. No. 2641/84 'on the strengthening of the common commercial policy with regard in particular to protection against illicit commercial practices' OJ 1984, L252.

89. *Id.*, Art. 1(a).

90. Art. 2.1. 'For the purposes of this Regulation, illicit commercial practices shall be any international trade practices attributable to third countries which are incompatible with international law or with the generally accepted rules.'

B. THE IMPOSITION OF Q.R.'S OR THE ESTABLISHMENT OF SURVEILLANCE IN THE TRADE WITH NON STATE-TRADING COUNTRIES

1. BASIC PROVISIONS

The imposition of q.r.'s may take place directly, or via the intermediate step of the so-called surveillance procedure. Products subject to surveillance 'may be put into free circulation only on production of an import document'.[91] Such a document is to be issued by the Member States free of charge for any quantity requested within five working days of an application being made by any Community importer.[92] The provisions governing the imposition of surveillance measures resemble those regarding quantitative restrictions. The surveillance measures still maintained on a national basis, *i.e.* by the Member States, are listed in Annex II of Regulation 288/82.[93] The procedure which might give rise to either measure is triggered by information on import trends being supplied by the Member States to the Commission.[94] Consultations regarding the information received and measures to be taken shall take place within eight working days at the request of either the Commission or (a) Member State(s) within the committee set up for this purpose under the Regulation.[95] The committee consists of representatives of the Member States and is chaired by the Commission. The purpose of the consultation is to decide whether an investigation procedure is justified in the light of the evidence made available.

It is worth noting that, contrary to Regulation No. 2176/84 on protection against dumped or subsidized imports and Regulation No. 2641/84 on protection against illicit commercial practices, the general import Regulations do not contain a private (industry) right of complaint to petition for import relief.

The investigation procedure is subject to a number of rules laid down in the Regulation[96] and gives rise to both rights and obligations for the parties involved. However, the fact that under certain conditions mentioned in Article 7(4) a formal investigation appears optional only, can be considered a defect of the Community's import regime. Without a public airing of opposing viewpoints and due consideration of all relevant arguments, EEC decision-making in the area of safeguard measures is incomplete regarding an essential element. Given the Community's institutional structure, decisions to impose safeguards (*i.e.* to tax EC corporations and consumers who benefit from unrestricted access to imports) are necessarily of an administrative nature. A

---

91. Reg. 288/82, *supra* n. 56, Art. 11(1).
92. In this way the volume of intended imports of a particular product can be ascertained for the coming period. Surveillance is also used to check adherence to voluntary export restraint agreements, *e.g.* Reg. 873/83 OJ 1983, L96/8.
93. Art. 19(e).
94. Art. 3.
95. Arts. 4 and 5.
96. Arts. 6–9.

public proceeding could avoid charges that the Community's administration is covertly catering to particular interests.[97] It may also restore to a certain extent the confidence of the more liberal Member States in the EEC trade policy process, and persuade them to delegate more powers in this field from the Council to the Commission.

The opening of an investigation is to be announced in the Official Journal giving a summary of the available information and stipulating that interested parties shall supply their views to the Commission within a given period. Interested natural and legal persons who have applied should be heard orally provided they have shown they have special reasons for this and that it is likely that they will be affected by the outcome of the procedure.[98]

As each investigation is likely to involve confidential information, safeguards protecting the interests of the parties involved are included in the Regulation to the extent that disclosure by the Community authorities is conditional upon specific authorization from the supplier. If, however, the request for confidentiality appears unjustified and no permission for disclosure is granted, the information concerned will be disregarded.[99]

The investigation is closed by the Commission submitting to the committee its report containing the result of the investigation of the trend of the imports concerned and the terms and conditions under which they take place.[100] It should also show the resulting injury to Community producers.[101] The establishment of injury (the injury test) is to take place on the basis of the following particulars,[102] each one of which is *mutatis mutandis* identical to the factors involved to establish injury in cases of dumping or subsidization:

1 . . .

(a) the volume of imports, in particular where there has been a significant increase, either in absolute terms or relative to production or consumption in the Community;

(b) the prices of the imports, in particular where there has been a significant price undercutting as compared with the price of a like product in the Community;

(c) the consequent impact on the Community producers of similar or directly competitive products as indicated by the trends in certain economic factors such as:

– production
– utilization of capacity
– stocks

97. See the Leutwiler report, *op. cit.*, n. 8.
98. Art. 6.
99. Art. 8.
100. Art. 7(1).
101. Art. 9(2).
102. Art. 9(1). See *e.g.* Reg. No. 1087/84 introducing protective measures in respect of certain electronic piezo-electric quartz watches with digital display, *op. cit.* nt. 69.

– sales
– market share
– prices (*i.e.* depression of prices or prevention of price increases which would normally have occurred)
– profits
– return on capital employed
– cash flow
– employment.

(2) . . .

According to the respective Regulations, in the case of dumping or subsidization *material* injury should result from a *significant* increase in imports whereas in the case of safeguard measures the *substantial* injury should be caused by *greatly increased* imports. Despite these terminological differences which signify heavier requirements on the imposition of safeguard measures the requirements on injury in the case of dumping or subsidization[103] are more difficult to satisfy as injury caused by other factors such as volume and prices of imports not dumped (or subsidized) or contraction in demand should not be attributed to the dumped or subsidized imports. This is rightly so as dumping and subsidization give rise to the right to impose a *selective* countermeasure. The exclusion of extraneous factors like contraction in demand is not required explicitly in safeguard procedures. In practice this has been counterbalanced to some extent by requiring high increases in imports and penetration levels.[104] However, q.r.'s cannot be applied in cases of injury being solely attributable to contraction in demand when the level of imports remains equal in volume.[105] Although this is possible under the terms of the Regulation, Article XIX GATT requires the injury to be caused by increased quantities of imports *and* the conditions upon which imports take place.[106]

If the Commission, on the basis of the information obtained, decides that no action by the Community is necessary, it places a notice to this effect in the Official Journal, after having consulted the Committee.[107] In case, however, the conditions are shown to be fulfilled and the Commission considers Community action necessary it shall make the required proposals to the Council to lay down an appropriate measure to remedy the situation.[108] The Council is, however, not required to act if it considers such action would not be

103. Art. 4 of Reg. No. 2176/84, *supra* n. 86.
104. See *e.g.* Reg. 3528/82 re stoneware and Reg. 1087/84 re quartz watches (part E) *op. cit.* nt. 69.
105. The Commission applied this view in Reg. 3528/82 where import penetration rates of articles of common pottery had remained stable and therefore import relief measures refused.
106. In fact all EEC safeguard measures instituted so far on the basis of Reg. 288/82 concerned cases of substantial price undercutting. In the quartz watches procedure imports of analogue electronic watches (*i.e.* with hands) were not hit by quotas as the large majority of imports were not undercutting similar and directly competing Community made watches. See Reg. 1087/84 part F, *op. cit.* nt. 69.
107. Art. 7(2).
108. Art. 7(3) and Art. 16.

in the Community interest;[109] it appears, in the terms of the Regulation, to have an absolute discretion to adopt protective measures where conditions have been fulfilled. The competence to lay down protective measures is not restricted to the Council. The Commission may take measures itself either on request of a Member State or on its own initiative. Measures can only be taken if the conditions outlined above have been fulfilled and in addition if the interest of the Community calls for immediate intervention.[110]

The Community interest requirement may be defined as the balance of the various interests involved in the application of safeguard measures; interests such as, apart from the importer's, the interests of the users and consumers whose overriding priority may lie in the lowest possible price rather than in the protection of a (uncompetitive) Community industry. Also, the effect of an import relief measure on the Community's international trade relations might be such that it is preferable that other measures are pursued instead. On several occasions the Court has established that the Commission has a wide margin of discretion where measures of economic policy are concerned.[111] In the light of this case law it will not prove easy for e.g. Community importers to attack the validity of Commission protective measures on the ground of incompatibility with the Community's interest.

A Commission measure is immediately effective but will not become definite for one month in the sense that every Member State has the right to refer it to the Council for further decision. The Council may either confirm, amend or revoke the measure within three months. If it doesn't the measure is considered revoked.[112]

As already mentioned; contrary to the nature of the EC as a customs union, EEC safeguard measures may be restricted to one or more Member States only (Article 15(3)a) and in fact all measures applied so far were restricted in this way. See further the contribution by Timmermans, Chapter Five, para. 10.

The investigation procedure of Regulation 288/82 is without prejudice to the adoption, at any time, of surveillance or protective measures where required by an emergency situation.[113]

2. FURTHER PROVISIONS REGARDING SURVEILLANCE AND PROTECTIVE MEASURES

According to Article 17, Member States can also institute, on an interim basis,

109. Art. 16. See for a discussion of the Community interest in the quartz watches case Reg. 1087/84, part I. For the reasons given there the German watch industry was not protected but the French industry was.
110. Art. 15(1).
111. E.g. Case 5/73, *Balkan-Import-Export* v. *Hauptzollamt* (1973) ECR 1091 *et seq.* at 1107.
112. Art. 15(5) and 15(6). *Cf.* Commission Reg. No. 873/83 re automatic import authorizations for stoneware articles from South Korea, *supra* n. 92, as confirmed by Council Reg. No. 2050/83, OJ 1983, L200/43.
113. Art. 7(4).

import relief measures, regardless of the status of the product under the Community import regime; *i.e.* (i) liberalized on Community level, or (ii) not subject to quotas or (iii) subject to national quotas.[114] Article 17, however, only applied until 31 December 1984 as far as products liberalized at Community level are concerned. The Commission proposed the necessary amendments to Article 17 as required, on which the Council was to act before the final date. The Commission proposals were, howver, not accepted by the Council. Thus, because of the final date of application, Article 17 at present only applies to products still subject to national quotas in one or more Member States *i.e.* liberalized in the remaining Member States only. The latter provision applies until 31 December 1987. After this date Member States will only be allowed to restrict imports on a national basis 'where such measure is justified by a protective clause contained in a bi-lateral agreement between the Member State and a third country'.[115] The national measures have an interim character in the sense that their notification to the Commission is considered to be a request to take measures at the Community level. If the resulting Commission measure, if any, does not have the same protective effect as the national one the Member State may refer the Commission measure to the Council for further decision as described above. The national measure can remain in force in this way for a maximum of three months. This is hardly consonant with the character of the Common Market and with the way in which this character is protected and preserved internally in the Community. This is the more so as the national measure remains in force during this period in spite of the decision of the Commission not to take any measure at all, or only one with a less protective effect, even where the Commission *can* take such measure for just a single Member State.

Apart from the procedures outlined above, Title VI of the Regulation authorizes particular Member States to maintain import licences and other requirements in relation to certain third states,[116] as well as, for all Member States, the adoption of measures on grounds of public morality, public policy or public security.[117] Title VI was substantially amended by Regulation No. 1243/86.[118]

C. COMPARISON BETWEEN REGULATION NO. 288/82 AND REGULATION NO. 1765/82 REGARDING THE APPLICATION OF SAFEGUARD MEASURES

The regulations mentioned in the heading are, apart from the differences already mentioned, largely similar. Further differences are that in the

114. Art. 17.
115. Art. 17(1)(b).
116. Art. 19.
117. Art. 21.
118. *Op. cit.* n. 70.

investigation procedure the Commission is to take into account the economic system pertaining in the State-trading countries.[119] This clause should be seen in the light of the resistance in the Council to the inclusion of a formal investigation procedure in the Regulations, it should enable the Commission to react in alert and effective manner in cases of adverse market developments as far as imports from State-trading countries is concerned.

Under Regulation No. 1765/82 the Council, when applying safeguard measures, is not tied as strictly to the same – practically identically worded – criteria as in Regulation No. 288/82. It may apply measures *in particular* when the criteria discussed above are fulfilled, but it may equally do otherwise.[120] The Council's discretion to act under Regulation 288/82 only comes into play once the stipulated conditions actually have been fulfilled. Similar considerations apply to the Member States.[121]

As was mentioned, under Regulation No. 288/82 Member States may impose interim national protective measures on the basis of a safeguard clause in national bi-lateral trade agreement. This latter possibility is not included in the State-trading Regulation as Community competence, with regard to conventional commercial policy measures, is also exclusive for this group of countries, and moreover *without* exceptions.

As regards the procedures for obtaining import licences the Member States have to inform the Commission of all relevant rules, particularly where these concern the conditions for the admissibility of applications. In this way the Commission is able to establish the conformity of the national procedures with the requirements of the Agreement on Import Licensing procedures concluded within the framework of the Tokyo Round.[122] This information requirement is only included in Regulation No. 288/82 as the State-trading countries are not parties to that Agreement.

D. REGULATION NO. 2641/84 ON THE STRENGTHENING OF THE COMMON COMMERCIAL POLICY WITH REGARD IN PARTICULAR TO PROTECTION AGAINST ILLICIT COMMERCIAL PRACTICES

'In the light of experience and of conclusions of the European Council of June 1982, which considered that it was of the highest importance to defend vigorously the legitimate interests of the Community in the appropriate bodies, in particular GATT, and to make sure the Community, in managing trade policy, acts with as much speed and efficiency as its trading partners, it has

---

119. Art. 9(2).
120. Art. 12(1).
121. Art. 13(1), see in this respect Van Bael and Bellis, *op. cit.* n. 66, p. 168.
122. OJ 1980, L71/102.

become apparent that the common commercial policy needs to be strengthened, notably in the fields not covered by the rules already adopted; . . .'[123]

The experience referred to in the above quotation from the preamble of Regulation No. 2641/84 is formed by the unilateral safeguard measures taken by the United States on steel imports from *inter alia* the Community and United States sanctions against the Community because of its exports for the construction of the Siberian natural gas pipeline.[124] Within two years the Council of Ministers acted on the stimulus provided by the European Council,[125] and provided the Community with two new courses of action, two new decision making procedures, in order to enable it, firstly, to respond 'to any illicit commercial practice with a view to removing the injury resulting therefrom'[126] and, secondly, to ensure 'full exercise of the Community's rights with regard to the commercial practices of third countries'.[127] The speed and efficiency mentioned by the European Council are supposed to have been achieved by including time limits for the various stages of the procedures[128] and by delegating certain decisions to the Commission.[129]

The scope of application of the Regulation is limited to cases not covered by other instruments of the CCP.[130] Either procedure may be started by a Member State's request substantiated by the necessary evidence.

However, private parties, can make use only of the Article 1(a) procedure against illicit commercial practices. The admissibility requirements put on private parties complaints, in order to ensure that the opening of an

---

123. Reg. No. 2641/84, *op. cit.* n. 88; preamble, seventh para.
124. Bourgeois and Laurent, 'Le "nouvel instrument de politique commerciale": un pas en avant vers l'elimination des obstacles aux echanges internationaux' 1985 *RTDE* 41–63 at 43 and Hilf and Rolf, 'Das "Neue instrument" der EG', 1985 *RIW* 297–311 at 298.
125. For the drafting history and comparative analysis of the Regulation see Bronckers 'Private Response to Foreign Unfair Trade Practices – United States and EEC Complaint Procedures' 1984 *Northw. J. of Int'l Law and Bus.*, 651 *et seq.*, at 714–726, reproduced in *Selective Safeguard Measures in Multilateral trade Relations: Issues of Protectionism in GATT European Community and United States Law* (Deventer, 1985) by the same author; Steenbergen 'The New Commercial Policy Instrument', 1985 *CMLRev.* 421–439 and Bronckers, TerKuile and Steenbergen 'Ondernemingen en handelspolitieke instrumenten' 1985 *SEW* 599–673.
126. Art. 1(a) of Reg. No. 2641/84.
127. *Id.*, Art. 1(b).
128. Art. 6(8) of Reg. no. 2641/84 charges the Commission with deciding as soon as possible on a request, once received, but normally within 45 days, or sixty days in special circumstances.
Art. 6(9) requires the Commission to present the outcome of the examination procedure within five months to the committee provided for under the Regulation, unless it concerns a complicated case when the period may be extended to seven months.
See also Art. 11. According to this Article decisions regarding measures to be taken or regarding termination of the procedure are, if taken by the Council, to be adopted within thirty days of receipt of the required Commission proposal.
See finally Art. 12. No time limits are laid down for Commission decisions foreseen in this Article. Commission decisions can be referred to the Council within ten days for revision. The Commission decision applies if the Council has not taken a decision within thirty days after referral.
129. See further *infra*.
130. Art. 13. Furthermore the Regulation is to act as a complement to the instruments of the CAP and those applicable to processed agricultural products.

examination procedure is justified, have been the object of some debate. It concerns mainly four aspects;
- the representation requirement
- the required evidence of injury
- the required evidence of the existence of an illicit commercial practice
- and lastly, the required Community interest involved.

The complaint concerned can be lodged by a natural or legal person as well as by an association not having legal personality as long as either is acting on behalf of a Community industry considering itself injured by the alleged illicit practice.[131] In Article 2(4) the term 'Community industry' is defined as *'all* Community producers,
- of products identical or similar to the product which is the subject of illicit practices or of products competing directly with that product, or
- who are consumers or processors of the product which is the subject of illicit practices',

Alternatively, the 'Community industry' may be formed by
- 'all those producers whose combined output constitutes *a major proportion* of total Community production'.

This (*i.e. the representation requirement*) looks like a formidable requirement particularly for smaller producers, as it either requires mobilisation of a larger part of the Community producers of the product concerned or of the branch organization. When there are few producers (or only one as was the case in the first complaint submitted under this Regulation)[132] the requirement may of course be less demanding. However, as Article 2(4)b has it the producers of a *region* of the Community also qualify if their output of the product in question constitutes *the* major proportion (*cf. a* major proportion if total Community production is involved) of the output of the Member State(s) within which the region is situated. Consequently the same applies to an association acting on behalf of those producers. The additional requirement made for regional application is that, if it concerns imports, the effect of the illicit practice is concentrated in the Member States of the region. Where it concerns a case involving Community exports it is required that a significant proportion of the output of the producers in the region is exported to the country maintaining the illicit practice. From the above it would seem obvious that the representation requirement may be more onerous for undertakings located in big Member States than for those in the smaller ones.[133]

The complaint lodged is to contain sufficient *evidence of* the existence of *an illicit commercial practice*. If applied very strictly this requirement can be a difficult one to fulfil, particularly where it concerns third country government's practices favouring local competitors. However, the wording of Article 3(2) leaves sufficient latitude for an interpretation in line with the purposes it serves *i.e.* justification of the opening of an examination procedure. The evidence

131. Art. 3(1).
132. OJ 1986, C25/2.
133. *Cf.* Bronckers *loc. cit.*, n. 125, at 735, Bronckers, Ter Kuile and Steenbergen, *loc. cit.*, n. 125, at 606 *ff.* and 642 *ff.*

justifying trade measures on the outcome of the procedure is to be, of course, of an entirely different nature and quality.

The complaint should also provide *proof of material injury* resulting from the illicit practice. The exchange of sensitive information between competitors brings with it a certain danger of exposure to charges of concerted practices.[134] In cases of direct complaints, the Commission, which receives the complaint, might therefore consider to be satisfied with proof of injury suffered by the submitting producer if the latter can show to have an average cost structure and competitive position compared to the Community or regional industry as a whole, as the case may be.[135] In general it can be said that the wording of the requirements put on private party complaints leaves sufficient room for a 'creative interpretation' in order to allow the Commission to entertain complaints by private parties. In this respect it should be emphasized that it concerns here the requirements of the *opening* of the examination procedure. This procedure allows for trade policy decisions by the Commission later on in the procedure. The admission of complaints is not bound to hard and fast rules although certain limits have to be respected. Commission decisions regarding complaints can be appealed to the Court of Justice like all procedural decisions under this Regulation and Regulation No. 2176/84 on anti-dumping and countervailing measures.

The *Community interest requirement* figures in two places in both procedures open under the Regulation. Firstly, this requirement is, obviously, to be fulfilled for the adoption of commercial policy measures whether taken to respond to an illicit commercial practice (Article 10(1)a) or to ensure full exercise of the Community's rights (Article 10(1)b). This is fully in line with the other procedures for the application of trade policy instruments of the Community.[136]

However, unlike in the other procedures the Community interest requirement is also to be fulfilled for the *opening* of the examination procedure. This would point to the fact that the opening of the procedure may also have certain trade policy implications or other effects on commercial relations with third states, even to such extent that possible legitimate complaints are not examined. If the opening of an examination procedure is refused by the Commission, on the ground of lack of Community interest, the weighing of the possible effects of the opening of the procedure against the

134. *Cf.* Ter Kuile, *loc. cit.*, n. 125, at 643.
135. In cases of complaints lodged during a period of increasing exports to a particular third country engaging in an illicit practice, a *threat* of injury could arguable satisfy the injury requirement where not a significant proportion of the output of those producers forming the Community industry is exported to the third country concerned (Art. 24(b)ii). If the third country forms in principle an attractive and expanding market the threat of injury should suffice to have the complaint accepted as the illicit practice threatens to injure those producers *intending* to export. In the course of the examination procedure a more solid case can than be constructed for the taking of definitive action.
136. Stanbrook 'The Impact of Community Interest and Injury Determination on Anti-Dumping Measures in the EEC' in Hawk (ed.) *Anti-Trust and Trade Policy in the United States and the European Community*, Annual Proceedings of the Fordham Corporate Law Institute, 1985 (St Paul, 1986), pp. 623–640.

content of the complaint takes place even before the full facts of the case are known. A negative decision on such grounds should be taken only in cases of clearly foreseeable substantial damage to an important Community interest.

The various elements mentioned so far have been further defined in Article 2. *Illicit commercial practices* are (1) international trade practices attributable to third *countries*, (2) which are incompatible with international law *or* with the generally accepted rules.

Whether a practice *attributable* to a third country is the same as a practice *of* such country is not certain.[137] The first notion might be wider and include government induced and perhaps even government permitted or sanctioned practices of non-governmental bodies or private parties.[138] However, strictly non-governmental practices do not qualify under the definition.[139]

Regarding the incompatibility with international law;[140] international commercial law or international law in the field of trade is found mainly in international treaty law consisting of a great number of bilateral treaties and a number of multilateral treaties. The latter include GATT, the instruments adopted in the GATT context, or, for example, in the context of the Customs Cooperation Council. Thus the Regulation offers a procedure for complaints and decision making, including time limits, which can be used by private parties or Member States against practices of countries with whom the Community has bilateral treaty relations which (also) cover the field of trade. Article 10(2) in that respect stipulates adherence by the Community to any international obligation in the form of consultation or dispute settlement procedures. This applies also to Member States' complaints about the breach of GATT rules by GATT members, which means that the time consuming GATT consultation and dispute settlement procedures will become part of the procedure foreseen in the Regulation.[141] The notion 'incompatible . . . with *the* generally accepted rules' in Article 2, being part of the definition of 'illicit commercial practice', appears at first sight somewhat puzzling. Truly generally accepted (bodies of) rules of public international law, in the strict sense of the word, in the field of international trade are few, if any. The only groups of rules that spring to mind are the GATT Agreement and possibly a CCC convention. In this way the GATT is also set as a standard of conduct for commercial relations with countries with whom the Community has no general treaty relations in this field, like a number of the State-trading countries. As the Community possesses this possibility already, on the basis of Article 113 of the EEC Treaty the effect of the Regulation is also in these cases to create a decision making procedure for dealing with the cases covered.[142]

137. *Cf.* Steenbergen, *loc. cit.* n. 125, at 433.
138. *Cf.* Bourgeois and Laurent, *loc. cit.* n. 124, at 50.
139. *Cf.* Steenbergen, *loc. cit.* n. 125, at 425.
140. *Cf.* Bourgeois and Laurent *loc. cit.* n. 124, at 50, Hilf and Rolf, *loc. cit.* n. 124, at 299 and Steenbergen *loc. cit.* n. 125, at 424.
141. Art. XXII and XXIII GATT respectively, and the clauses contained in many other GATT articles and in the Tokyo Round codes.
142. For further examples see Hilf and Rolf *loc. cit.* n. 124 at 301 and Bourgeois and Laurent *loc. cit.* n. 124 at 52.

In this respect the question has been raised whether the rules, breaches of which constitute an illicit practice in terms of the Regulation, are to be directly effective in order to enable a private party to file an admissible complaint based on such rules.[143] In cases of breaches of obligations in bilateral agreements between the Community and third countries this does not in principle appear to form a serious obstacle as the Court of Justice has on various occasions declared such treaties directly effective.[144] However, in case direct effect is conditioned by the Court this would mean a virtual erasion of breaches 'of the generally accepted rules' as a basis for admissible private party complaints, as the Court has so far consistently refused to hold the GATT directly effective in Article 177 EEC cases referred to it by national courts. Whether direct effect will also be required by the Court in *direct* actions has so far not been decided. The Court should not impose such a condition in these cases as it is not the legality of a Community act which is at stake but merely whether the Community authorities may be required to open an investigation upon a private party complaint or to choose a course of action against an illicit practice if all other conditions are fulfilled. Even then the wide Community discretion will remain unimpaired because of its decision on whether the requirement of the Community interest has been fulfilled.

The second procedure provided for under the Regulation, which can only be started on request of a Member State or by the Commission itself, concerns 'ensuring full exercise of Community's rights with regard to commercial practices of third countries'.[145] The community's rights are in Article 2(2) defined as 'those international trade rights of which it may avail itself either under international law or under generally accepted rules'. This procedure in principle concerns the same rules the infringement of which constitutes an illicit practice for the purpose of the first procedure.[146] There are, however, two important differences. Firstly, a 'complainable practice' is in the Regulation described as being *of* a third country rather than being *attributable* to it as is the case in the Article 1(a) procedure as outlined above. This difference limits the scope of the second procedure to government practices only, in contrast to the first one. The second difference is the absence of an injury requirement for starting an investigation or for the taking of measures. This is consistent with the fact that it is not necessarily practices which are incompatible with international law or generally accepted rules which are involved. This may also explain the absence of a private right of complaint.[147]

Apparently, this provision is concerned in particular with Community

---

143. Steenbergen, *loc. cit.* n. 125, at 426.
144. Case 87/75, *Bresciani* (1976) ECR 129, Case 17/81, *Pabst & Richarz* (1982) ECR 1331 and Case 104/81, *Kupferberg* (1982) ECR 3641. For comments on these cases see: Bebr 'Agreements concluded by the Community and their possible direct effect: from International Fruit Company to Kupferberg' (1983) *CMLRev.*, 35–73 and Völker 'The Direct Effect of International Agreements in the Community's Legal Order', *LIEI* 1983/1, 131–145.
145. Art. 1(b).
146. Steenbergen *loc. cit.*, n. 125 at 433.
147. Steenbergen, *ibid.* p. 433.

participation in international commercial decision-making procedures like GATT dispute settlement procedures.

The examination procedure to be followed once a complaint has been accepted, resembles *mutatis mutandis* the procedure in anti-dumping and countervailing cases. The subsequent phase differs however in two respects; the measures available for action and the decision-making procedure. In principle, 'any commercial policy measures may be taken which are compatible with existing international obligations and procedures'.[148] As examples are listed the suspension or withdrawal of trade policy concessions, the raising of existing customs duties, and 'the introduction of quantitative restrictions or any other measures modifying import or export conditions or otherwise affecting trade with the third country concerned'. In other words, just about any legal means is open for usage by the Community as long as its main effects concern the trade relations with the third country involved.

The final decisions *i.e.* decisions regarding measures to be applied are taken by the Council, on a proposal by the Commission within thirty days,[149] with the exception of 'decisions relating to the initiation, conduct or termination' of international consultations or dispute settlement procedures.[150] The latter decisions are taken by the Commission.[151] The Commission decides also if no measures are to be taken, except where such decision results from adequate measures being taken by the third country who's practice is being examined. In the latter case either the Commission or the Council may decide.[152]

E. COMMON RULES ON EXPORTS

The common rules for the Community's exports are found in Regulation No. 2603/69 adopted by the Council on the eve of the end of the transitional period; 20 December 1969.[153] The system laid down by the Regulation is a fairly simple one. It consists of a basic principle concerning Community exports, the exceptions thereto, and rules regarding the adoption of protective measures.

148. Art. 10(3). Also in Art. 1 the reference to 'compliance with existing international obligations and procedures' is found. Garcia Bercero raises the question whether such direct reference to the international obligations of the Community would entail direct effectivity of the international rules concerned allowing private parties an opportunity of challenging Community measures incompatible with them: 'Trade Laws, Gatt and the Management of Trade Disputes between the US and the EEC', *Yb. of Eur. Law* (1985) 149–189, n. 31.
149. Arts 10(2)b and 10(3).
150. Art. 11(2).
151. Art. 11(2)a and Art. 12. The latter provides for reference of the Commission decision to the Council by a Member State for revision within 30 days. If no Council decision is reached within this period the Commission decision applies.
152. Art. 9(2)a: 'When, after an examination procedure, the third country or countries take(s) measures which are considered satisfactory the procedure *may also* be terminated in accordance with the provisions of Article 11', which provides for a decision by the Council.
153. Reg. No. 2603/69 establishing common rules for exports, OJ 1969, L324.

The basic rule declares all EEC exports to be free from quantitative restrictions.[154] Exceptions to this rule are threefold:
- the restrictions applied according to the procedures provided for in the Regulation, which concerns the use of safeguard measures;[155]
- the group of products for which the Council has not provided common rules so far, these products are listed in the Annex to the Regulation and in Article 10, as amended;[156]
- the restrictions applied by the Member States on the grounds of public morality, public policy, public security, or for the protection of public health or national treasures.[157]

The procedure for the imposition of safeguard measures on exports is roughly similar to that for imports. Differences concern, first, the grounds on which measures can be taken. These are (i) avoiding a shortage of essential products within the EC and (ii) fulfilment of international obligations particularly in relation to primary products.[158] Secondly, the Regulation provides for the possibility of discriminatory application of export quotas *i.e.* limitation of such measures to exports to certain third countries only.[159] In the preamble to the Regulation no references are found to GATT although there are certain obligations binding on the Communities and the Member States in the field of export restrictions, particularly as regards MFN-treatment and non-discrimination. Although in the first general import Regulation,[160] dating from the same period, extensive reference to Article XIX obligations was made, the preamble to the general export Regulation only includes a general reference to the Community's international obligations. The group of products listed in the Annex, and as such exempted from the application of the principle of freedom of export, comprises at present some thirty headings which is half of the number in 1969. The Court declared in the *Bulk Oil* Case[161] that Article 10 and the Annex form a 'specific authorization' of the Member States by the

---

154. *Id.* Art. 1.
155. The provisions regarding the imposition of protective measures on exports are found in Title III.
156. Art. 10: 'Until the Council, acting by a qualified majority on a proposal from the Commission, has introduced common rules in respect of the products listed in the Annex to this Regulation, the principle of freedom of export from the Community as laid down in Article 1 shall not apply to those products for the Member States mentioned in the Annex or to the following products for all Member States: . . .' (the products listed consist mainly of crude oil and certain oil products as well as 'petroleum gases' and certain products thereof).
157. Art. 11.
158. Art. 7(1). Since the inception of the Regulation the first ground – avoiding shortage of essential products – has been used to impose export restrictions on ashes residues and scrap of non-ferrous metals, of which at present only these for copper remain.
The 1982 system of voluntary export restraints applied by the Community to the export of steel products to the United States was, as far as applicable to EEC products, not based on Reg. No. 2603/69 but directly on Art. 113 of the EEC Treaty. This appears to be correct given the absence of a proper ground for such measures in the Regulation; see Regulation No. 2870/82 'on the restriction of the exports of certain steel products to the United States of America', OJ 1982, L307.
159. Art. 6(3).
160. Reg. No. 2041/68, JO 1968, L303.
161. Case 174/84, *Bulk Oil.* v. *Sun International* of 18 February 1986, not yet reported.

Community in the terms of the *Donckerwolcke* Case[162] despite the fact that the Annex contains no specification other than the CCT heading of the products concerned. It does not specify the circumstances in which national measures may be taken nor the object or purpose of such measures. Nor is the Member State, country of export or any other modality specified; in fact one wonders in what way the 'authorization' could have been less specific. Any Member State is thus authorized to take whatever measure it sees fit at whatever moment with respect to the products listed in the Annex. This situation is more akin to a system of concurrent competences than to an exclusive power in the hands of the Community as was established for the whole field of the Common Commercial Policy by the Court in the *Donckerwolcke* Case.[163] In this way the requirement formulated in the *Donckerwolcke Case* of a specific authorization by the Community for measures of commercial policy of a national character has been substantially weakened.

Article 10 and the Annex were amended by Regulation No. 1934/82.[164] Oil and gas (products) are no longer listed in the Annex but included in the Article itself, while next to each product in the Annex the Member State(s) is listed which still applies export quotas. For the export of oil and gas (products) *each* Member State can still apply national measures.

---

162. Case 41/76, *Donckerwolcke, supra* n. 71.
163. See the Annotations to the *Bulk Oil* Case of Feenstra in 1987 *SEW* 145 and Völker in (1987) *CMLRev*. 99–109. As discussed the Court held in this case that the *implementation* of a national policy which aims at imposing quantitative restrictions on exports is a measure of equivalent effect even if the policy itself is not incorporated in legally binding decisions. As such 'such a policy . . . does not escape the prohibitions laid down by Community law . . .'. Subsequently the Court declared the national policy measure to be authorized by the Community as the product involved (crude oil) was included in the Annex to Regulation No. 2603/69. According to the Court: 'Article 1 of Regulation No. 2603/69 lays down the general rule that exports from the Community to non-member countries are free, that is to say, not subject to quantitative restrictions, . . . Article 10 of the Regulation limits the scope of that principle on a transitional basis with regard to certain products, until such time as the Council shall have established common rules applicable to them; . . . It must therefore be held, . . ., that Article 10 . . . and the Annex to that Regulation constitute a specific authorization permitting the Member States to impose quantitative restrictions on exports of oil to non-member countries, and there is no need to distinguish in that regard between previously existing quantitative restrictions and those which are subsequently introduced.' (paras 32 and 33) 'The answer . . . must therefore be that Regulation 2603/69 . . . does not prohibit a Member State from imposing new quantitative restrictions or measures having equivalent effect on its exports of oil to non-member countries.' (para. 36) This might raise the question, as Feenstra points out, whether, with the coming into force of Regulation 2603/69, all national measures with equivalent effect as q.r.s which were *not* applying to products listed in the Annex were prohibited. If so, this would constitute a fundamental difference with the system applying to imports. In the *EMI* Case ((1976) ECR 811) the Court held '. . . the provisions of Reg. No. 1439/74 introducing common rules for imports, . . . relate only to quantitative restrictions to the exclusion of measures having equivalent effect.'
164. OJ 1982, L211.

F. ADMINISTERING QUANTITATIVE RESTRICTIONS

The procedures dealt with so far may lead to the imposition of either Community or national q.r.'s. The latter will be administered according to the procedures laid down under national law and might as such be subject to Community scrutiny under Article 19(3) of Regulation No. 288/82. The Community does not itself have at its disposal an administrative apparatus capable of administering Community q.r.'s *vis-à-vis* individual importers in the Member States. Regulation No. 1023/70[165] lays down a procedure whereby Community q.r.'s, established by the Council under the various Regulations discussed, are divided into national quota shares. The national quota shares are to be published in the Official Journal unless it is decided otherwise.[166] The Regulation lays down provisions for the administration of national quotas and the issuing of import or export licences, as the case may be, by the authorities of the Member States.

Certain aspects of the system provided for may lead to a repartitioning of the Community market along the lines of the national markets, *i.e.*:
– every Member State can refuse to honour applications for import or export licences of non-residents[167] and
– licences issued are only valid in the issuing Member State.[168]

Although these two provisions were planned to remain in force until 31 December 1972 at the latest they have so far not been replaced by the Council with a system more compatible with the requirements of the Common Market. In practice the procedure provided for in this Regulation is not often used. It appears that Community q.r.'s are split up over the Member States by the Council *ad hoc* by which different systems of allotment of the 'reserve quota' over the Member States which have 'spent' their shares are used. For the accompanying problem of the application of Article 115 authorizations to avoid parallel imports refer to the contribution by Timmermans in Chapter Five.

CONCLUSION

The Common Commercial Policy, as it stands at the moment, presents a divided picture. On the tariff side the common policy is more or less complete; outside the tariffs imposed by the Community, which together make up the Common Customs Tariff, no national tariffs remain (apart from the ECSC

---

165. Reg. No. 1023/70 establishing a common procedure for administering quantitative quotas, OJ 1970, L124.
166. *Id*. Art. 3.
167. Art. 14(2).
168. *Ibid*. A similar effect as that of the latter provision is created by requiring that all transactions made under licence shall be charged against the quota share of the Member State issuing the licence, as is done in Art. 6(3).

tariffs, in the formal sense). Compared to the internal market the difference which remains is the treatment of charges with equivalent effect, which are subject only to a standstill requirement and a case by case Community scrutiny. The relevant common customs legislation contains the necessary elements for the uniform application of the CCT.

As regards quantitative restrictions the picture is rather different. In the trade with non-State trading countries a certain amount of national quotas still exist. Amendments to those quotas are made by the Member States themselves, unless the Commission proposes a Community measure to the Council instead. New national measures can still be applied, if a safeguard clause in a national bilateral trade agreement makes this possible.

Liberalisation of the trade with the group of State trading countries is in general pitched at a much lower level than in the trade with non-State trading countries; many national quotas still exist, although there are substantial differences from Member State to Member State and between imports from individual State trading countries. Amendments of national quotas are laid down by the Commission, unless it concerns an urgent measure.

The position of measures with equivalent effect as quantitative restrictions is not yet clear; they are covered by Article 113 of the EEC Treaty but excluded from the application of the general import regulations, for the rest we are awaiting further rulings of the Court of Justice.

The legality of a number of major elements of the CCP in the light of certain GATT obligations is doubtful to say the least. This concerns in particular preferential trade policy measures (*e.g.* the agreements with the EFTA countries) and other bi-lateral policy measures such as passive and active voluntary export restraint arrangements as well as the remaining *national* trade policy measures. The latter, moreover, pose a constant threat to the unity of the Common Market since they form the basis for Article 115 authorizations by the Commission allowing Member States to exclude certain products from community treatment.

ANNEX I. REGULATION 3286/80 ON IMPORT ARRANGEMENTS IN RESPECT OF STATE-TRADING COUNTRIES

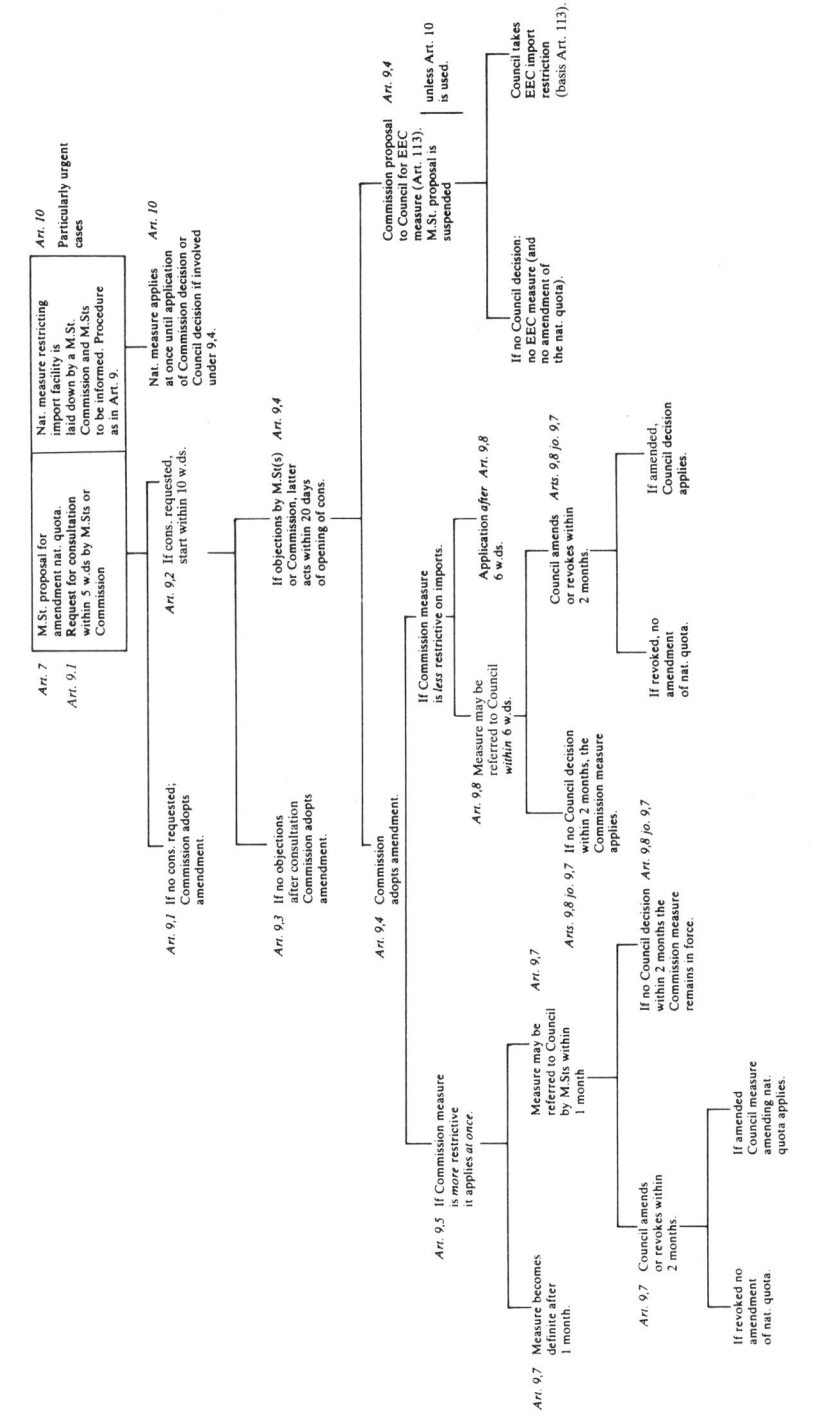

PROCEDURE FOR THE AMENDMENT OF IMPORT ARRANGEMENTS MAINTAINED BY THE MEMBER STATES: ARTICLES 7, 9 AND 10 OF THE REGULATION

Art. 7 / Art. 9.1: M.St. proposal for amendment nat. quota. Request for consultation within 5 w.ds by M.Sts or Commission

Art. 10: Nat. measure restricting import facility is laid down by a M.St. Commission and M.Sts to be informed. Procedure as in Art. 9.

Art. 10: Particularly urgent cases

Art. 9.1 If no cons. requested, Commission adopts amendment.

Art. 9.2 If cons. requested, start within 10 w.ds.

Art. 9.3 If no objections after consultation Commission adopts amendment.

Art. 9.4 If objections by M.St(s) or Commission, latter acts within 20 days of opening of cons.

Art. 9.4 Commission adopts amendment.

Nat. measure applies at once until application of Commission decision or Council decision if involved under 9.4.

Art. 9.5 If Commission measure is *more restrictive* it applies *at once*.

If Commission measure is *less restrictive* on imports.

Art. 9.7 Measure becomes definite after 1 month.

Measure may be referred to Council by M.Sts within 1 month

Art. 9.8 Measure may be referred to Council within 6 w.ds.

Application *after* Art. 9.8 6 w.ds.

Arts. 9.8 jo. 9.7 If no Council decision within 2 months, the Commission measure applies.

Art. 9.8 jo. 9.7 If no Council decision within 2 months the Commission measure remains in force.

Art. 9.7 Council amends or revokes within 2 months.

Council amends or revokes within 2 months.

Arts. 9.8 jo. 9.7 If amended, Council decision applies.

If revoked, no amendment of nat. quota.

If amended Council measure amending nat. quota applies.

If revoked no amendment of nat. quota

Art. 9.4 Commission proposal to Council for EEC measure (Art. 113). M.St. proposal is suspended

If no Council decision: no EEC measure (and no amendment of the nat. quota).

unless Art. 10 is used.

Council takes EEC import restriction (basis Art. 113).

ANNEX II. REGULATION 288/82 ON COMMON RULES FOR IMPORTS

PROCEDURE FOR THE AMENDMENT OF IMPORT ARRANGEMENTS MAINTAINED BY THE MEMBER STATES IN THE TRADE WITH NON-STATE-TRADING COUNTRIES: ARTICLE 20 OF THE REGULATION

Art. 20, sub 1   M.St. intention of change of nat. quota. Request for consultation by M.Sts or Commission within 5 w.ds.

In extremely urgent cases the nat. amendment applies at once and does not await consultation with Commission or M.Sts if requested.

Art. 20, sub 4   This emergency procedure can only be used where it concerns additional quota for not more than 20% of an exhausted quota.

sub 2,a & 2,c   Request for consult. within 5 w.ds. Consult. to start within 5 w.ds.

sub 2,b   If no consultation requested within 5 w.ds nat. measure becomes effective.

sub 3,a   If no objections remain after consult. nat. measure becomes effective.

If objections are raised.

sub 3,b   Commission proposal to Council for EEC measure (legal basis Art. 113) within 3 wks of start of consult.

sub 3,c   Nat. measure effective after three wks of start of consult.

Commission proposal adopted by the Council.

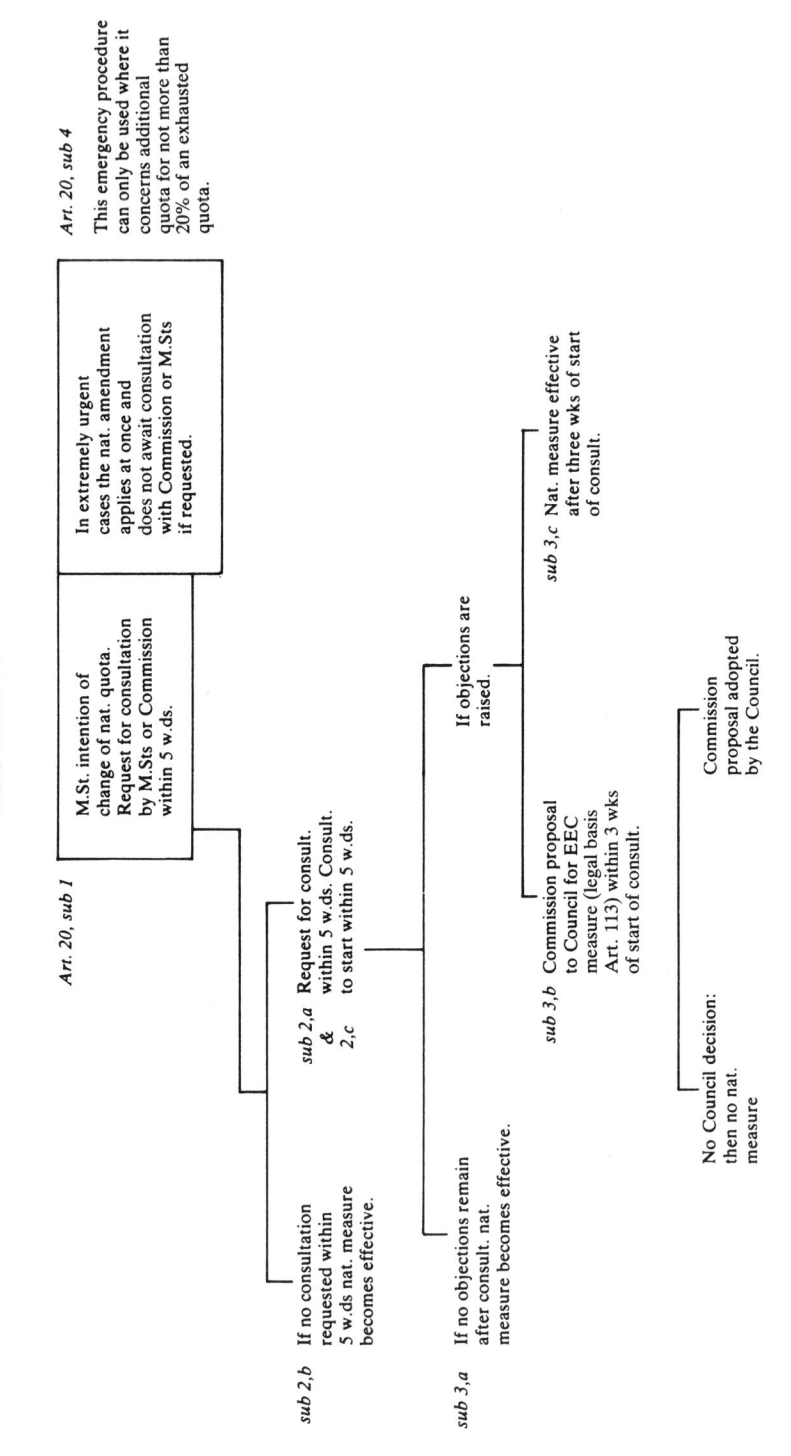

No Council decision: then no nat. measure

CHAPTER THREE

A LEGAL ANALYSIS OF PROTECTIONIST MEASURES AFFECTING JAPANESE IMPORTS INTO THE EUROPEAN COMMUNITY – REVISITED

By Marco C.E.J. Bronckers[*]

> 'Publicity is justly recommended as a remedy for social and industrial diseases. Sunlight is said to be the best of disinfectants; electric light the most efficient policeman' – Louis D. Brandeis, *Other People's Money* 92 (1914)

INTRODUCTION

Trade relations between the European Community and Japan continue to be strained. In the Community and elsewhere, the unrelenting inflow of Japanese goods is bringing increasing calls from national industries for protective measures. At the same time complaints about poor sales opportunities for European products in the Japanese market, and corresponding requests for retaliatory measures against Japan, are growing in volume and acerbity.

A notable response in the Community to such pressures has been a proliferation of trade restrictions. It is by no means easy, however, to judge the legality of existing restrictions on Japanese imports and to determine which authority is competent to impose new ones. What complicates matters is, first of all, the lack of a Community trade policy *vis-à-vis* Japan. The result is that with respect to Japan a whole array of both Community and especially national measures have been taken. A second complication is the paucity of information on trade restrictions affecting Japanese imports. The public at large, which is taxed by trade restrictions, often receives little or no pertinent information

---

[*] Member of the Rotterdam Bar.

from the EEC or national authorities about limitations on Japanese imports. That is particularly disturbing. It puts into doubt not only the legality, but also the propriety of these restrictions.

The purpose of this study is to set out the broad lines of the legal issues raised by protectionist measures affecting Japanese imports into the Community. First, an outline will be given of the development of trade relations between the Community of Twelve and Japan, within the context of GATT. An analysis of the authority under Community law to issue protective measures against Japanese imports within the EEC follows. We then examine generally the validity of the Community's trade restrictions on Japanese products in the light of the GATT. The next part inquires whether there are provisions in the Community's domestic legal order that secure compliance of EEC and national trade measures with GATT principles.

Complaints about trade barriers in Japan also spark protectionist pressures in the Community. In this connection we will discuss the pending GATT dispute settlement proceeding which the EEC initiated against Japan in 1982. The main complaint of the Community has been that Japan does not offer sufficient access to Community exports of manufactured products. A brief look at how the Community may approach new trade negotiations with Japan in GATT concludes this analysis.

Two preliminary remarks are in order:

1. This contribution does not discuss the application of anti-dumping and countervailing duties on imports from Japan. Such levies are applied to products of which the export price is distorted in one way or another. No further account is taken here of this phenomenon.

2. Nor does this study examine the compatibility of import restrictions on Japanese products with the ECSC and Euratom Treaties.

I. THE DEVELOPMENT OF TRADE RELATIONS BETWEEN THE EUROPEAN COMMUNITY AND JAPAN WITHIN GATT

Trade relations among over 100 countries are governed by the General Agreement on Tariffs and Trade (GATT), which dates from 1947, and by the permanent consultations within the GATT framework.[1] The twelve EEC Member States and Japan are also signatories to the GATT. Considerable difficulties were experienced, however, before the GATT rules were actually

---

1. GATT numbers 92 contracting parties. See GATT 32d Supp. BISD VIII (1986) (to which survey Hong Kong and Mexico should be added as new members). In addition, some 30 countries apply the provisions of the GATT on a *de facto* basis. Notably absent in the GATT are most of the communist countries. Recently, however, China has applied for membership and the Soviet Union has expressed an interest in participating in the upcoming GATT round of trade negotiations.

applied to relations between the Community and Japan. This chapter deals with the obstacles that for a long time separated the European and Japanese trading partners from each other. The GATT did not become operational in trade relations between the Community of Nine (as it then was) and Japan until 1975. In the meantime, the EEC had come to represent the individual Member States within GATT. We shall also deal briefly with this substitution.

A. BACKGROUND[2]

Most of the EEC Member States became GATT signatories at an early date and without any friction.[3] When, however, the signing of the Peace Treaty with Japan in 1951 was followed in the autumn of that year by approaches from that country, serious problems arose. Taking the lead from the United Kingdom, the Benelux countries and France, among others, opposed Japan's request to be allowed to attend GATT meetings as an observer. Their objections to Japan's full participation in international trade – objections still repeated under many different guises – were directed against allegedly aggressive Japanese competition in certain sensitive sectors. Frequent references were made to differences in labour relations, as a result of which Japan could charge keenly competitive prices for labour-intensive products (textiles, footwear, clothing, china and toys were cited as examples). Nowadays the Japanese are still condemned for 'attacks' on certain industries that play an essential part in the economies of many countries (such as steel, the car industry and shipbuilding), or would play a more important role if Japanese imports were not putting pressure on countries' own efforts (in such areas as electronics, *e.g.* chips; chemicals, *e.g.* pharmaceuticals; and high-tech machinery, *e.g.* energy-saving plants).

The opposition to observer status for Japan was of no avail, and in October 1951 the country was invited to attend GATT meetings in that capacity. Japan remained undaunted and nine months later formally applied to accede to the GATT as a contracting party. The feelings of disquiet, particularly among the European countries, came to the fore once more. The Europeans called for

---

2. The historical facts set out in the two sections which follow are taken partly from the authoritative and candid work by Gardner Patterson, who later became Deputy Director-General of GATT, *Discrimination in International Trade: The Policy Issues (1954–1965)*, 271–322 (1966). See also Lowenfeld, *VI International Economic Law (Public Controls on International Trade)*, 84–91 (1979).

3. The Benelux countries, France and the United Kingdom are among the original contracting parties to the GATT. Denmark, Germany and Greece joined GATT in 1950, Italy in 1951, Portugal in 1962, Spain in 1963 and Ireland in 1967. See the *Third Analytical Index (notes on the drafting, interpretation and application of the Articles of the General Agreement)*, 192–193 (3d rev. 1970).

far-reaching safeguard clauses to protect themselves against Japan's exports.[4] In order to break the deadlock that resulted, Japan requested in the autumn of 1953 that it be considered for 'temporary membership'. On this occasion too Japan was supported by the United States, which after the Second World War had become very involved in that country's recovery and had thus built special interests there. Finally a two-stage solution was decided on. Japan was invited to take part in the meetings of the GATT Contracting Parties, although without having the right to vote. Then a number of the contracting parties issued a declaration in which they stated that they were prepared to apply the GATT to Japan in anticipation of its accession.[5] Among the present-day EEC Member states, France and the United Kingdom refused to sign this declaration.

In July 1954, Japan announced that it wished to hold tariff negotiations with a view to formally acceding to the GATT. In the spring of 1955 seventeen of the Contracting Parties were in agreement on this. In mid-1955, all the contracting parties finally voted for Japan's accession to the GATT.[6] At the same time, however, fourteen contracting parties, which accounted for 40% of Japan's exports to all GATT signatories, invoked a provision of the General Agreement that made the GATT régime inapplicable in their trade relations with Japan. The following section deals with the application *vis-à-vis* Japan of this provision (Article XXXV) by countries which were to become members of the EEC.

B. RELIANCE ON AND ABANDONMENT OF GATT ARTICLE XXXV IN TRADE RELATIONS BETWEEN EEC MEMBER STATES AND JAPAN; BILATERAL AGREEMENTS OF MEMBER STATES WITH JAPAN

Article XXXV of the GATT stipulates that at the time a country accedes to the GATT, contracting parties may refuse to apply the Agreement in their trade relations with that country. As was to be expected, the Benelux countries, France and the United Kingdom invoked this provision, despite having voted for Japan's accession to the GATT. Although they could not oppose Japan's membership any longer, they did manage to limit the consequences of its

---

4. A number of contracting parties considered that Article XIX of the GATT (the most prominent safeguard clause) did not lay down clearly enough the permissibility of safeguards which affect the products of just one particular contracting party (in this case Japan). The controversy surrounding the (non-)discriminatory application of Article XIX was circumvented by a GATT working party, which had been instructed to study the problems concerning Japan's accession. See GATT Doc. L/76 (1953), discussed in Bronckers, *Selective Safeguard Measures in Multilateral Trade Relations: Issues of Protectionism in GATT, European Community and United States Law*, 19–20 (1985). The application of Article XIX GATT is examined below in Part III.B. 1 and 2.
5. See GATT, 2d Supp. BISD 30–32 (1954); Trb. 1966, Nos. 27 and 28.
6. The text of the Protocol of Accession for Japan is contained in GATT, 4th Supp. BISD 7–10 (1956); Trb. 1966, No. 35.

membership. From the outset, Japan endeavoured to gain true recognition as a GATT contracting party from the 'Article XXXV countries'. What seemed to matter most to Japan was removing an all too conspicuous prejudice. It did not so much object to the practices of many other GATT contracting parties that had not invoked Article XXXV but nevertheless continued to discriminate against Japanese imports.[7]

Japan was particularly displeased with the refusal by industrialized countries, including the future Member States of the EEC, to apply the GATT to its exports. When at the end of 1959 the Community of Six (as a customs union) opened negotiations under GATT Article XXIV(6) to adjust tariff concessions previously granted by the individual Member States, and also took part in the preparations for a new comprehensive round of GATT tariff negotiations (the Dillon Round), Japan went on the offensive. It warned that if France and the Benelux countries did not withdraw their recourse to Article XXXV, Japan would put a number of questions to the GATT Contracting Parties concerning the methods and legal implications of the Community negotiations with Japan. This was a reference to the anomaly that the tariff concessions Japan negotiated with four of the six Member States under GATT would not be protected by the GATT rules.[8]

To direct the strong feelings along positive channels, the Contracting Parties assigned the GATT Secretariat and a special working party the task of investigating the background to the recourse to Article XXXV vis-à-vis Japan.[9] An important conclusion of this study was that while most of the 'Article XXXV countries', including the four EEC Member States, did in fact give Japan most-favoured-nation treatment as regards tariff concessions, they reserved the right to impose discriminatory import restrictions on Japanese products.[10] The then Community of Six and Japan evidently settled their dispute over recourse to Article XXXV during the Dillon Round, because they actually did conduct tariff negotiations on that occasion. Formally, however, the EEC Member States relinquished their recourse to Article XXXV in respect of Japan only after several obstacles had been surmounted.

In 1961, agreement was reached on a multilateral textile arrangement which has since been extended and amplified several times.[11] Provision was made for bilateral agreements between exporting and importing countries designed to keep textile exports down, where necessary, to levels agreed on in advance as

7. The Federal Republic of Germany and Italy did not invoke Article XXXV against their former ally, but Italy in particular continued to discriminate against Japanese imports just the same. Patterson, *op. cit.*, n. 2, pp. 286–287.
8. See GATT Doc. L/1245 (1959).
9. Japan's request for these studies is reproduced in GATT Doc. L/1391 (1960). The results of the factual study by the Secretariat are contained in GATT Doc. L/1466 (1961). The working party's report is set out in GATT Doc. L/1531 (1961); GATT, 10th Supp. BISD 69–74 (1962).
10. See in particular paras. 4–5 of the working party's study. This study has been discussed in Dam, *The GATT: Law and International Economic Organization*, 349 (1970).
11. Patterson, *op. cit.* n. 2, p. 310 *et seq.* The Multifibre Arrangement, which also covers man-made fibres, was extended for another five years in August 1986. See the contribution of Van Dartel to this book, Chapter Four.

in 1951, importing countries were especially worried about an unrestrained flow of textile-imports from Japan. Not long afterwards the United Kingdom,[12] France[13] and the Benelux countries[14] abandoned their recourse to Article XXXV, having reached bilateral agreements with Japan regarding potentially discriminatory safeguard clauses that could affect only Japanese imports if applied.[15]

When Spain and Portugal acceded to the GATT in the early 1960s, they also invoked Article XXXV in respect of Japan. Both Spain and Portugal ceased to invoke this provision in the early 1970s,[16] well before they joined the European Community in 1986. While still applying Article XXXV GATT, Spain and Portugal negotiated bilateral trade agreements with Japan in 1966, authorizing them to maintain discriminatory import restrictions on Japanese products.[17] It is interesting to note that Japan apparently did not insist that Spain and Portugal abandon their recourse to Article XXXV, in exchange for these bilaterally negotiated discriminatory trade restrictions on Japanese exports. Interesting as well is the fact that, after Spain and Portugal did withdraw their claim to Article XXXV, they allowed their bilateral agreements with Japan to expire. The exact status of these agreements and of the discriminatory restrictions incorporated therein is rather controversial at the time of this writing (fall of 1986).

Lastly, mention should be made of a characteristic complication in the Community's trade relations with Japan. In late 1967 Ireland acceded to the GATT and had recourse to Article XXXV *vis-à-vis* Japan.[18] In 1974, after Ireland had become a member of the European Community, Japan succeeded in convincing that country that its recourse to Article XXXV could be withdrawn. Ireland, knowing itself to be bound by the exclusive powers of the Community in external trade relations,[19] put the question before the Commission. The Commission felt that it would be inopportune at that

---

12. GATT Doc. L/1992 (1963); subsequently the United Kingdom abandoned its recourse to Article XXXV with respect to certain overseas territories. GATT Doc. L/2208 (1964); Doc. L/2896 (1967).
13. GATT Doc. L/2129 (1964).
14. GATT Doc. L/2308 (1964).
15. See the First Protocol to the Treaty of Commerce, Establishment and Navigation between the United Kingdom and Japan dating back to 1962; discussed in Patterson, *op. cit.*, n. 2, p. 294–296. France and Japan included a similar safeguard clause in a protocol to their bilateral trade agreement of 14 May 1963; this protocol was elaborated in an 'interpretation' agreed upon on 30 March 1968. The link between the abandonment of recourse to Article XXXV and the agreement upon a bilateral safeguard clause is clearly set out in the Agreed Minutes to the 1960 bilateral trade agreement between the Benelux countries and Japan. Trb. 1960, No. 152; entered into force in 1962, Trb. 1962, No. 60. In 1963 the link was incorporated in a Protocol, Trb. 1963, Nos. 110–111; this came into effect in 1964, Trb. 1964, Nos. 166–167 (see also Trb. 1965, No. 2).
16. GATT Doc. L/3646 (1971) (withdrawal by Spain); GATT Doc. L/3690 (1972) (withdrawal by Portugal).
17. The agreement between Spain and Japan dates from 22 February 1966; that between Portugal and Japan from 29 July 1966.
18. GATT Doc. L/2954 (1967).
19. See text, *infra*, at n. 30 *et seq.*

moment for Ireland to withdraw its recourse without a *quid pro quo* from Japan.

Back in 1970 the Council had authorized the Commission for the first time to conduct negotiations with Japan with a view to concluding a trade agreement.[20] These negotiations were soon deadlocked, primarily because Japan did not want to grant the Community's request for a bilateral (discriminatory) safeguard clause for the entire Community.[21] The exchange of five Member States' safeguard clauses for a Community safeguard clause was obviously not sufficiently attractive for Japan. It would appear that the Commission entertained the hope for some time that in negotiations on the abandonment of Ireland's recourse to Article XXXV it could still persuade Japan to accept a 'selective' safeguard clause for the Community of Nine. This hope proved false however, and in the summer of 1975 the Council withdrew on Ireland's behalf the recourse to Article XXXV *vis-à-vis* Japan.[22]

This course of events also reflects that the Community replaced the individual Member States within GATT. The following section briefly discusses this substitution.

C. THE REPLACEMENT OF THE EEC MEMBER STATES BY THE COMMUNITY WITHIN GATT

The European Court of Justice decided that the Community replaced the Member States within GATT in several cases in which the validity of Community rules was contested by an appeal to the GATT. In its *Third International Fruit Company* judgment the Court upheld the view that, insofar as the EEC Treaty covered the field of application of the GATT, the Community had taken the place of the Member States at the entry into force of the Common Customs Tariff on July 1, 1968, and was bound by the GATT.[23] In the subsequent *Douaneagent* judgment the Court abandoned this reservation and accepted full Community substitution.[24] Most recently, the Court reasserted full Community substitution in the *SPI/SAMI* judgment.[25]

It may be asked whether the Court's judgments on full Community substitution in GATT do not require further qualification. A number of GATT provisions could be seen as extending beyond the Community's sphere of

---

20. See the *Fourth General Report* of the EEC Commission, point 448 (1970).
21. See the *Fifth General Report* of the Commission, point 460 (1971); *Sixth General Report*, point 437 (1972).
22. GATT Doc. L/4215 (1975).
23. Joined Cases 21–24/72, *International Fruit Company and others* v. *Produktschap voor Groenten en Fruit*, (1972) ECR, 1219 (para. 18).
24. Case 38/75, *Douaneagent der N.V. Nederlandse Spoorwegen* v. *de Inspecteur der Invoerrechten en Accijnzen*, (1975) ECR, 1439 (para. 21).
25. Joined Cases 267–269/81, *Amministrazione delle Finanze dello Stato* v. *Società Petrolifera Italiana SpA (SPI) and Spa Michelin Italiana (SAMI)*, (1983) ECR, 801 (para. 19).

competence, for example Articles XII (restrictions to safeguard the balance of payments), XV (exchange arrangements) and XXI (issues of national security). The counterargument, however, would be that whenever the EEC Member States want to resort to measures which are covered by GATT, those measures must be considered trade policy actions. And pursuant to Article 113 of the EEC Treaty the Community does have – exclusive – competence over any trade policy action taken in the EEC.

In any event, in practice the other GATT contracting parties recognize that the Community has assumed the duties and obligations of the individual Member States, even absent a formal decision or amendment to the General Agreement. The EEC therefore signed all the agreements drawn up during the Tokyo Round.[26] By the same token, if a GATT contracting party such as Japan were to object to Community or national trade measures of the Member States, it is the Community which would ultimately have to account for them to the GATT Contracting Parties. The Court explicitly confirmed this with respect to national measures in the *SIOT* Case.[27]

In this connection, finally, it should be mentioned that the Community has assumed exclusive competence over the external trade relations of its new Member States such as Spain and Portugal from the day of their accession. The transitional rules provided for in their Treaty of Accession do not delay this transfer of authority to Brussels.[28] Accordingly, any complaints Japan were to raise in GATT about (existing) trade-related measures of the new EEC Member States would have to be addressed to the Community.

II. THE PARADOX IN TRADE RELATIONS WITH JAPAN: COMMUNITY POWERS, NATIONAL MEASURES

Although the Community's powers in trade policy are incontestable, it is the protective measures taken by individual Member States against Japanese imports that matter. This paradox is a major feature of the Twelve's trade relations with Japan and is the starting point for the following analysis. We shall

---

26. Notwithstanding protests from the Commission, the Member States too signed the Codes on Technical Barriers to Trade and on Trade in Civil Aircraft, since certain governments did not consider the matters governed by these Codes to be under sole Community jurisdiction. See the reply by the Commission to Parliamentary Questions Nos. 1444/79 (OJ 1980, C105/31) and 1689/79 (OJ 1980, C137/35). See also Steenbergen, 'De Tokyo Ronde', 28 *SEW* 1980, 752 *et seq.*, at 764–765.

27. Case 266/81, *Società Italiana per l'Oleodotto Transalpino (SIOT)* v. *Ministero delle Finanze et al.*, (1983) ECR, 731 (para. 28). See, *e.g.*, the disposition in GATT of Hong Kong's complaint about quantitative restrictions maintained by France on quartz watches and a number of other products. GATT, 30th Supp. BISD 129 (1984).

28. See Articles 177 *et seq.* (with respect to Spain) and Articles 364 *et seq.* (with respect to Portugal) of the Treaty of Accession. OJ 1985, L302/9.

first look generally at the problems that have arisen in the exercise of the Community's powers in relations with Japan. We shall then examine whether national restrictions on Japanese imports are in conformity with Community law; the restrictions on imports of Japanese cars will serve as an illustration. Lastly, we shall discuss the legal instruments available to the Community, and in particular to the Commission, for creating a genuine Community trade policy *vis-à-vis* Japan.

A. COMMUNITY POWERS BUT NO POLICY ON TRADE RELATIONS WITH JAPAN

Whereas in other spheres of external relations it is far from self-evident that the Community has exclusive powers – indeed in some cases this can be only judicially pronounced[29] – the *Donckerwolcke* judgment[30] removed all doubts that the Community has had sole powers in commercial policy since the end of the transitional period (31 December 1969). The Court nevertheless acknowledged in that same judgment that the Community's commercial policy had at that stage not yet been fully established. Although there has been progress in the creation of the Community commercial policy, it is still incomplete. Apart from the application of tariffs, trade relations with Japan in particular have hitherto been governed largely by national measures.

According to the *Donckerwolcke* judgment the Community must grant specific authorization for all national measures that come under the heading of commercial policy; this requirement the Court deduced from Article 113 of the EEC Treaty.[31] Consequently, in order to assess the legality of national measures affecting trade with Japan, two[32] questions must be considered. Does the measure come within the scope of Article 113 of the EEC Treaty? If so, is it expressly covered by a Community authorization?

1. THE SCOPE OF ARTICLE 113 OF THE EEC TREATY

Frictions with Japan centre on the Community's considerable and growing deficit of trade in goods with this country (ECUs 18 billion in 1985, ECUs 10.9

---

29. Thus, the Latin adage *in foro interno, in foro externo* acquired, in hindsight, new significance in the famous *AETR* judgment. (Case 22/70), (1971) ECR, 272.
30. Case 41/76, *Donckerwolcke* v. *Procureur de la République*, (1976) ECR, 1921 (para. 32).
31. Recently, the Court again cited this decision approvingly in Case 174/84, *Bulk Oil* v. *Sun Oil*, 18 February 1986, not yet reported (para. 31) (this recent judgment suggests that the Court is inclined to construe its 'specific authorization' requirement rather liberally).
32. In this Part only the conformity of national measures with Community law as such is discussed. Part III.B contains an examination of the compatibility of national restrictions on Japanese imports with GATT law.

billion in the first half of 1986; both figures for the Community of Twelve). Some might characterize these frictions as a trade policy problem and expect the Community to play a central rôle in resolving them, since it enjoys exclusive competence over trade policy by virtue of Article 113. That analysis, however, wrongly suggests that the principal remedy to reduce the deficit is to take trade policy action against Japan (*e.g.*, import restrictions on Japanese products imposed by the EEC to protect European industries and/or to retaliate against Japanese trade distortions).

There are various factors that contribute to the trade deficit. Consider for instance the differing macro-economic policies adhered to by Japan and by its trading partners[33] or the relative lack of competitiveness of certain European industries. To the extent there are governmental instruments to influence these factors, they are available to the Member States. Without an economic (*e.g.*, fiscal and monetary) policy of its own, the Community cannot effectively participate in the continuing international discussions on Japan's economic environment. Furthermore, government support to increase the competitiveness of European industries by and large is a matter for the Member States, not the Community (consider, *e.g.*, tax régimes, export credits and guarantees).[34]

Nevertheless, it is clear that many in the Community consider import restrictions a suitable means to reduce the trade deficit with Japan. Pursuant to Article 113 of the EEC Treaty such defensive trade policy action falls within the preserve of the EEC institutions. Yet even on this defensive side the Member States have retained the initiative.

First of all, some Member States have resorted to actions reducing Japanese imports, which actions are arguably incompatible with Community law. Notable examples are the voluntary export restraints (VERs) on Japanese cars which government officials of Belgium, allegedly on behalf of the Benelux, and Germany negotiated with the Japanese government in 1981. As a result of these arrangements, which typically were never published, Japan froze its 1981 car exports to the Benelux at the 1980 level. With respect to Germany it appears that the Japanese government agreed not to allow car exports in 1981 to rise by more than 10% compared to the volume shipped in 1980.

The Commission has repeatedly asserted that since the end of the transitional period the Member States are no longer authorized to take protective measures independently or to elicit and then accept 'voluntary export restraints' (VERs). This would hamper, if not cut across, a Community policy regarding such measures, contrary to Article 113 of the EEC Treaty. In

---

33. See generally Saxonhouse, 'Japan's Intractable Trade Surpluses in a New Era', 9 *World Economy* 1986, 239.

34. One way in which the Community seeks to reinforce European industrial competitiveness, on a relatively limited scale, is by sponsoring common research and development projects such as ESPRIT (information technology), BRITE (basic technological research and application of new technologies), and RACE (advanced communication technologies). See OJ 1984, L67/54 (ESPRIT); OJ 1985, L83/8 (BRITE), and OJ 1985, L201/24 (RACE).

the Commission's view, those Member States that have negotiated safeguard clauses in bilateral agreements with Japan also can no longer take independent action against imports from that country.[35]

The Commission did not, however, take any steps against the VERs on car exports which the Benelux and Germany negotiated with Japan in 1981. That is not all that surprising. In challenging these VERs the Commission might have scored points on the principle of Article 113, but would probably have lost credit with Member States. Suggestions that the Commission was currying favours with Japanese interests in discouraging the national VERs could well have damaged its image, since the prevailing political climate in the Community at that time supported restrictive action against Japanese car exports.[36]

2. THE LACK OF AN ALL-EMBRACING COMMUNITY TRADE AGREEMENT WITH JAPAN; BILATERAL AGREEMENTS OF THE MEMBER STATES

For the most part the Community has until now had to content itself with periodical authorizations to extend the periods of validity of the trade agreements concluded by Member States with Japan. This Community authorization covers the safeguard clauses which the Benelux countries, France and the United Kingdom agreed with Japan in the early sixties (discussed above, in Part I.B).[37] It also covers a bilateral trade agreement between Germany and Japan of 1960 (without a safeguard clause), and 'agreed minutes' between Italy and Japan of 1969 (without a safeguard clause, but incorporating various mutual trade restrictions).[38]

The only formal bilateral trade agreement negotiated and concluded with

---

35. The most concise expression of the Commission's thoughts on this issue is to be found in an unpublished transcript of a verbal communication of the late Th. Hijzen, at that time Director-General for External Relations of the Commission, during a meeting of the Second Committee of Permanent Representatives on 17 June 1976 (commonly referred to as the 'Hijzen Statement'). See also, *infra*, text at n. 65.

36. Thus in May 1981, barely a month before Belgium and Germany negotiated their VERs, the Council had noted with approval the Commission's intention to begin discussions with Japan on the unilateral restriction of car exports to the Community. Bull. of the EC 1981, No. 5, 1.3.8.

37. Most recently, Council Decision 86/456/EEC (safeguard clauses of the Benelux and France), OJ 1986, L266/32; Council Decision 86/19/EEC (safeguard clause of the United Kingdom), OJ 1986, L29/26. This possibility of extension was established by way of derogation from the Council Decision of 9 October 1961 (see *infra*, n. 41) in Council Decision 69/494/EEC on the progressive standardization of agreements concerning commercial relations between Member States and on the negotiation of Community agreements. OJ 1969, L326/39.

38. See Council Decision 86/456/EEC, *id*. The 'agreed minutes' between Japan and Italy of 1969 apparently reflect the last of a series of confidential understandings envisaged by 'agreed minutes' of 1961, which in turn could perhaps be retraced to a commercial protocol signed by Japan and Italy in Rome on 18 October 1955.

Japan at the Community level is an agreement under the Multifibre Arrangement.[39] This agreement liberalized the importation from Japan of the categories of textile products coming under the Multifibre Arrangement as of 31 March 1977.[40]

The Community never wanted its role to be confined to giving passive approval to the national commercial policy instruments which the Member States present to it from time to time. At the very beginning of the transitional period the Council established a working programme for achieving uniformity in the commercial policies of Member States *vis-à-vis* other countries.[41] It did not, however, prove possible to implement fully by the end of the transitional period what in retrospect is seen to have been an ambitious programme.

From 1963 onwards the Commission urged that negotiations for a trade agreement be opened with Japan,[42] and finally in July 1970 it received the necessary authorization from the Council.[43] We have already noted that the actual negotiations became deadlocked after some time. On the Japanese side, major objections were raised to the inclusion in the agreement of a safeguard clause which resembled the bilateral agreements with the Benelux countries and France (and the United Kingdom). The bone of contention now was that the Community as a whole was seeking the possibility of taking selective protective measures against Japanese imports, without at the same time keeping competing products from other exporting countries off its market.

In 1973 it was decided to include these and other issues in the Multilateral Trade Negotiations (MTN), which were then starting under GATT auspices. As it turned out, however, the Tokyo Round failed to produce any agreement on a new Safeguards Code. While negotiations on a GATT Safeguards Code have continued and may intensify during the upcoming new round of GATT negotiations (see below, Part III.B.2), the proposals for an encompassing bilateral trade agreement between the Community and Japan were shelved.

---

39. The agreement was concluded by Council Reg. (EEC) 1989/76, OJ 1976, L219/1.

40. The following year imports from Japan of all textile products falling within Chapters 51 to 62 of the Common Customs Tariff (CCT) were liberalized as from 1 January 1978 by Council Reg. (EEC) 2127/77, OJ 1977, L248/1. In the Community the only restrictions which still officially apply to imports of Japanese textile products are a number of Italian quotas on certain articles of natural silk. See Chapter 50 of the CCT on List 1 annexed to the common import régime laid down in Council Reg. (EEC) 228/82, which is discussed in Part II.B.1.

41. Council Decision of 25 September 1962, OJ 90, 5 October 1962, p. 2353/62. See also the Council Decision of 9 October 1961, OJ 71, 4 November 1961, p. 1273/61 concerning a consultation procedure for the negotiation of agreements concerning commercial relations between Member States and third countries and for changes in the state of liberalization in relation to third countries.

42. See the *Seventh General Report* of the EEC Commission, point 295 (1964).

43. Bull. of the EC 1970, No. 9/10, point 82 (p. 93).

3. THE 1983 EXPORT RESTRAINT ARRANGEMENT BETWEEN JAPAN AND THE EEC; THE COMMISSION'S AUTHORITY TO NEGOTIATE VERs

Quite recently, in February of 1983, Japan agreed for the first time to restrain exports of 10 products to the Community as a whole (rather than to Member States individually, as was Japan's customary practice). The product lines affected by this export restraint arrangement between the Japanese government and the EEC Commission were videorecorders, colour TV tubes, cars, motorcycles, machine tools, light commercial vehicles, quartz watches, forklift trucks, colour TV sets and hi-fi equipment.[44]

In public the Commission has always remained secretive about the details of these VERs. It appears that they varied in nature, depending on the product involved. Thus the VERs on videorecorders and colour TV tubes allegedly were quite specific as to 'maximum' volume and 'minimum' prices, whereas the other restraint commitments were more loosely defined.

Publicly the EEC Commission did herald these VERs as a major breakthrough. It regarded their negotiation as a sign that Japan (as well as the EEC Member States!) had come to recognize that trade frictions ought to be resolved at the Community level.[45] With hindsight the Commission probably was too optimistic at that, because the VERs do not appear to have brought a Community trade agreement or policy *vis-à-vis* Japan any closer. Moreover, the economic success of the VERs is very doubtful. For instance, according to one recent estimate, the VER on videorecorders (the most prominent of the 1983 package) raised consumer prices in the EEC by at least 15% in the first year. At the same time, this VER did very little to protect the then fledgling European videoformat (V2000), which was subsequently abandoned by the Community's producers of videorecorders.[46]

Both the legality and the propriety of the 1983 VERs are questionable as well. It appears that the Commission did not seek or receive authorization from the Council to negotiate and agree on export restraints with the Japanese government. Yet Article 113 EEC Treaty prescribes that the Council must authorize the Commission to open negotiations on trade agreements with third countries; and it is the Council which concludes such trade agreements pursuant to Article 114 EEC. The decisive issue here of course is whether export restraint arrangements constitute a trade agreement within the meaning of these Treaty provisions.

In this as well as in other cases the Commission has characterized VERs as a unilateral measure taken by the exporting country. Yet that argument often is not convincing, because the pressure to restrain trade through VERs usually originates from – negotiations with – the importing country. The duplicity of characterizing VERs as a unilateral measure of the exporting country was

44. Bull. of the EC 1983, No. 2, at 8–11.
45. Wyles, 'Brussels jubilant on Japan deal', *Financial Times* of 15 February 1983, at p. 4.
46. See generally Hindley, 'EC Imports of VCRs from Japan: A Costly Precedent', 20 *J. World Trade L.* 1986, 168.

highlighted in the *Korean stoneware* Case. In that Case the Commission first claimed that a Korean commitment to restrain exports was a unilateral measure. Subsequently, however, the Commission authorized complementary, national restrictions on intra-Community trade of Korean stoneware; its authorization could only be justified if the Korean VER constituted a trade agreement with the Community.[47]

Assuming that the 1983 VERs of Japan represented a trade agreement which the Commission negotiated without the Council's prior fiat, one can still think of arguments favouring their legality under Community law. The VER on videorecorders might have been portrayed as a 'settlement agreement', prompted by the antidumping complaint of Philips and Grundig against their Japanese competitors.[48] Furthermore, without making any distinction between the different VERs, it is conceivable that the Council would have formally sanctioned the Commission's initiative on the basis of Article 114 after the fact. Alternatively, the Commission might have argued that it has independent authority to negotiate agreements with third countries restricting exports to the EEC. Because the latter argument potentially offers the most extensive legal basis for the Commission to negotiate VERs, it merits closer examination.

Under the Community's import régime (Council Regulation (EEC) 288/82) the Commission is empowered to impose quotas unilaterally in order to safeguard a Community industry against increasing import competition.[49] On various occasions the Commission has taken the position that its authority to impose quotas unilaterally includes authority to negotiate VERs with third countries. According to the Commission this is justified because it considers VERs a lesser evil (in that they are less binding on exporting countries) than unilateral restrictions. Its view seems to have been endorsed by the Court in the *First Dürbeck* Case.[50] It is not persuasive, however.

---

47. This issue turns on an interpretation of Commission Decision 80/47/EEC, OJ 1980, L16/14, implementing Article 115 of the EEC Treaty. See Van Dartel, 'De Algemene Invoerverordeningen van de EEG', 32 *SEW* 1984, 406 *et seq.*, at 420.

48. At the request of Philips and Grundig the Commission initiated an antidumping investigation concerning imports of Japanese videorecorders in December 1982. OJ 1982, C338/27. Subsequently, Philips and Grundig withdrew their complaint, following the VER on videorecorders negotiated in February 1983. Thereupon the Commission terminated the antidumping investigation in March 1983, OJ 1983, L86/23. In this decision the Commission did not characterize the VER as an 'undertaking', a settlement agreement within the meaning of the antidumping regulation (compare art. 10 of the current antidumping regulation, Council Regulation (EEC) 2176/84; OJ 1984, L201/1). Rather, it referred to the 'unilateral' decision of Japan to moderate the quantities and to institute a system of 'floor prices' regarding exports of videorecorders.

It is doubtful whether the Commission (if it had so desired) could have justified the VER on videorecorders as a 'settlement agreement'. For instance, the combination of price revisions and quantity limitations set forth in the VER is not envisaged by the antidumping regulation. See Van Bael & Bellis, *International Trade Law and Practice of the European Community*, 102 n. 18 (1985).

49. Art. 15 of Council Regulation (EEC) 288/82, OJ 1982, L35/1. See also the contribution by Völker on this point, Chapter Two.

50. Case 112/80, *Dürbeck v. Hauptzollamt*, (1981) ECR 1095 (para. 39). See Sack, 'The

This view ignores that VERs, contrary to unilateral trade restrictions, escape international discipline in GATT (discussed below, in Part III.B.2). Moreover, most VERs are not subject to domestic scrutiny either. Very frequently the details of VERs, such as the 1983 package negotiated with Japan, remain secret. The affected consumers as well as the public at large in the EEC can only guess at their objective and effect.[51] These aspects make VERs particularly troublesome and tend to create more 'evil' than do publicity and legal discipline surrounding unilateral trade restrictions. The fundamental question regarding the Commission's exercise of safeguard authority of course is not the extent to which it forces third countries to reduce their exports (through more or less binding measures), but whether the Commission should have sought export reductions to begin with. When the Commission resorts to VERs, Community nationals all too often cannot answer this question. Interest groups other than the particular domestic producer which benefits from a VER are prevented from influencing or challenging the Commission's judgement. That taints any attempt to legitimize independent forays of the Commission into VERs.

Obviously the same criticism applies to all VERs that are negotiated outside regular, predetermined procedures (*e.g.*, VERs negotiated by EEC Member States). Proper procedures at least should encourage opposing interests to make their case for or against import reductions – which amount to taxation of the public at large for the benefit of particular domestic producers. There may be political justifications for redistributing welfare through the negotiation of a VER, but welfare redistribution ought not be left to the untrammeled discretion of administrative authorities. Consider in this connection a rather unfortunate statement of the Commission that it is not prepared to make any cost-benefit analyses, showing *inter alia* the (price) effects on consumers, of the trade restrictions which the Community maintains in various industrial sectors (among others the videorecorder sector where the Commission negotiated a VER with Japan).[52]

With respect to trade restrictions that may be adopted following formalized investigation procedures (*e.g.*, in antidumping and countervailing duty actions), such cost-benefit analyses conceivably could be undertaken by private interest groups that oppose these measures. Yet even here there is merely a possibility that private parties are able to finance and compile a

---

Commission's Powers under the Safeguard Clauses of the Common Organization of Agricultural Markets', 20 *CMLRev* 1983, 757 *et. seq.*, at 763–764.

51. In response to Parliamentary Question No. 214/85 the Commission gave a broad overview of the existing export restraint arrangements which the Community concluded with third countries. OJ 1985, C341/5. Though commendable as a first step, this response is still much too vague to afford the public any insight into the goals, operation and effects of VERs.

52. See answer of the Commission to Parliamentary Question No. 1289/84. OJ 1985, C113/4. Thus the Commission seems to oppose a major recommendation of the important Leutwiler report *'Trade Policies For A Better Future'* (Geneva 1985), drawn up by seven outside experts at the request of the GATT's Director-General. The Leutwiler report, at p. 35, proposes that in each country the costs and benefits of trade policy actions, existing and prospective, should be analyzed through a 'protection balance sheet'.

comprehensive analysis. This possibility does not absolve the Community authorities of their independent responsibility to gauge and publish the effects on the economy as a whole whenever they resort to trade restrictions. If there is any justification for governmental trade restrictions, including VERs, they should be able to withstand the scrutiny of the public and the taxpayer.[53]

Meanwhile, the 1983 export restraint arrangement with Japan (or rather, the Commission's interpretation of this arrangement as a unilateral measure taken by Japan) remained undisputed in the Community. The VERs appear to have expired in December 1985. Since then the Japanese authorities have continued to express their intention to moderate exports generally and to supervise exports of sensitive products to the Community.[54] The EEC on the other hand unilaterally raised the customs duty on imports of videorecorders from 8% to 14%,[55] and maintained surveillance of imports of most of the products covered by the 1983 VERs.[56]

B. NATIONAL RESTRICTIONS ON JAPANESE IMPORTS

Currently, there are no unilateral Community restrictions on Japanese imports in force (other than regular tariffs or antidumping duties). The lack of a Community trade agreement with Japan provides only a superficial explanation; the true cause lies deeper.

The Community has been unable to define a common approach to what is seen as the 'Japanese problem'. There are too many conflicting interests and viewpoints among Member States which cannot be reconciled at the Community level. Still, it must be acknowledged that, largely at the Commission's instigation, Community strategies are being contemplated.[57] Regular high-level consultations are held between Community and Japanese delegations. These steps, however, have not yet produced any concrete results in terms of the abolition or at least the standardization of unilateral national restrictions on imports of Japanese products.

National restrictions on Japanese imports with which an interested party is

53. 'A major reason why things have gone wrong with the trading system is that trade policy actions have often escaped scrutiny and discussion at the national level. Clearer analysis and greater openness in the making of trade policy are badly needed . . .'. Leutwiler report, *id.*, at p. 35.
54. Answer of the Commission to Parliamentary Question No. 2011/85, OJ 1986, C150/7.
55. Council Reg. (EEC) 3679/85, OJ 1985, L351/2. This is discussed below, in Part III.B.3.
56. Council Reg. (EEC) 130/86. OJ 1986, L18/21.
57. See notably the Commission's recommendations in COM (86) 60 final, and its more analytical and historical survey of EC–Japanese trade relations in COM (85) 574 final. The latter document is discussed in Maillet, 'L'amélioration des relations économiques CEE–Japon: aux Européens de jouer', 29 *Revue du Marché Commun*, 1986, 3.

See also the Moorhouse-report on commercial and economic relations between the Community and Japan drawn up on behalf of the European Parliament's Committee on External Economic Relations, Doc. A2-86/86.

confronted can take two forms. A Member State can limit direct imports from Japan at its national frontiers; it can also restrict indirect imports of Japanese products via another Member State by means of intra-Community restrictions. The legal grounds for these two kinds of restrictions will be examined below.

1. NATIONAL RESTRICTIONS ON *DIRECT* IMPORTS OF JAPANESE PRODUCTS: REGULATION (EEC) NO. 228/82

Imports of industrial products into the Community from other countries are governed by Council Regulation (EEC) 288/82, establishing the Community's common import régime.[58] Völker analyzes this Regulation in Chapter Two of this book. His analysis shows how the Community authorities (*i.e.*, the Council or the Commission) could take trade restricting action against Japan. Here we will only highlight the national restrictions permitted under the common import régime, since these are of particular relevance to the trade with Japan.

As a matter of principle, the importation of foreign industrial products into the European Community is free of quantitative restrictions. Yet there are exceptions to this rule, both on the Community and national levels. In several ways the common import régime, either implicitly or explicitly, allows Member States to impose new or retain old trade restrictions.

a. A *'negative list'* is annexed to Regulation (EEC) No. 288/82 of products that are subject to national, unilateral quantitative restrictions ('quotas').[59] The list merely mentions the existence of quotas, and provides few particulars. Though controversial, it is often assumed that these national quotas are compatible with Community law by virtue of inclusion in this list. This issue turns on whether the inclusion by the Council of national quotas in the 'negative list' represents an authorization which is specific enough to satisfy the Court's *Donckerwolcke* doctrine.[60]

The 'negative list' is considered to be exhaustive. Among others, it contains a number of references to national quotas which are exclusively directed at Japanese imports. Though these quotas may be compatible with Community law, they carry a presumption of illegality when viewed against the GATT's principles (see below, Part III.B.1).

Member States applying national quotas can change (*e.g.*, reduce) them, after notifying and consulting with the other Member States and the

---

58. OJ 1982, L35/1. The Regulation does not apply to imports from State-trading countries, China or Cuba, or to imports of textile products, since these are subject to special Community import arrangements.
59. A second list enumerates the Community's surveillance measures, subjecting imports to a licensing system. An update of this list and of the 'negative list', including the national quotas maintained by Spain and Portugal, was recently published in OJ 1986, C213/1.
60. See, *supra*, text at n. 30, and the analysis by Timmermans, Chapter Five.

Commission. They can also by independent decision expand a quota up to 20%.[61]

b. Under certain limited circumstances Member States can impose new quotas as an *interim safeguard measure*, should they decide that a national industry requires immediate protection against an increase in foreign import competition.[62]

Member States retain this interim authority until 31 December 1987 with respect to products that are subject to national quotas. Thus, until the end of 1987 Germany could impose a safeguard restriction on Japanese cars, because Italy for many years now maintains a quota thereon.[63] This authority applies to those Member States which have recourse to safeguard clauses in bilateral agreements, notably with Japan, without any time or product limitation. Accordingly, in view of their bilateral agreement with Japan, the Benelux countries could resort to safeguard restrictions on Japanese car imports even after 1987 (Germany cannot, because its commercial agreement with Japan does not contain a safeguard clause).

All interim restrictions imposed by a Member State, including those based on a bilateral safeguard clause, are subject to a Community authorization procedure.[64] That is a significant reflection of the shift in powers which occurred on 1 January 1970, when 'Brussels' assumed exclusive competence over the Community's external trade relations pursuant to Article 113 of the EEC Treaty. This shift in powers emerged only gradually. As late as 1973 the Benelux countries independently adopted safeguard measures against imports of a number of Japanese electronic products, without consulting the Community.[65] It was not until the *Donckerwolcke* judgment of 1976 that the consequences of the transfer of national responsibility for commercial policy to Brussels were clearly set out.

c. Without time or product limitations the Council has empowered the Member States to impose quotas on grounds of *public policy* (health, safety etc., including protection of intellectual property), foreign exchange formalities or formalities resulting from international agreements in accordance with the Treaty.[66] The unresolved issue is whether the Council's provision is declaratory (reflecting residual, independent powers of the Member States), or whether it is to be interpreted as a Community authorization of national commercial policy measures. This is discussed in Bourgeois' contribution, Chapter One under IV.

61. Art. 20 of Reg. (EEC) 288/82; see also Annex II of Chapter Two.
62. Art. 17 of Reg. (EEC) 288/82.
63. See, *infra*, text at n. 73.
64. Art. 17(4) of Reg. (EEC) 288/82.
65. See the Netherlands Official Gazette, the *Staatscourant*, of 12 April 1973, No. 73/1. The Benelux countries' import restrictions on Japanese imports of electronic goods are discussed in de Groot, 'Nieuw Protectionisme in Nederland', 46 *Maandschrift Economie* 1982, 156 *et seq.*, at 171–172; 16 *Euromarkt Nieuws* 1973, 120.
66. Art. 21 of Reg. (EEC) 288/82, which was recently amended by Council Reg. (EEC) 1243/86, OJ 1986, L113/1.

d. Aside from the actions permitted under *b.* and *c.*, the Member States can no longer unilaterally impose quotas on products for which importation into the Community has been liberalized, an exception being an Italian *'experimental list'*. Italy agreed to the liberalization of these listed products of Japanese origin only if it was empowered to (re)introduce quantitative restrictions on their importation under certain circumstances. The Council granted Italy's request by an unpublished decision of 25 May 1970. To date, Italy apparently has not made any use of these 'experimental' powers.

Italy may also refuse to authorize the importation, *e.g.* from Japan, of certain machinery and equipment which is in poorly maintained condition, whether used or new.[67] The Commission has no record that Italy ever invoked this provision.

e. The common import régime does not contain a prohibition of, or even a reference to *measures having equivalent effect* as quantitative restrictions. That would seem to leave leeway to the Member States to impose quota-equivalent restrictions on imports from third countries. Indeed, the Court has rejected several challenges to such national restrictions. In these cases the Court held that the Treaty's rules prohibiting measures having equivalent effect on intra-Community trade (Articles 30–36 EEC) cannot as such be transposed to relations with non-Member States, even if there is a directly effective bilateral trade agreement between the Community and a third country which contains similar provisions.[68]

While reviewing national measures having equivalent effect in these cases, the Court was not asked and did not inquire whether these measures were specifically authorized by the Community. Accordingly there is a tension between these cases and the Court's *Donckerwolcke* doctrine, since one ordinarily has to assume that national quota-equivalent restrictions are of a commercial policy nature and – hence – fall within the ambit of Article 113 EEC. It will not be easy to resolve this discrepancy, especially as long as the common import régime remains silent on measures having equivalent effect.

An interesting test-case occurred in October 1982, when the French government decided to change the customs clearance procedures regarding imports of videorecorders ('VCRs'). All VCR imports henceforth had to be transported several hundred miles inland to *Poitiers*, where they were funneled through a customs bureau staffed by only two inspectors who 'went by the book'. This move was prompted by French concern about sharply rising VCR imports from Japan. Within a matter of weeks 150,000 VCRs were held up in Poitiers.[69]

The Commission promptly initiated proceedings against France pursuant to Article 169 of the EEC Treaty.[70] In the Commission's view the change in

---

67. Art. 19(2) of Reg. (EEC) 288/82, as amended by Council Reg. 1243/86.
68. Cases 51/75, 86/75, 96/75, *EMI* v. *CBS*, (1976) ECR, 811 (paras. 20, 20 and 12 respectively); Case 225/78, *Procureur de la République Besançon* v. *Bouhelier*, (1979) ECR, 3151 (para. 6); Case 270/80, *Polydor* v. *Harlequin*, (1982) ECR, 329 (para. 19).
69. Ball, 'France's Risky Protectionist Fling', 107 *Fortune* 1983, 76–77.
70. Bull. of the EC 1982, No. 12, 3.3.2.

customs clearance procedures constituted a measure having equivalent effect as a quantitative restriction, in violation of France's obligations under the EEC Treaty. Interestingly, however, the Commission focused its infringement action on the barriers created by the French measure to intra-Community trade (*i.e.*, principally the imports of EEC-made VCRs). It relied exclusively on Articles 30–36 of the Treaty.

Conspicuously absent in its arguments was any reference to Article 113 of the EEC Treaty and to the effects of the Poitiers-measure on trade with third countries (*i.e.*, the imports of Japanese VCRs which had triggered the French ploy). The Commission may well have wanted to avoid the appearance of any association with Japanese interests. Similar concerns possibly explain why so far the Commission has never challenged national measures of equivalent effect which Member States apply to direct imports from third countries.

The Commission's reluctance to challenge the French restriction, to the extent it affected Japanese VCR imports, became even more pronounced in early January 1983. By that time the Poitiers-measure no longer applied to EEC-made VCRs. It continued to apply to Japanese VCRs, even to those that had first been imported into other Member States. Although this restriction on indirect imports of Japanese VCRs clearly infringed Article 30 of the EEC Treaty on which the Commission had originally based its action, it allowed the infringement proceedings against France to slow down.[71]

Ultimately, it was the French Poitiers-measure in particular which appears to have persuaded Japan to negotiate the VER on videorecorders with the Commission in February of 1983 (discussed above, in Part II.A.3).[72] Subsequently, France disassembled the Poitiers-operation and reverted to the usual customs clearance procedures for VCR imports. The Commission did not pursue its infringement action on the basis of Article 169 EEC against France.

Illustration: National Restrictions on Imports of Japanese Passenger Cars

The flow of Japanese passenger cars into the Common Market continues to receive much attention from the media and in political statements. (In 1985 846,000 Japanese units were newly registered in the Community of Ten, representing 9.5% of all new car registrations). We shall review the most important protective measures taken against Japanese car imports. It must be stated at the outset that imports of Japanese cars presently appear to be unrestricted in the Benelux, Denmark, Germany and Ireland. Greece no longer maintains formal import restrictions on cars, but Japanese exporters

---

71. Maresceau, 'The GATT in the Case-Law of the European Court of Justice' in *The European Community and GATT* (Hilf, Jacobs & Petersmann eds.), 113 (1986).

72. *E.g.*, statement of Masaaki Morita, Vice-President of Sony, cited in 'Sony over export-afspraken video: "In Europa zo snel mogelijk terug naar correcte situatie"', *Financieele Dagblad* of 19/21 March 1983, at 11.

have occasionally complained that the Greek authorities informally require them to assume countertrade commitments, obliging them to buy Greek products in exchange for import authorizations. In addition, Japanese exporters have encountered difficulties with the application of Greek type-approval requirements regarding cars.

(a) Italy's country-specific quota

Apparently in response to MITI's refusal in 1961 to allow Fiat in cooperation with Mitsubishi to market small passenger cars in Japan, Italy placed a quota of less than 1,000 units exclusively on imports of Japanese cars in the early sixties. Soon afterwards it became obvious that this quota, originally a retaliatory measure, conveniently served to protect the Italian car industry against Japanese import competition. Over the years Italy increased the quota only in driblets. For quite a long time no more than 2,200 Japanese cars could be imported into Italy. At the economic summit of seven industrialized countries, held in Tokyo in May 1986, Italy agreed to expand this quota to 3,300 units.[73]

This restriction was repeatedly acknowledged by the Community following the transitional period and is now to be found in the 'negative list' annexed to Regulation (EEC) No. 288/82 under CCT tariff subheading 87.02. The Italian restriction is therefore incontestable in Community law, if one assumes that the 'negative list' constitutes a specific authorization by the Community of these national quotas within the meaning of the Court's *Donckerwolcke* doctrine.

(b) Spanish and Portuguese global quotas

The 'negative list' indicates that both Spain and Portugal maintain global quotas on car imports from third countries (see CCT heading 87.02). As usual, the details have to be found elsewhere.

With respect to Portugal there is a specific Protocol regarding car imports from third countries attached to its Treaty of Accession to the Community.[74] This Protocol applies exclusively to countries with which Portugal does not have bilateral trade agreements (*e.g.*, it does not apply to its former EFTA-partners). The Protocol distinguishes between imports of fully assembled and knocked-down motor vehicles. Because Portugal favours local assembly of cars (also for the benefit of local parts producers) only very limited quantities of fully assembled cars may be imported from third countries.

---

73. By decree of 20 June 1986 the Italian government increased all its officially recognized quotas on Japanese imports by 50%. See *Gazzette Ufficiale* of 9 July 1986.
74. Protocol no. 23, OJ 1986, L302/463.

Knocked-down motor vehicles can, interestingly enough, be imported solely from Japan, because the Protocol stipulates quota shares (expressed in maximum import value) only with respect to Japanese car manufacturers. The Protocol is due to expire on 31 December 1987.

With respect to Spain there is no specific Protocol regarding car imports from third countries. Japanese cars can still be imported without restriction in the Canary islands and the two Spanish free ports in Northern Africa, Ceuta and Melilla. A different régime applies to the Iberian peninsula and the Balearic islands. Prior to Spain's accession to the EEC no Japanese cars could be imported into these territories. In May of 1986, however, Spain established a contingent allowing imports of 1,000 passenger cars from third countries during six months.[75] It appears that the largest share of this quota (900 units) was subsequently allocated to Japan, the remainder being divided mainly among Brazil and the United States. According to Spanish officials similar six-month contingents, perhaps slightly increased, will be opened in 1987.

(c) Measures introduced by France having an effect equivalent to import restrictions

France has never formally placed an import quota on Japanese cars, but it is a notorious fact that Japanese manufacturers' share of the market cannot exceed 3%. It is suggested that Japan 'voluntarily' limits its exports to France. The French authorities keep track of the situation themselves in any event by delaying, where necessary, the completion of customs formalities such as the type-approval procedures used to determine whether a given model meets certain technical requirements.[76] The fact that these type-approval procedures for cars have not yet been harmonized throughout the Community plays into the hands of the French.

From the point of view of Community law, France's policy is dubious if not illegal. If France's manipulation of the type-approval procedures could be termed a quantitative restriction, the infringement of Community law would be evident, since Regulation (EEC) No. 288/82 does not list a French import quota on Japanese cars. If, however, the French restriction is seen as a measure having equivalent effect, then its status under Community law is less clear.[77]

Apart from these considerations, the application of French customs formalities, such as type-approval procedures, to imports of Japanese cars can perhaps be construed as an infringement of a Community rule based on the

---

75. The global contingent was established pursuant to a Ministerial decree of 6 May 1986, published in the *Bulletin Official del Estado* of 19 May 1986.

76. For example, in the spring of 1981 it was reported that over 9,000 Japanese cars were awaiting clearance and type-approval in French ports. See the reports in *Le Républicain Lorrain* of 6 February 1981.

77. See text, *supra*, at n. 68.

Tokyo Code on Technical Barriers to Trade.[78] In view of the sparse information on the actual execution of French type-approval procedures, which makes it difficult to judge whether Japanese cars receive less favourable treatment compared to cars imported into France from other third countries, this potential legal challenge can merely be indicated here.

(d) Export-restraint arrangements between British and Japanese car industries; antitrust and government action

For years there have been informal arrangements between the British Society of Motor Manufacturers and the Japanese Automobile Manufacturers Association, limiting Japan's share of the UK car market to between 10% and 11%.[79] These arrangements undoubtedly have an effect on competition in the Community, and on first sight they appear to come within the scope of Article 85 of the EEC Treaty according to the interpretation given to this provision by the European Court of Justice[80] and the Commission.

In an interesting decision from 1975 concerning *Canned Mushrooms*, the Commission declared an export limitation agreement between Taiwanese and French producers of canned mushrooms to be in violation of Article 85 EEC.[81] The Commission was of the opinion that even if the French producers had reason to fear market disruption caused by an unrestrained increase of imports from Taiwan, this could not justify the export restraints they negotiated with the Taiwanese producers. It reserved to itself the exclusive right to take appropriate safeguard measures in those circumstances. Indeed, the Commission had imposed a safeguard measure against imports of canned mushrooms into the EEC six months before invalidating the producers' agreement, but a full year and a half after the conclusion of that agreement.[82]

The Commission handed down a similar decision in 1984, when it

78. The Code was published as an annex to the EEC Council Decision concerning the conclusion of the Tokyo Round negotiations. OJ 1980, L71/29. The Council then laid down implementing measures comprising provisions on the introduction and implementation of technical regulations and standards. Council Decision 80/45/EEC, OJ 1980, L14/36. See Bourgeois, 'The Tokyo Round Agreements on Technical Barriers and on Government Procurement in International and EEC Perspective', 19 *CMLRev.* 1982, 5.

79. See, *e.g.*, the article on p. 7 of the *Financial Times* of 28 May 1982, 'Japan car sales in UK agree with forecast', in which reference is made to a 'gentleman's agreement' between the British and Japanese car industry. Differences of opinion concerning the interpretation of this arrangement are being discussed at regular high-level meetings of industry officials. See the article 'Datsun protests about "distortion" of Japanese car import figures' on p. 11 of the *Financial Times* of 19 May 1982.

80. See Case 22/71, *Béguelin Import Co.* v. *G.L. Import-Export S.A.*, (1971) ECR, 949 (para. 11) (this concerned an exclusive dealing arrangement between a Japanese and Belgian/French firms); Case 71/74, *Frubo* v. *Commission*, (1975) ECR, 563 (para. 38); *EMI* v. *CBS, supra*, note 68 (paras. 28, 25 and 14 respectively).

81. OJ 1975, L29/26.

82. OJ 1974, L218/54 (this measure struck imports of canned mushrooms originating in all third countries, but since it was taken with a view to protect the French market in particular, it is safe to assume that imports from Taiwan were affected especially).

condemned a cartel agreement between Eastern- and Western-European traders and producers of *Aluminium* as violative of Article 85.[83] The objective of this agreement was to increase prices of aluminium exported from Eastern-Europe, among others through market sharing arrangements. One of the arguments used by participants to defend this cartel was that governmental measures, such as anti-dumping duties, would have been ineffective to protect the Western-European producers against low-priced ('dumped') imports of Eastern-European aluminium. The Commission flatly rejected this contention: 'The alleged impracticality of (trade) legislation is a matter for legislative correction and does not justify the making of restrictive agreements by undertakings.'[84]

Already in 1972 the Commission had sounded a warning note in an extraordinary opinion.[85] It advised those concerned that arrangements under which imports of Japanese products into the Community are limited or otherwise 'regulated' might well be prohibited by Article 85(1) of the EEC Treaty and recommended that these arrangements be notified to the Commission. The private UK–Japan arrangements on cars have never been notified, however. An interested party, or the Commission itself, could therefore claim that these arrangements are null and void, without taking into account the exceptions to the EEC ban on cartels laid down in Article 85(3) of the EEC Treaty.[86]

Caution is nevertheless called for here. The arrangement between the Japanese and UK car industries will not have escaped the notice of the respective authorities. Insofar as these arrangements are to be attributed to government intervention on the Japanese or UK side, it is questionable whether they are covered by Article 85 of the EEC Treaty.

The Commission recognized this problem in a 1974 decision in which it declared that a French–Japanese *Ballbearings* cartel was contrary to the antitrust provisions of the EEC Treaty.[87] The deal involved a 'unilateral' promise from a number of Japanese producers to their French competitors that they would raise the prices of ballbearings exported to France to the price level of ballbearings produced in France. On this occasion the Commission declared that measures 'imposed' on Japanese undertakings by the Japanese authorities were outside the scope of Article 85. That Article could, however, be applied to measures 'merely authorized' by the Japanese authorities.

In intra-Community relations, however, the Court at one point seemed to be more sympathetically inclined towards industries when government authorities

83. OJ 1985, L92/1. See also the *Zinc producers* Case, OJ 1984, L220/27.
84. *Aluminium* decision, at 45.
85. Commission communication concerning imports of Japanese products to which the Treaty of Rome is applicable. OJ 1972, C111/13. This communication was set in a broader context by Aarts, 'Mededingingspolitiek en Economische Crisis', 28 *SEW* 1980, 16 *et seq.*, at 27–28. The Commission also underscored the distinction between privately negotiated export limitations and its own negotiations with third countries on export restraints in its answer to Parliamentary Question No. 295/77. OJ 1977, C270/10.
86. See Arts. 4(1), 5(1) and 25 of Council Reg. 17/62. OJ 1962, 204.
87. OJ 1974, L343/19 and in particular 23.

intervene in private actions in ways that restrict competition. In the *Suiker-Unie* judgment[88] the Court declared null and void the part of a Commission decision describing the selling and purchasing practices of a number of French, Belgian, German and Italian sugar buyers as conduct agreed between them which ran counter to Article 85 of the EEC Treaty.[89] The Court based its judgment on two considerations. Firstly, it took the view that the Italian rules (which were among the measures designed to implement the common organization of the market in sugar) left very little opportunity for competition, and that consequently the arrangement among the industries could not appreciably impede competition. Secondly, the Court considered that the Italian rules and their manner of implementation[90] had had 'a determinative effect' on the conduct of the industries concerned, so that had it not been for these regulations and their implementation, the challenged co-operation would not have taken place.[91] In other words, the Court seemed prepared to recognize an appeal for immunity under Article 85 when the industries concerned can prove that if the authorities had not intervened, their conduct would have been different.

In the more recent *Stichting Sigaretten Industrie* ('SSI') judgment, however, the Court may have changed its tack.[92] In this case the tobacco industries, participating in price arrangements condemned by the Commission, argued extensively that the Dutch government had played a decisive rôle in bringing about these arrangements. On its face the Court refrained from considering to what extent intervention from government authorities may have the effect of removing agreements entered into by private enterprises from the ambit of Article 85. The Court dismissed SSI's defense for lack of factual proof that the authorities, in discussing with SSI the objectives they wished to see achieved, had indicated that those objectives should be achieved by the disputed price arrangements.[93]

The summary fashion in which the Court reviewed and dismissed this defence of the tobacco industries is not altogether satisfying. For reasons of their own choosing Member States quite often seek to influence marketing strategies of industries informally, through 'administrative guidance'. In practice industries may find it very difficult to resist these informal pressures, if only because in present-day mixed economies they depend in many ways on the

88. Joined Cases 40–48, 50, 54, 56, 111, 113–114/73, *Suiker Unie et al.* v. *Commission*, (1975) ECR, 1663.
89. OJ 1974, L140/17.
90. The Court had previously noted that the Italian Government had requested Italian buyers to meet their import requirements in a rationalized way, 'that is to say by concerted action', and had urged the suppliers 'to harmonize supplies'. See paras. 54–55 of the judgment.
91. *Id.*, paras. 67–72.
92. Joined Cases 240–242, 261–262, 268–269/82, *SSI et al.* v. *Commission*, judgment of 10 December 1985, not yet reported.
93. See para. 40 of the judgment. The Court's *SSI* judgment did not come as a complete surprise. In the earlier *Fedetab* Case as well the Court held that the Belgian government's involvement was insufficient to immunize contested conduct of Belgian tobacco manufacturers from antitrust liability. *Van Landewijck et al. (Fedetab)* v. *Commission* (Joined Cases 209–215 and 218/78, (1980) ECR, 3125 (paras. 126 *et seq.*).

good-will of government authorities. At the same time industries often will be hard-pressed to present specific evidence as to the extent of such informal government intervention if their conduct is challenged (not infrequently the governments concerned are reluctant to specify their involvement).

It is unfortunate if antitrust authorities ignore the realities of manifold government interventions in industrial market behaviour. When industrial conduct in which governments have intervened raises antitrust concerns, the appropriate inquiry probably should be into the *effective* cause of the contested conduct. Admittedly, this approach is casuistic, not very predictable and quite possibly fraught with problems of proof. Yet it can have the distinct advantage of addressing the actual state of affairs in the marketplace.

For example, when the national authorities strongly encourage producers to conclude arrangements with their Japanese counterparts rather than take up the cudgels themselves with the Japanese (or the EEC!) authorities over commercial policy, this 'encouragement' ought to immunize these producers from proceedings, or at least fines, under Article 85 of the EEC Treaty. The Commission, on the other hand, would want to grant immunity only in those cases where the government formally 'imposes' certain actions on private industry.[94] The advantage of its 'hard and fast rule' is that the parties concerned know better where they stand.

A measure introduced by a Member State which contributes towards export-restraint arrangements between national and Japanese undertakings could itself prove contrary to the EEC competition rules. Some authors have interpreted Article 90 of the EEC Treaty as prohibiting the Member States from abetting industries in infringing the EEC rules on competition.[95] They seek support for this position from the *Inno/Atab* judgment in which the Court, apparently on the basis of Article 90 of the EEC Treaty, held that the Member States could not take any measures enabling undertakings to evade the rules on competition contained in the EEC Treaty.[96]

---

94. See apart from its 1974 *Ballbearing* decision, the Commission's 1984 decision in the *Aluminium Cartel* case, *supra* note 83, at para. 10.2 (p. 39): 'The fact that the UK government, in pursuit of its own legitimate interests, permitted a private restriction upon competition within the Community does not mean that it either sought or desired a breach of the law within the Community and still less that it favoured that breach. Even if the UK Government had intended such a breach (which the Commission does not believe was ever the case), that would not alter the position of the undertakings . . . The Commission has the duty to enforce the EEC Treaty and therefore does not accept that any encouragement given by the UK Government could be a defence for the acts of the UK-based undertaking so far as those acts violated Community law . . .'.

95. Meal, 'Government Compulsion as a Defence under United States and European Community Law', 20 *Columbia Journal of Transnational Law* 1981, 5 *et seq.*, at 127 n. 267 (with refrerences to other works). See also Marenco, 'Government Action and Antitrust in the United States: What Lessons for Community Law?', to be published in 12 *L.I.E.I.* 1986/2.

96. Case 13/77, *NV Gb-Inno-Bm* v. *Atab*, (1977) ECR, 2115 (para. 33). It is not completely clear whether the Court indeed referred to Article 90, or to the more general obligations deriving from Article 5 of the EEC Treaty. In a later judgment on the same point the Court explicitly made reference to Article 5. Case 229/83, *Leclerc* v. *Au Blé Vert*, judgment of 10 January 1985, not yet reported (para. 14). See also, most recently, in Joined Cases 209–213/84, judgment of 30 April 1986, not yet published (paras. 71 *et seq.*).

Final remark

The different responses of the Member States to Japanese car imports illustrate how difficult it can be to forge a consensus in the Community on foreign trade relations. Several Member States, some such as Germany having their own car industry, generally favour unrestricted access of Japanese car imports. Others for quite some time have had recourse to limitations. By now the various national restrictions on Japanese cars seem to be entrenched in the Community's fragmented trade relations with Japan. Even the Commission appears to accept this.

A recent Parliamentary Question cited a study which concluded that abolition of the Italian, French and British car restrictions, while taking into account significant job losses (17,000 man years in Italy, 11,000 man years in France, and 19,000 man years in the United Kingdom), would yield a net welfare increase of $1.5 billion. On this basis the Parliamentarian, Ms. Boot, inquired whether the Commission would be willing to bring about a relaxation of these restrictions for the benefit of consumers. In its answer the Commission did not evaluate the study's conclusions, but merely emphasized the high priority it attaches to employment protection. The Commission went on to refer to the VER on cars it had negotiated with Japan in 1983, indicating that its measure did not affect the existing restrictions maintained by Member States. This answer suggests that the Commission is reluctant to invest political capital in uniform Community-wide treatment, let alone liberalization, of Japanese car imports.[97]

2. INTRA-COMMUNITY RESTRICTIONS MAINTAINED BY MEMBER STATES ON *INDIRECT* IMPORTS OF JAPANESE PRODUCTS: ARTICLE 115 OF THE EEC TREATY

If a Member State introduces a quota on direct imports of specific Japanese imports, this does not mean its market is hermetically sealed. On the basis of the principle of free movement of goods within the Community,[98] an importer should still in theory be able to obtain his supplies without any trouble from an intermediary in another Member State (provided of course imports from Japan are not restricted in that Member State and demand does not exceed supply there). Consequently, to be sure that its market is not flooded by Japanese products coming in via another Member State, the Member State in question will also want to protect internal frontiers.

Article 115 of the EEC Treaty authorizes the Commission to permit an exception to the free movement principle where differences in national commercial policy measures cause a deflection of trade or where these

---

97. Answer of the Commission to Parliamentary Question No. 1289/84. OJ 1985, C197/2.
98. Arts. 30 *et seq.* of the EEC Treaty.

differences cause other economic difficulties in one or more Member States. This Treaty provision addresses the problems caused by the incomplete state of the EEC's common commercial policy. (For a detailed analysis of this provision see the contribution by Timmermans in Chapter Five). The Commission, the only Community body empowered to act here, laid down further rules on the application of Article 115 of the EEC Treaty in a separate Decision.[99]

The application of Article 115 is controversial. The critical question is when the Community's commercial policy can be considered as sufficiently developed to bar the use of Article 115. The concern is that intra-Community trade restrictions derogate from a fundamental Treaty principle (free movement of goods within the Common Market), and may themselves hinder the implementation of the common commercial policy. In view of these concerns, the Court has concluded that as a rule Article 115 must be interpreted narrowly.[100]

In practice, however, it appears from both the Court's and the Commission's case law that there is still quite some room to apply Article 115. Thus in the recent *Tezi* judgments the Court upheld the application of Article 115 to national shares of a Community quota imposed within the framework of the Multifibre Arrangement.[101] The Court rejected Tezi's argument that the Community quota evidenced a common commercial policy regarding textile imports which precluded intra-Community trade restrictions, designed to complement national sub-quotas on third country imports of textiles, pursuant to Article 115.[102] In the Court's view the application of Article 115 was justified, because the conditions surrounding textile imports varied from Member State to Member State.

In *Tezi* there was at least the appearance of a common commercial policy because the EEC authorities started out by imposing a Community-wide restriction. Even that appearance of commonality is lacking in instances where national restrictions originate in Member States (*e.g.*, the restrictions included in the 'negative list' annexed to Regulation (EEC) No. 2288/82). Accordingly, following the *Tezi* line of reasoning, there is *a fortiori* no sufficiently developed common commercial policy here. In those instances the only issue in determining whether the Commission can justifiably apply Article 115 would then seem to be, whether there exists a national restriction on direct

99. Commission Decision 80/47 EEC, OJ 1980, L16/14.
100. *Donckerwolcke* judgment, *supra*, n. 30 (para. 29).
101. Case 59/84, *Tezi Textiel B.V.* v. *Commission*; Case 242/84, *Tezi Textiel B.V.* v. *Ministerie van Economische Zaken*, judgments of 5 March 1986, not yet reported. See on these judgements particularly the contribution by Timmermans, Chapter Five.
102. See also the exchange between the Commission and the Council on the application of Article 115 to national subquotas of a Community-wide tariff quota in Case 218/82, *Commission* v. *Council*, (1983) ECR, 4063 *et seq.*, at 4069. Contrary to the Commission, the Council argued that Article 115 would be inapplicable because the Community tariff quota was based on a regulation issued pursuant to Article 113 and because its subject-matter formed part of the common commercial policy. The Court did not decide this point then because no Article 115 decision had in fact been issued in that case.

imports which has been imposed in accordance with the Treaty. That issue turns on whether the national restriction has been specifically authorized by the Community within the meaning of the *Donckerwolcke* judgment.

The Commission appears to take the position that the national quotas enumerated in the 'negative list' have been specifically authorized by the Community. Thus on many occasions it has permitted Italy by virtue of Article 115 to impose intra-Community restrictions so as to seal off that country's notorious quota on direct Japanese car imports.[103] Spain recently received a similar authorization from the Commission to prevent indirect imports of Japanese cars.[104] Still, the Commission's view as to whether a national restriction is consistent with Community law and may be supplemented by an Article 115-measure is not final.

In the rather curious *Ilford* Case, the President of the Court by summary judgment suspended an Article 115-decision of the Commission, which had authorized Italy to impose restrictions on intra-Community imports of non-sensitized colour photograph films originating in Japan.[105] The President found some support for the Italian importer's view that there was in fact no Italian measure restricting *direct* imports of these films from Japan! In that case, of course, there would have been no basis whatsoever for an Article 115-measure. The President concluded that, in any event, there was not sufficient certainty of a national restriction consistent with Community law which could warrant application of Article 115.

3. ORIGIN RULES AND NATIONAL IMPORT RESTRICTIONS

If a Member State maintains a quota on direct imports of Japanese widgets, the Japanese manufacturer may try to circumvent this quota by establishing an assembly operation of widgets using only Japanese parts in country X (outside the EEC). Assuming that widgets from X can be freely imported in the Member State, the Japanese company could then try to enter these widgets in this Member State by claiming that their country of origin is X.

The Member State does not have to accept this claim of origin at face value. The Council has established general rules to determine the origin of products,

---

103. *E.g.*, OJ 1986, C91/3. France and the United Kingdom apparently are able to prevent inroads caused by indirect imports on their unofficial restrictions on direct Japanese car imports via other means than Article 115. Because their restrictions are not acknowledged in the 'negative list', the Commission would not authorize intra-Community restrictions on Japanese cars pursuant to Article 115 at their request.

104. OJ 1986, C161/3. Interestingly, Portugal at the time of this writing had not requested permission from the Commission pursuant to Article 115 to block indirect imports of cars from third countries.

105. Case 1/84R, *Ilford Spa* v. *Commission*, (1984) ECR, 423. The case was withdrawn during the main proceedings. Sometime afterwards the Commission again authorized Italy pursuant to Article 115 to impose restrictions on intra-Community imports of these colour photograph films originating in Japan. OJ 1986, C93/3.

and for particular products the Commission has issued specific implementing rules.[106] Pursuant to the Council's general rules, the country of origin of the widget imports in our hypothetical case remains Japan. The imports could hence be restricted by the Member State unless the assembly in country X constitutes a 'substantial process or operation that is economically justified' and results in 'the manufacture of a new product' or 'represents an important stage of manufacture'.[107] These requirements are open to varying interpretations, depending mainly on whether and to what extent subsequent manufacturing stages add value to or change the tariff classification of the intermediate product.

The determination of origin can also play a rôle in the application of restrictions to intra-Community imports which are imposed pursuant to Article 115. Instances have been reported where a Member State, maintaining restrictions on imports of Japanese products, refused entry as well to like products which were manufactured in another Member State by local subsidiaries or joint-ventures of the Japanese producer. (Local investment in the EEC is, of course, an obvious way for Japanese companies to by-pass import restrictions). Ordinarily, products that are manufactured in a Member State can be freely marketed anywhere in the Community. Yet in these instances the Member State concerned took the position that, although the products were manufactured elsewhere in the EEC, they should nevertheless be considered of Japanese origin and subjected to restriction. Two examples may illustrate this.

In 1982 the Triumph Acclaim was introduced as the first result of British–Japanese cooperation in car manufacturing. Italy immediately branded this car as a Japanese product. It announced that any shipments from Great Britain (where the Acclaim was manufactured) into Italy would count towards its national quota, which then permitted imports of only 2,200 Japanese units per year.[108] This quota on direct imports from Japan had been supplemented by Italian restrictions authorized pursuant to Article 115 on indirect imports of Japanese cars via other Member States. Following an increase in the number of UK components in the Acclaim, coupled with strong protests from the British government, Italy allowed the Acclaims to pass its borders without restriction.

Earlier a more complicated but telling case had arisen in connection with zippers. In 1973 the EEC Commission initiated antidumping proceedings

---

106. Council Reg. (EEC) 802/68 concerning the Community definition of 'country of origin', OJ 1968, L148/1. The Commission has adopted implementing regulations to determine the origin of particular products such as radio and television receivers, taperecorders, textiles and ball and roller bearings.

107. Art. 5 of Council Reg. 802/68. (See on this Regulation the contribution by Völker, Chapter Two.) Note that Art. 6 of Reg. 802/68 provides that manufacturing operations whose object is to circumvent measures applicable to goods from specific countries shall under no circumstances confer origin. There is, however, no guidance on how this provision to deter abuse of the origin rules is put into effect.

108. See generally the editorial of the Financial Times of 26 April 1982, 'What makes a car European', on p. 22.

against imports of Japanese zippers produced by Yoshida Tokyo. After Yoshida Tokyo had, among other things, agreed to restrain voluntarily its zipper exports to Italy, the Commission terminated these proceedings. Still, imports of zippers in Italy continued to increase. This time the zippers originated mainly from Yoshida's manufacturing subsidiaries in the Netherlands and Germany. The Commission then issued a Regulation narrowing the definition of origin specifically with respect to zippers.[109] As a result, the Yoshida subsidiaries no longer received certificates designating their zippers, which incorporated Japanese parts, to be of Community origin.

The lack of these certificates caused problems for the European Yoshida subsidiaries in their exports to third countries. They also found that exports to Member States (such as Italy) were being obstructed, even though the Commission had not authorized intra-Community restrictions pursuant to Article 115. The Yoshida subsidiaries could have tried to prove the existence of illicit, unauthorized, national restrictions on intra-Community traffic of Japanese zippers. Such action, however, would not have forestalled a formal authorization by the Commission of national restrictions on Japanese zipper imports pursuant to Article 115, and would not have removed the impediments to their exports to third countries. Therefore, the Yoshida subsidiaries directly challenged the Commission's Regulation defining the origin of zippers. This challenge was successful. The Court invalidated the Commission's narrow definition of origin, holding that the Commission had exceeded its powers by using criteria which were extraneous to the objectives of the Council Regulation laying down the general rules on origin determinations.[110]

With persistent concern over Japanese imports and the low level of Japanese investments in European manufacturing operations, complications regarding the definition of origin are likely to recur. The Commission reported recently that at present only a fifth of Japanese investments in the Community are for manufacturing or assembly, and of this only a fraction involves a significant amount of value added locally. Yet Member States, in a drive to attract as much investment in manufacturing as possible, more and more seem to be outbidding each other in offering subsidies and other incentives to foreign investors, notably to Japanese companies.[111]

---

109. Commission Reg. (EEC) 2067/77. OJ 1977, L242/5.
110. Case 34/78, *Yoshida Nederland B.V.* v. *Kamer van Koophandel en Fabrieken voor Friesland*, (1979) ECR, 115; Case 114/78, *Yoshida GmbH* v. *Industrie and Handelskammer Kassel*, (1979) ECR, 151.
111. Commission report on EC–Japan relations, COM (86) 60 final, at 11. These subsidies and incentives often will be covered by the Community's régime on state aids. See Articles 92 (ff) of the EEC Treaty. The Commission, when it decides to approve such state aids, may require Japanese investors to transfer technology to local European producers. See the Commission's Answer to Parliamentary Question No. 1833/84, OJ 1985, C248/2.

C. WAYS IN WHICH THE COMMISSION CAN FORGE COMMON POSITIONS IN EEC TRADE POLICY VIS-À-VIS JAPAN

Paralysis tends to afflict the Council's decision-making when the interests of the Member States diverge sharply, as is so often the case in trade relations with Japan. The Commission therefore seems preeminently suited to bring about common positions in EEC trade policy with respect to Japan. As we have seen, however, the Commission in exercising its authority is unlikely to ignore the political sentiments prevailing in the Member States.[112] Still it seems useful to mention some of the means available to the Commission for the purpose of reducing fragmentation and improving consistency in Japanese–EEC trade relations.

1. It could refuse to continue to present further proposals to the Council authorizing Member States to extend their bilateral trade agreements (including safeguard clauses) with Japan. This might encourage the Member States (*casu quo* the Council) to concentrate once again on Community negotiations with Japan for a trade agreement. Yet, in view of the political power struggle between the Community institutions and the fact that the Commission depends on the Council to achieve a wide variety of objectives, it is doubtful whether the Commission would persist in its refusal if the Council emphatically requested proposals for authorization.

2. In proposing revisions to the Council of the common import régime, which is due for reassessment by the end of 1988,[113] the Commission might press for changes in the 'negative list' of national quotas on Japanese imports. For example, the Commission could propose to replace national quotas by a system of Community surveillance, followed by Community restrictions should a dramatic increase in Japanese exports create any untoward effects. The Council, of course, is not obliged to adopt any such proposals of the Commission, and can amend them by unanimous vote pursuant to Article 149 of the EEC Treaty.

3. If the Commission lacks the power to eliminate national quotas, it does have authority to empty them of meaning. In order to be effective, national restrictions on direct imports frequently have to be complemented by intra-Community restrictions on indirect imports of the

---

112. *E.g.*, the Commission did not take action against the VERs on car exports which the Benelux and Germany negotiated with Japan in 1981 (text, at n. 36); the Commission did not pursue its challenge in 1983 of the French 'Poitiers'-restriction, designed to curtail imports of Japanese videorecorders, under Art. 113 (text, at nn. 69–72); the Commission seems to have acquiesced in the current national restrictions on Japanese car imports, among which notably the French and British restrictions are of dubious legality also under Community law (text, nn. 76–96).

113. See Art. 19(1) of Reg. 288/82, as amended by Council Regulation (EEC) 1243/86. OJ 1986, L113/1.

same product shipped via other Member States. Acting under its discretionary powers pursuant to Article 115, the Commission could henceforth refuse to sanction intra-Community restrictions on indirect imports of Japanese imports.

Indeed, as part of its plans to complete the Community's internal market by 1992, the Commission has announced that it intends to render Article 115 inoperative. It expects that if Article 115 were no longer available, any import restrictions would have to be applied on a Community-wide basis. That is still in the future, however, as the Commission recognizes.[114]

At the present time a more subtle, gradual approach might be for the Commission to grant Article 115-authorizations only after the national quota has already been exceeded through indirect imports by a considerable amount. In this way the Commission would effectively substitute its judgement for that of a Member State as to what extent a national industry should be protected against import competition. Having recognized this, the industries concerned (and, perhaps as a result, their governments) might then come to accept full Community authority over trade restrictive measures.

4. The Commission could conduct a more active competition policy *vis-à-vis* cartel agreements and other arrangements that are more difficult to classify, such as voluntary export restraints between European and Japanese industries (and *vis-à-vis* any government measure underlying these private arrangements) under Article 85 *et seq.* of the EEC Treaty. The Commission would be treading on sensitive ground where these private industry arrangements are prompted by national government authorities.

5. The Commission could bring before the Court the bilateral export restrictions which some Member States occasionally negotiate independently with Japan as an infringement of Community powers in respect of the common commercial policy (action under Article 169 on the ground of an infringement of Article 113 of the EEC Treaty). The risk here is naturally that the Court may not go along with the Commission (all the way), and so to a certain extent legitimize initiatives by individual Member States. If one looks only at the legal merits of the case, however, the Commission's arguments appear to carry sufficient weight to justify Court proceedings.

Thought should be given to the fact that the Member States' divergent trade measures cannot but give Japan the impression that the Community is unable

---

114. *Completing the Internal Market*, white paper from the Commission to the European Council, COM (85) 310 final, at 11–12. See Crossick & Clough, 'Is the European Community's Commercial Policy Protectionist? Article 115 – A Shield or a Sword', 20 *International Lawyer* 1986, 293 *et seq.*, at 302.

to carry its own weight. Common positions of the EEC with respect to Japan are needed to fortify the Community's negotiating stature. Thus, should fragmentation remain the rule, there is no doubt that the Community's efforts to remove the barriers which EEC-made exports must surmount in Japan will continue to suffer.

III. COMPATIBILITY WITH THE GATT OF RESTRICTIONS ON IMPORTS FROM JAPAN

The restrictions applied in the Community to imports of Japanese products do not only pose problems relating to Community law. As we have seen, trade relations between the EEC Member States and Japan have come to be governed by GATT rules, albeit after some hesitation on the part of certain Member States. As a result of its substitution for the Member States as of 1 July 1968, the Community as such is now bound by the GATT.[115] Consequently, both national and Community restrictions on Japanese imports, at least as a matter of international law,[116] have to be compatible with GATT rules.

Below we will examine broadly whether some of the more prominent restrictions imposed in the EEC on Japanese imports are in fact consistent with GATT obligations. First it is useful to recall some of the basic principles and attitudes of the GATT and its contracting parties which are especially relevant to this analysis.[117]

A. SOME GATT BASICS

The GATT is predicated on the desirability of reducing government intervention in international trade. Nevertheless, the GATT's rules do not impose on member countries a *laissez-faire* philosophy. What the GATT

---

115. See, *supra*, text at nn. 23–28. Whether the EEC Member States are now bound by the GATT by Community law (Art. 228(2) EEC Treaty) and/or by virtue of their original, individual accession is still a matter of some debate. Because the substitution of the Community for the Member States has not been formally recognized by the GATT contracting parties, who have never discharged the Member States from their individual responsibilities to comply with the GATT's obligations, the better view seems to be that the Member States are bound to observe the GATT both under international law by virtue of their individual accession and under Community law by virtue of the Court's interpretation of Art. 113 of the EEC Treaty.

116. Whether national and Community trade measures have to be compatible with GATT as a matter of EEC law is discussed below, in Part IV.

117. Lucid discussions of the GATT framework as a whole can be found in Jackson, *World Trade and the Law of GATT* (1969); Dam, *op. cit.*, n. 10. Particularly helpful is the comparative analysis of GATT rules and US and EEC trade laws and practices in McGovern, *International Trade Regulation* (2d ed. 1986).

prescribes is that the contracting parties use the most efficient policy instrument whenever they do intervene in international trade.[118]

Accordingly, the GATT as a matter of principle directs that its contracting parties must not discriminate between the trade to or from different countries.[119] The primary objective of the GATT's non-discrimination principle is to promote economic efficiency, to the extent possible, in government interventions. Thus, when an import restriction does not discriminate between supplying countries, the most efficient suppliers will retain their competitive advantage. As a result the importing country can satisfy its import needs at the lowest cost.

All this helps to explain why the GATT generally favours tariffs as the means for governments to restrict international trade, if they do. Global import duties, for example, saddle all foreign producers with the same competitive disadvantage on the importing government's market. These duties leave the underlying market (*i.e.*, price) mechanism as such intact and preserve the relative competitive position of the most efficient foreign exporters. Global tariffs therefore constitute a genuinely non-discriminatory means of government intervention in external trade.

In contrast, the GATT as a rule outlaws quantitative restrictions, as is evidenced by Article XI. Early on it was recognized that quantitative restrictions are inherently discriminatory in effect.[120] The reason is that they disrupt the price mechanism. Thus prevalent quota-systems under which the importing government divides a global quota into import shares between supplying countries cannot but discriminate. These country-allocated quota shares arbitrarily change the relative competitive position of different suppliers. Efficient exporters will almost always find that the quota shares reduce their access to the importing country's market more sharply, at least in relative terms, compared to less efficient suppliers.

The actual practice of the GATT contracting parties does not quite resemble these guiding principles to which they originally committed themselves. Particularly in the last 10 or 15 years, the GATT contracting parties have mostly resorted to quota-type restrictions whenever they granted import relief.[121] In addition, there are still various quota-type restrictions in existence dating back to the GATT's early days, when certain mostly transitional waivers

---

118. See generally Roessler, 'The Scope, Limits and Function of the GATT Legal System', 8 *World Economy* 1985, 287 *et seq.*, 292 (ff). While the GATT's rules do not oblige Member States to adopt *laissez-faire* policies, they rest on the belief that the market mechanism generally is best suited to allocate economic resources efficiently. This is reflected in the policy advice to the contracting parties emanating from the GATT Secretariat. See notably Wolf, 'Tower of Babel: Conflicting Ideologies of Adjustment', 2 *World Economy*, 1979, 481.

119. Another central reflection of the GATT's non-discrimination principle is the requirement of Art. III that imported goods receive treatment similar to the treatment governments accord to national products. For a full survey of GATT provisions incorporating the principle of non-discrimination see Jackson, *op. cit.* n. 117, at p. 255.

120. *E.g.*, Haberler, *Quantitative Trade Controls – Their Causes and Nature*, 20–27 (1943) (League of Nations study); Heuser, *Control of International Trade*, 80–110 (1939).

121. GATT, *International Trade 1983/84*, 19 (1984).

exempted them from the prohibition of Article XI.[122] Even now quantitative restrictions to some extent may legally be justifiable, because the GATT provides for various exceptions to its principles. A notable exception is embodied in Article XIX, the main safeguard clause, which among others suspends the prohibition on quantitative restrictions in the event a contracting party has cause to protect a domestic producer temporarily against an unforeseen and significant increase in import competition.

Still, taking into account the established exceptions, it is fair to assume that many quota-type restrictions which the contracting parties currently maintain are inconsistent with GATT rules. So far, however, the affected countries have only challenged relatively few quota-type restrictions through GATT dispute settlement proceedings, set out in Articles XXII and XXIII. The dearth of formal objections reflects in large part the traditional view of the GATT as a consensus-seeking body, where conflicts are preferably resolved through negotiation – even though this leaves many issues unresolved. This traditional view, espoused in particular by the EEC, is more and more subject to criticism. There is, for instance, increasing resistance from at least some quarters (notably the United States) to continue negotiations on the elimination of quantitative restrictions that are GATT-inconsistent; negotiations in which the restricting countries may request concessions from others in exchange for lifting their quotas.[123]

Even if the contracting parties would adopt a more principled position on the elimination of GATT-inconsistencies, however, the Japanese government might still be reluctant to take the lead in enforcing GATT law. Given its considerable and controversial trade surplus with major GATT contracting parties such as the EEC and the US, Japan politically is in a delicate position to insist on removal of trade barriers and increase its surplus further. Moreover, Japan has rarely initiated and never fully pursued a dispute settlement proceeding against trade measures of others in GATT. Instead, Japan has opted for quiet though persistent diplomacy. Yet, as a matter of law, nothing in the GATT precludes Japan from formally disputing import restrictions on its products in the future.

---

122. The history of these so-called 'residual restrictions' is recounted in Dam, *op. cit.* n. 10, at pp. 163–166. The policy clashes preceding the GATT's prohibition on quantitative restrictions are described in Jackson, *op. cit.* n. 117, at pp. 308–314.

123. These differing viewpoints are brought out in the latest report of the GATT working group on quantitative restrictions. GATT, 32d Supp. BISD 91 (1986). The mere fact that GATT-inconsistent trade restrictions have remained undisputed for a long time does not make them invulnerable to attack. The panel decision in the *quartz watches* Case, cited, *supra*, in n. 27, suggests that the GATT contracting parties can still successfully challenge each other's 'old' violations (see para. 29 of the decision).

B. REVIEW OF CERTAIN TYPICAL RESTRICTIONS ON JAPANESE IMPORTS

Restrictions on Japanese imports in the EEC typically include country-specific quotas, voluntary export restraints and modifications of tariff concessions. The issues these restrictions raise under GATT law will now be broadly sketched.

1. COUNTRY-SPECIFIC QUOTAS

Of the import quotas maintained by Member States, many apply globally, to different exporting countries. These global quotas often also affect imports from Japan. If they do not benefit from a specific exception, they violate Article XI GATT. Yet these global quotas do not represent the most prominent bone of contention in EEC–Japanese trade relations.

In this context most attention is focused on the so-called 'discriminatory quotas'. Because quotas are inherently discriminatory in effect, this expression is pleonastic. It fails to highlight the particularly offensive feature of these quotas, which is that they apply only to the products of one or several – among many – exporting countries. A better way to refer to these quotas is that they are country-specific. As a matter of principle, country-specific quotas are inconsistent with the GATT (notably Articles XI and XIII).

EEC Member States retain a number of country-specific quotas that are targeted exclusively and explicitly[124] on imports from Japan. These are enumerated in the 'negative list' annexed to Regulation No. 288/82. A notorious example is the Italian restriction on Japanese cars, discussed above. By way of exception there are several justifications in GATT law for country-specific quotas.[125] Yet these exceptions are quite narrow, and it is fair to assume that not all of the restrictions which Member States maintain on Japanese imports satisfy their conditions.

Significantly the GATT's principal safeguard clause, Article XIX, does not

---

124. Note that if and so long as Japan is the sole producer in the world of a particular product, an importing country can safely restrict the imports of this product through a global quota without identifying its target, Japan. In that case the importing country does not run afoul of the GATT's prohibition on country-specific quotas.

125. See notably Arts. XIV (balance-of-payments restrictions), XIX (3)(a) (retaliatory restriction following a global safeguard measure), XX and XXI (general and security exceptions), XXIII (2) (retaliatory restriction following a finding of 'nullification or impairment'), XXV (5) (specific waiver).
   Consider also that certain old country-specific quotas of the Member States might be exempted from GATT obligations by virtue of a 'grandfather clause'. Virtually all contracting parties have acceded to the GATT by means of a protocol which incorporates a 'grandfather clause'. Pursuant to this clause the contracting parties are obliged to apply Part II of the GATT (containing, among others, the rules on quantitative restrictions) 'to the fullest extent not inconsistent with existing legislation'. Accordingly, country-specific quotas that predate a country's accession to the GATT arguably do not have to comply with Arts. XI and XIII. See generally McGovern, *op. cit.* n. 117, at pp. 15–19.

permit country-specific quotas. By notifying a quota to GATT under Article XIX, a GATT contracting party can only suspend the prohibition on quantitative restrictions of Article XI. It cannot suspend the rules set forth in Article XIII on how quantitative restrictions are to be administered.

Article XIII first lays down the ground rule that quotas must apply globally, to *all* supplying countries.[126] Furthermore Article XIII contains a number of guidelines which GATT contracting parties must observe in implementing import quotas. For instance, with respect to the most prevalent quota system under which the importing government allocate quota shares to the main supplying countries, Article XIII requires that these shares reflect the quantities these suppliers have traditionally imported (without prescribing the criteria, however, to delineate a representative historic period).

Oddly enough, its heading suggests that the guidelines of Article XIII aim at a non-discriminatory administration of quantitative restrictions. This reflects the common misunderstanding that quotas, and especially country-allocated quota shares, can in some way be administered consistent with the economic precepts of the GATT's non-discrimination principle. Yet the operability of the non-discrimination principle depends on the price mechanism – which quotas ordinarily disrupt. The only way in which non-discrimination could be achieved under a quota system, by leaving the price mechanism intact at least among the foreign suppliers, would be for the importing government to organize an auction of import licenses in which all suppliers can participate. Article XIII, however, does not even mention the auction method of administering quotas. For various reasons, that are unrelated to considerations of economic efficiency, most GATT contracting parties have resisted the idea of auctioning import licences.[127]

If anything then, the notion of non-discrimination expressed in Article XIII is a legal fiction. It does not preserve the relative competitive advantage of the most efficient suppliers when they are faced with quantitative import restrictions. On the other hand, the guidelines of Article XIII to some extent do curb the discretion of importing governments in administering quantitative restrictions (this is a salutary objective in its own right because unfettered discretion easily provokes unpredictability and favouritism). Thus Article XIII clearly prohibits country-specific quotas.

In July 1983, the GATT condemned a country-specific quota which France had maintained for many years on imports of (quartz) *watches* and other products from Hong Kong. Because France (*casu quo* the EEC) did not rely on any of the GATT's exceptions, it was held that the French quota violated

---

126. Note that this rule of Art. XIII, as well as the general prohibition on quantitative restrictions of Art. XI, also applies to export restrictions.

127. See generally Bronckers, *op. cit.* n. 4, at 96–97. Rumour has it that at the time Article XIII was being negotiated, right after the Second World War, several Western European governments refused to accept auction systems. They felt that auctions would prevent them from exercising discretion in administering quotas, and thereby from rewarding the support of certain trading interests. In the words of one observer 'import licenses were used to finance political recovery'.

Article XI. Given this violation, an evaluation of Article XIII was considered unnecessary.[128]

Interestingly, within a year of the GATT's ruling the EEC Commission replaced the contested country-specific restriction with a global restriction on imports into France of quartz watches.[129] This time the Commission was careful to design a global quota, allocating quota shares to all main suppliers, so as not to run afoul of Article XIII. In addition the Commission notified this quota to the GATT pursuant to Article XIX in order to benefit from the suspension of Article XI.[130] The quantity of quartz watches which Hong Kong could export to France pursuant to its quota share under the Commission's global quota, was virtually the same as the quantity which France had previously allowed Hong Kong under the country-specific quota.[131] It therefore appeared as if Hong Kong had merely scored a Pyrrhic victory in challenging the country-specific quota in GATT. Indeed, one Parliamentarian critically questioned the Commission's actions.[132]

Yet the gains to Hong Kong of its GATT complaint were quite significant. First, Hong Kong established a point of principle with precedential value. For example, France dismantled the other disputed quotas more rapidly than could otherwise have been anticipated. Secondly, the Commission's quota was limited to digital quartz watches. Henceforth Hong Kong was free to export analogue quartz watches to France. Thus, the Commission's quota in fact added considerably to the quantity of digital quartz watches which Hong Kong could export to France. Thirdly, with respect to its exports of digital quartz watches covered by the Commission's quota, Hong Kong had the legal security of multilateral discipline. This quota could not be arbitrarily reduced by the Community or France. Moreover, in line with the temporary nature of safeguard measures envisaged by Article XIX GATT, the Commission's quota is due to expire at the end of 1986.

Lastly, one might have expected that Hong Kong was able to charge higher prices under the Commission's global quota than under the French country-specific quota, because the latter permitted the other non-restrained exporters of digital quartz watches to increase their sales to France at the expense of Hong Kong. Assuming that as a result of the Commission's global quota the total supply of foreign quartz watches on the French market decreased, or at least expanded less rapidly than would otherwise have been the case, it is possible that Hong Kong as well as the other exporters could have charged a higher price for their products. Whether Hong Kong actually secured this

---

128. GATT panel report cited, *supra*, in n. 27. There was also some question as to whether the French quota did single out imports from Hong Kong.
129. Commission Reg. (EEC) 1087/84. OJ 1984, L106/31. The Commission issued this Regulation pursuant to its safeguard authority under art. 15 of Reg. 288/82.
130. GATT Doc. L/5645 (1984).
131. As of 1981 France allowed Hong Kong to import 440,000 quartz watches annually. In 1984 the Commission allowed Hong Kong to import 440,000 digital quartz watches, which quantity was to be increased by 5% both in 1985 as well as in 1986.
132. Answer of the Commission to Parliamentary Question No. 1418/84. OJ 1985, C111/21.

economic benefit is doubtful, however, because it appears that Hong Kong was never able to fill its quota share allocated by the Commission. This may simply be a reflection of market conditions, because consumers have increasingly shown a preference for analogue quartz watches in recent years. Yet there have also been complaints of Hong Kong producers that France restrained imports of digital quartz watches through manipulations with import licences.

2. VOLUNTARY EXPORT RESTRAINTS

For some time now VERs have been a source of considerable controversy in GATT. They are seen as the epitome of the trend towards bilateralism in international trade relations. Because VERs represent quantitative restrictions and because they are country-specific ('discriminatory'), there are those who argue without much ado that VERs violate Articles XI and XIII GATT.[133] In fact, however, these simplified arguments have had little effect in terms of subjecting VERs to GATT discipline.

a. The law as it stands

The first complication is that VERs appear in many different guises. Sometimes the only or primary actors appear to be industries (*e.g.*, in the arrangement between the British and Japanese car manufacturers discussed above). The GATT offers no authority to regulate industrial participation in VERs, because it lacks provisions on restrictive business practices.[134] At other times the involvement of government in VERs is more pronounced. Yet the spectrum of government involvement in VERs ranges widely, from unilateral and allegedly non-committal 'forecasts' of future trade patterns by the exporting country's government, to formal and binding arrangements approaching treaty status between the governments of the importing and exporting countries concerned (these are occasionally referred to as 'orderly marketing arrangements').

A major problem with any legal analysis of government involvement in VERs lies in their paradoxical nature. The pressure to restrict trade originates in the importing country, yet translates into a voluntary trade restriction

---

133. *E.g.*, Petersmann, 'International and European Foreign Trade Law, GATT Dispute Settlement Proceedings Against the EEC', 22 *CMLRev* 1985, at 441 *et seq.*, 445, 451, 454 and 476.
134. Early on in the GATT's existence there has been some debate as to whether the GATT's waiver (Art. XXV) or dispute settlement (Art. XXIII) provisions could not be applied to private restrictive business practices. No firm conclusions were drawn at the time and no actions against restrictive business practices have ever been taken in GATT. *See* Jackson, *op. cit.* n. 117, at pp. 522–527. The issue does resurface now and then in GATT discussions.

imposed by the exporting country. This paradox seems to elude the principles of GATT Articles XI (prohibition on quantitative import and export restrictions) and XIII (obligation to apply permissible quantitative import and export restrictions globally).

In case the importing country does not become involved in the implementation of the VER, the rules on import restrictions of Articles XI and XIII are difficult to apply (which is an important reason why importing governments frequently are inclined to deny any specific involvement in VERs). On the other hand it is not appropriate to apply the rules on export restrictions of Article XI and XIII to VERs, because these rules were written with a view to guarantee importing countries equal access to the products of other GATT contracting parties.[135] In the case of VERs the importing countries involved obviously are not interested in having unrestricted access to foreign products.

A related problem of VERs is that of enforcement. Who is going to complain that VERs violate GATT principles? The importing and exporting governments that are at both ends of the bilateral restraint are unlikely complainants, because they obviously perceive the VER to be in their best interests under the circumstances – albeit for different reasons. Third countries seem better suited to request a GATT review, but then they have to come to grips with the paradox posed by VERs (and with the possibility that a complaint may expose them to counterclaims in the event they have participated in VERs themselves).

There are several ways in which VERs can affect third countries. The exporting country that restrains its exports to certain importing countries, may try to divert its trade surplus to other countries, thereby putting pressure on the domestic producers of these countries. Yet these third countries cannot very well hold the exporting country responsible for a violation of Articles XI and XIII GATT. If anything, they receive more than their fair share as defined in Article XIII of the exporting country's trade. And they cannot fault the importing country for violating Article XI, if the latter is not involved in the implementation of the VER.[136]

Third countries have only successfully intervened in instances where their exports were unilaterally restricted by an importing country that had also elicited VERs from other suppliers (Note that the direct involvement of the importing country in these VERs was beyond dispute). In those cases,

---

135. On the *ratio legis* of the GATT's prohibition on export restrictions see Quick, *Exportselbstbeschränkungen und Artikel XIX GATT*, 262 (1983); Jackson, *op. cit.*, n. 117, at pp. 497–506.

136. A third country that *can* demonstrate the importing country's active involvement in a VER, could conceivably charge the importing country with a violation of Art. XI without having to prove injury due to trade diversion. In the event a complaining country succeeds in establishing that the respondent has failed to carry out its obligations under the GATT, there is a presumption that the respondent's action has 'nullified or impaired' the benefits accruing to the complainant within the meaning of Art. XXIII (1)(a) GATT. See paragraph 5 of the Agreed Description of the Customary Practice of the GATT in the Field of Dispute Settlement. GATT, 26th Supp. BISD 215, 216 (1980).

concerning *Norwegian restrictions on textile imports* and *EEC restrictions on apple imports*, the complainants did not challenge the legality of the VERs. They only claimed that their import share was inferior to the import shares accorded to the suppliers which had voluntarily restrained their exports. Here the GATT Contracting Parties first characterized the VERs as quantitative *import* restrictions within the meaning of Article XI. Secondly, they held that, for purposes of comparing the quantity of the unilaterally imposed import quota with the quantities of the quotas agreed to under the VERs, the guidelines of Article XIII did apply and had to be observed by the *importing* country.[137]

These rulings are of limited value in subjecting VERs to GATT discipline. They do not prevent GATT contracting parties from engaging in VERs as long as the involvement of the importing country is obscure(d). For example, in the summer of 1986 the Japanese government urged its car makers to restrain exports to the EEC. Japanese officials explained this move as an attempt to head off further trade frictions with the Community.[138] At the same time Commission officials denied that they requested a VER on cars from Japan, similar to the arrangement which existed between 1983–1985; they characterized the Japanese move as a precautionary, unilateral decision. On the assumption that both sides' statements are correct, it is submitted that neither the Community nor the Japanese government have contravened Articles XI and XIII GATT as they currently stand.

Consider also that to hold otherwise would be to forbid exporting countries like Japan to take measures avoiding a trade conflict with a pressured importing country, and would force them to risk unilateral import restrictions. Such a revisionist interpretation of the GATT's prohibition on export restrictions in Article XI is unrealistic.

A separate question is whether an exporting country X that chooses to limit its exports by way of precaution *vis-à-vis* country A, may try and divert its excess output to country B. As a matter of GATT principles nothing is wrong with that. In fact, when the supply of exports to country B increases, their price may decrease to the benefit of consumers in country B. In other words, the trade diversion of country X does not burden but benefits the overall economic welfare of country B. Yet the political costs of trade diversion in country B may be high, because the domestic producers which must compete with the extra supply of exports are likely to suffer adjustment problems. These producers will call on their government for protection. And in the event the competitive pressure of increasing exports becomes intolerable for its domestic producers, the government of country B could resort to safeguard restrictions pursuant to Article XIX GATT (or to antidumping duties by virtue of Article VI, if the diverted exports are priced unfairly low).

Before one condemns the possibility of such a chain reaction of trade

---

137. *Norwegian Restrictions on Hong Kong Textile Imports*, GATT, 27th Supp. BISD 119 (1981); *EEC Restrictions on Imports of Apples from Chile*, GATT, 27th Supp. BISD 89 (1981).
138. See the article 'Japan's Auto Makers Observe Tokyo's Export Limits to EC', *Wall Street Journal* of 25 August 1986.

restrictions and attributes this to the VER of country X, one ought to recognize that a unilateral import restriction of country A would also have prompted country X to try and divert its excess output to country B. Once again, this goes to show that the problems created by VERs originate in the importing countries concerned. This point bears emphasis in any attempt to discipline the use of VERs.

b. *Proposals for reform*

At present VERs escape the checks and balances which the GATT imposes on government measures designed to grant import relief to domestic producers. It is therefore not surprising that much of the discussion on VERs focuses on Article XIX GATT, the principal safeguard clause. This provision of the GATT defines the conditions governing import relief measures that may be exempted from certain GATT obligations (*e.g.*, Article XI). Many argue that VERs should be subject to GATT discipline, and appear to believe that a mere revision of the conditions of Article XIX could bring VERs back into the GATT's fold. Yet their narrow focus on the GATT safeguard clause and a possible new Safeguards Code is misplaced.

At the outset it is important to stress that Article XIX sets forth an exception to certain GATT principles for the benefit of importing countries that wish to protect their domestic producers with trade restrictions against an unforeseen rise in imports. By providing for temporary derogations from certain GATT obligations, Article XIX serves to increase the confidence of governments to carry out existing and assume new obligations. Politically, Article XIX serves as a 'fail safe' mechanism for GATT contracting parties.[139]

Apparently, however, the potential beneficiaries of Article XIX (the importing countries) find its present conditions, which are thought to aid the interests of the affected exporting countries, too stringent.[140] Hence the pressured importing governments seek relief outside Article XIX, and they succeed whenever the exporting country voluntarily restricts its trade. In that case the trade restraint is not or not effectively covered by GATT prohibitions (notably Articles XI and XIII) and the importing countries concerned do not have to invoke the exceptions to GATT principles set forth in Article XIX, nor do they have to satisfy the conditions attached to these exceptions. Given the proliferation of VERs, the 'success-rate' of countries in obtaining import relief

---

139. Robertson, *Fail Safe Systems for Trade Liberalization*, 5–6 (Thames Essay No. 12, 1977). There is serious doubt, however, whether the different objectives that importing governments ascribe to safeguard actions are consistent and feasible. For a concise and critical examination see Pearson, *Emergency Protection in the Footwear Industry*, 10–13 (Thames Essay No. 36, 1983).

140. Notable conditions of Article XIX that deter importing countries are (a) the showing of a causal connection between domestic injury and import competition, (b) the lack of a provision for country-specific restrictions and (c) the possibility of retaliation by the restricted suppliers.

outside the GATT régime is high. The fact that VERs often grant considerable benefits to the exporting country concerned, in the form of 'quota rents' (higher revenues), also explains their multiplication.

This background suggests a number of things for proposals to reform the present situation. To the extent importing countries do not become involved in the implementation of a VER, and cannot be deemed to have instituted an import restriction themselves, it would seem that no GATT rule can be devised to hold them responsible for the trade restraint. How could importing countries be faulted under the GATT in case they do not take trade-related measures themselves in connection with a VER? On the other hand, as was indicated above, forbidding exporting countries to engage in VERs is an unrealistic option. Accordingly, the conclusion seems inescapable that the GATT cannot prohibit VERs as such. One can only try to contain their use.

Basically there are two conceivable ways to achieve containment of VERs. The pressures in importing countries that provoke VERs from exporting countries should be controlled. That is primarily a question of domestic law. Furthermore, the GATT régime ought to be revised so as to reinforce the position of exporting countries that wish to preserve their market access in importing countries. To this end mere adaptations of the GATT safeguard clause are inadequate. Thus, tightening the conditions of Article XIX is not going to reinforce the position of exporting countries and help them resist demands for VERs. If the possibility to obtain exemptions from GATT obligations through Article XIX is simply made more difficult, this will create an even greater incentive for importing countries to circumvent the GATT prohibitions on trade restraints. On the other hand, should the conditions of Article XIX be relaxed to the point where existing VERs can satisfy them, exceptions to GATT prohibitions on trade restraints will become the rule. Such wholesale legitimation of VER-type measures would effectively eliminate any GATT discipline over import relief. It would also weaken the bargaining position of exporting countries who are faced with demands for VERs.

Very briefly put, recommendations for curbing the proliferation of VERs are the following.

First of all, reinforce the position of exporting countries by strengthening the GATT regime throughout. An important reason why exporting countries 'voluntarily' restrain their trade to some extent is that GATT rules currently permit importing countries to restrict trade unilaterally even more sharply. For example, the GATT (notably Articles XIX and XIII) fails to prescribe that importing countries cannot reduce imports below a certain base level. Furthermore, the GATT broadly authorizes contracting parties to restrict unilaterally injurious imports of subsidized imports, without providing clear guidelines as to which subsidies are and are not countervailable.[141] At the present time, when government subsidies abound even in market-oriented

---

141. The lack of guidance is particularly acute with regard to domestic subsidies that are not specifically targeted on exports. See generally Horlick, Quick & Vermulst, 'Government Actions Against Domestic Subsidies', 12 *L.I.E.I.* 1986/1, p. 1.

economies, the threat of unilateral countervailing action launched by an importing country often persuades exporters to restrain voluntarily their allegedly subsidized trade. Indeed, the GATT Subsidies Code explicitly makes provision for such settlement arrangements![142] Moreover, the GATT dispute settlement proceedings can be quite cumbersome. They may not provide an effective remedy, even when the GATT-inconsistency of a trade restriction is fairly obvious. Rather than awaiting the outcome of dispute settlement proceedings sometime in the future, and losing their market position in the meantime, exporting countries often prefer a quick settlement through a VER.[143] Finally, on the GATT level, the conditions of Article XIX ought to be reconsidered from the perspective of an importing government, so as to determine whether they can be loosened without undue damage to exporting interests.

Secondly, revisions of the GATT régime alone will not eradicate VERs. Importing countries command powers which fall beyond the GATT's scope, but which may very well persuade exporting countries to self-impose trade restrictions (*e.g.*, development aid, political support etc.). Accordingly, it is necessary to devise domestic constraints as well on a government's inducement of trade restrictions from others.[144] To this end the domestic trade policy process must be made transparent, so as to allow public debate and appropriate consideration of opposing interests whenever the government is considering demands for import restrictions.[145]

A final but important point is that one should be clear about the objectives of reform. The above-mentioned recommendations to curb the use of VERs correspond with the objective of maximizing the access of exporting countries to importing countries' markets. As said before, however, VERs may offer significant benefits to the exporting countries concerned. Self-imposed restrictions on the quantity exported are likely to raise the price of the remaining exports to the restricted market, and allow the exporters to collect the extra revenue ('quota rents') resulting from such price increases. If, therefore, the objective of reform is to maximize the pecuniary returns of exporting countries, different considerations apply. In fact, compared with trade restrictions that are envisaged by the GATT, VERs may then appear to be a preferable alternative.[146]

---

142. See Art. 4 (5)(a) of the Subsidies Code. GATT, 26th Supp. BISD 56, 62 (1980).
143. This consideration was highlighted as an important factor, contributing to the multiplication of 'grey area' measures such as VERs, in a recent report of the Chairman of the GATT's Safeguard Committee. GATT, 30th Supp. BISD 216, 218 (1984).
144. See generally Bronckers, *op. cit.* n. 4, at pp. 79–110; Völker in Chapter Two of this book.
145. See, text, *supra*, at n. 53.
146. See the thought-provoking analysis of Hindley, 'The VER System and GATT Safeguards', paper presented at a World Bank conference on the *Role and Interests of Developing Countries in the Multilateral Trade Negotiations*, 30 October–1 November 1986, Bangkok (forthcoming publication).

3. MODIFICATIONS OF TARIFF CONCESSIONS

Though decreasing in importance as a result of successive GATT negotiations on their reduction, tariffs are still a trade barrier to be reckoned with. And while the general trend of the last decades has indeed been to reduce tariff levels, reversals have occurred as well. In the Community's trade relations with Japan two recent tariff changes are worth mentioning: the EEC's increase of import duties levied on videorecorders (as of 1 January 1986) and on compact-disc players (as of 1 January 1984). Particularly the latter created a stir in the GATT, the implications of which extend beyond this one case.

By way of introduction, the relevant GATT rules on tariffs can be summarized as follows. The GATT does not oblige its contracting parties to abolish or lower their tariffs. It does, however, encourage them to do so through multilateral negotiations, as is reflected in Article XXVIII bis. Any tariff concession granted by a contracting party on a certain product is referred to as a 'binding'. Bindings are recorded in the tariff schedule of the contracting party concerned, and apply indiscriminately to all GATT contracting parties pursuant to Article II (1)(a) of the GATT.[147]

Relatively few of the products traded by the GATT contracting parties (especially by the EEC) remain 'unbound'. The customs duties on these products can lawfully be increased at will. On the other hand, the tariffs on 'bound' products can only be raised in accordance with GATT rules.

Tariff concessions (i.e. reductions of customs duties on 'bound' products) can be suspended by virtue of an appeal to Article XIX. In this way the customs duty of a certain 'bound' product may be temporarily increased. Bindings can also be withdrawn in connection with the modification of the tariff schedule of a contracting party. Article XXVIII governs these comparatively permanent increases of customs duties.

The procedures of Article XXVIII are fairly complex.[148] For present purposes it suffices to remark that once a country expresses its wish to modify its tariff schedule, the GATT Contracting Parties will designate the countries with whom the applicant must negotiate the modification, *i.e.* the countries with whom the applicant initially negotiated the concession or who have a principal or substantial supplying interest (para. 1). In these negotiations the applicant country and the affected suppliers must 'endeavour' to maintain the overall tariff level (para. 2). In practice this balance is achieved through compensatory concessions: the applicant country grants new or increases existing concessions to offset the withdrawal of other concessions. If agreement cannot be reached, the applicant country is authorized to withdraw

---

147. This is not the place to describe the practical problems of tariff negotiations, conducted on a 'most-favoured-nation' basis in accordance with Article I, and of the interpretation of schedule-commitments. See generally Jackson, *op. cit.* n. 117, chapter 10; McGovern, *op. cit.* n. 117, at pp. 176–183.
148. See the procedural guidelines adopted by the GATT Contracting Parties in 1980. GATT, 27th Supp. BISD 26 (1981).

or modify the tariff concession unilaterally. Thereupon the affected suppliers may retaliate unilaterally, even though both unilateral moves could well raise the overall tariff level (para. 3). Finally, among several other GATT contracting parties, the European Community traditionally has reserved the right to initiate modifications of its tariff concessions at any point in time (para. 5).

Significantly, in contrast to other GATT remedies that permit protective action, Article XXVIII does not require the applicant country to justify its unilateral actions. The applicant does not have to show, for example, that the domestic industry which benefits from the upward revision of a tariff is suffering from an unforeseen rise in import competition (compare Article XIX); or that the selling price of the imported products is distorted and unfair (compare Article VI).

Nevertheless, when the Commission proposed to the Council in June 1985 to modify the tariff concession on *videorecorders* pursuant to Article XXVIII, it did volunteer some justifications for internal use. The Commission pointed out that the VER on videorecorders it had negotiated with Japan in 1983 was due to expire at the end of 1985. It favoured replacement of the VER by a tariff increase, because the latter constituted a transparent measure which would be more agreeable to the GATT. In addition, the Commission believed that an increase in the customs duty on videorecorders (a finished product), coupled with compensatory reductions on semiconductors (a semifinished product) represented a modest step towards the restructuring of the Common Customs Tariff with regard to electronic products. The underlying rationale appeared to be an attempt to stimulate the manufacture of finished products in the Community.[149] Interestingly, the Commission did not indicate whether these considerations (transparency of trade restrictions and structure of the Community's tariff profile) should guide future applications by the EEC of Article XXVIII as well.

When the Community failed to reach agreement with Japan on compensatory tariff reductions, it increased the customs duty on videorecorders from 8% to 14% and introduced some compensatory reductions unilaterally (*e.g.* by lowering the import duty on semiconductors from 17% to 14%), effective 1 January 1986.[150] Interestingly, the Community did reach agreement with Japan on compensatory concessions later on. When the mutually agreed concessions were published, it appeared that the Community had withdrawn(!) some of its previous, unilateral concessions (notably on pocket calculators).[151] There appears to have been a connection with the Community's approval of a contemporaneous modification by Japan of its tariff concession on imports of leather and leather footwear.[152] Both parties seem to have been more concerned with agreeing on mutually

149. COM (85) 349 def.
150. Council Reg. (EEC) 3679/85. OJ 1985, L351/2.
151. Council Reg. (EEC) 1069/86. OJ 1986, L99/1.
152. See GATT Doc. L/5978 (1986).

acceptable restrictions, than with maintaining an overall low level of tariff concessions following their respective modifications.

Although the videorecorders case raises questions from the GATT's perspective, the Community's earlier modification of the tariff concession covering *compact disc* (CD) *players* was even more controversial. It will be recalled that Philips originally developed this product, and that Sony participated in the end phase of this development. Even before the CD-players were put on the market, however, the Community notified the GATT that it intended to raise the applicable import duty (by creating a separate sub-classification in the tariff heading for sound recording and reproduction appliances). Prompted by Philips, and in turn by the Benelux countries, the Community thereby intended to secure a satisfactory sales position for EEC-made compact disc players on the Common Market. Japan objected strenuously to this application of Article XXVIII. As a matter of policy Japan argued that such a pre-emptive tariff raise would jeopardize the development of new, particularly high-technology, products. In terms of Article XXVIII Japan argued that it was not possible to identify the interested suppliers and to determine the compensatory concessions to which they could lay claim in case the 'binding', covering a new product, was modified.[153] Several countries, including the United States, endorsed Japan's objections.[154]

The Community went ahead anyway, and effective 1 January 1984 increased the customs duty on CD-players unilaterally from 9.5 to 19% (it did announce at the time that the duty would be gradually reduced from 1987 onwards).[155] In protest Japan refused to negotiate compensatory concessions with the Community, but did not retaliate.

Significantly, the European Parliament recently appeared rather taken with the possibility of modifying the Community's tariff concessions, and increasing the customs duties on a variety of imported products, as a means to reduce the trade deficit with Japan. It particularly recommended an 'intelligent use of pre-emptive tariffs' by the Community in the context of newly-developed products. The Parliament stated that any such tariff strategy would have to be consistent with the Community's GATT obligations. Yet it did not address the GATT controversies which the implementation of its proposals would stir up.[156]

---

153. *E.g.*, GATT Doc. TAR/W/45 (1984) (working paper of the Japanese Delegation to GATT).
154. GATT Doc. TAR/M/11, at 5–11 (1984).
155. Council Reg. (EEC) 3506/83. OJ 1983, L351/1. Useful background information on the CD-player case, which raised some thorny questions from a Community law perspective as well, can be found in 27 *Euromarkt-Nieuws*, 1984, 11–14.
156. Parliamentary Resolution on trade and economic relations between the European Community and Japan, adopted on 11 September 1986, at paras. 16–19 (not yet reported).

IV. STATUS AND SUPERVISION OF GATT PRINCIPLES IN THE COMMUNITY'S LEGAL ORDER

The EEC could be brought into a GATT dispute settlement proceeding both for national or Community restrictions on Japanese imports that are inconsistent with GATT rules (the GATT's dispute settlement procedure is discussed below, in Part V.A). Being the directly affected supplier, Japan is the most eligible party to challenge GATT-inconsistent restrictions before the GATT. As already indicated, however, the Japanese government so far has never fully pursued a formal challenge of restrictions on its exports in GATT. Private parties, such as exporters or importers of Japanese products, have no access to the GATT's dispute settlement machinery. Any suggestions in that direction still meet with firm resistance from governments.[157]

It is within the discretion of the Japanese government whether or not to dispute trade restrictions in the GATT forum. Political considerations, relating to possible repercussions of contentious diplomatic action in view of its controversial trade surplus, may to some extent explain the Japanese government's reticence in this respect. Yet in the absence of formal challenges in GATT, one wonders whether there are safeguards within the Community's legal order designed to secure the GATT's observance by EEC institutions and Member States with regard to Japan. Are the GATT's rules part of Community law? Does Community law offer a remedy to private parties to challenge infringements of GATT rules by Community institutions or Member States in court? If not, should private parties have such a remedy?

These have proven to be sensitive questions that defy easy answers. It would go beyond the scope of this paper to address this subject in detail. Fortunately, the reader can be referred to a recently published collection of essays of various authors who bring out the conflicting viewpoints.[158] Here we will confine ourselves to a summary of their findings and some comments.

A. SOME FINDINGS

The original GATT agreement antedates the creation of the European Communities. This agreement has never been transformed by a separate act into Community law, and the Court has never said in so many words that the GATT as such has become an integral part of Community law.[159] Yet it is often assumed that it has.[160] On the other hand, the Community itself has concluded

---

157. *E.g.*, Answer of the Commission to Parliamentary Question No. 1439/85. OJ 1985, C353/19.
158. *The European Community and GATT* (Hilf, Jacobs & Petersmann eds. 1986) with contributions on this subject from Ehlermann, Everling, Hilf, Maresceau, Pescatore, Petersmann and Tumlir.
159. Hilf, *id.*, at 161 (citing authorities who doubt that it has); Maresceau, *id.*, at 125.
160. Ehlermann, *id.*, at 138; Petersmann, *id.*, at 56.

various agreements within the GATT framework (notably, most of the 1979 Tokyo Codes) and these are considered to be an integral part of Community law by virtue of Article 228(1) of the EEC Treaty.[161]

The Court has never addressed itself explicitly to the rank of an international agreement concluded by the Community. Yet certain of its rulings are interpreted as meaning that rules of international law which are binding on the Community (treaty law and general principles of international law) are subordinate to the founding Treaties, but take precedence over Community secondary legislation. There is no doubt that international law, to the extent it is binding on the Community, takes precedence over inconsistent national law of the Member States.[162] The Court has held several times that the Community is bound by the GATT, and these principles are therefore thought to apply to GATT rules as well.[163]

Despite their binding nature, the Court so far has consistently denied 'direct effect' to GATT rules.[164] It has thereby precluded private litigants from relying on GATT principles when they challenge trade restrictions imposed by Community institutions or Member States in national court proceedings or in related actions before the European Court of Justice (compare Article 177 of the EEC Treaty). This case law has found both staunch defenders as well as strong opponents.[165]

The Court has as yet not had occasion to decide whether private litigants can request it to review Community acts against GATT rules pursuant to a direct appeal under Articles 173 or 215 of the EEC Treaty where 'direct effect' arguably is not an issue. Should this be permitted, there are those who would urge the Court to exercise self-restraint and to refrain from assuming a creative role in the interpretation of GATT provisions.[166] In their view the Court should also adopt a cautious attitude if the Commission were ever to initiate an infringement action under Article 169 of the EEC Treaty against a Member State for violating a GATT rule.[167]

---

161. Hilf, *id.*, at 164.
162. This leaves open the possibility that dualist Member States require transformation of international law, which is not binding on the Community, before this can take precedence over prior inconsistent national law.
163. Ehlermann, *op. cit.* n. 158, at 131–132; Hilf, *id.* n. 158, at 162.
164. Most recently in the *SPI/SAMI* judgment, *supra*, n. 25.
165. Ehlermann, *op. cit.* n. 158, at 135 (pro); Maresceau, *id.*, at 124 (pro); Hilf, *id.*, at 173–182 (contra); Petersmann, *id.*, at 58–59 (contra); Pescatore, *id.*, at xvii (apparently contra); Everling, *id.*, at 97–98 (citing relevant considerations).
166. Ehlermann, *id.*, at 139; Maresceau, *id.*, at 117.
Note that the Court may shortly find occasion to interpret GATT principles in an appeal brought under Article 173 EEC against a Commission decision refusing to investigate a complaint pursuant to the new EEC trade policy instrument, discussed *infra* at note 183. See the appeal lodged by Fediol with the European Court of Justice on 6 March 1987. (Case 70/87), OJ 1987, C96/8.
167. Maresceau, *id.*, at 113.

B. SOME COMMENTS

It has been argued that the GATT's lack of direct effect does not necessarily mean that the GATT totally lacks a legally binding character or confers no protection in the Community's legal order.

In this connection mention is made of the fact that the Community's secondary foreign trade legislation sometimes implements certain GATT rules,[168] or prescribes that protective measures will only be adopted 'with due regard for existing international obligations'.[169] Furthermore, it is pointed out that, even though the Court has not endowed the GATT with 'direct effect', the Community institutions as a matter of EEC law must observe GATT obligations and must ensure that it is observed by the Member States. In addition the possibility has been raised that, while denying 'direct effect' to the GATT, the Court of Justice might be willing to interpret Community law or national law so as to bring it into conformity with GATT law.[170]

1. AWKWARD RESULTS

The fact remains, however, that both Community institutions and Member States have ignored and continue to ignore the GATT without being restrained by its 'binding' status in the Community's legal order. References to 'existing international obligations' in secondary trade legislation, and the general principle that they must observe GATT obligations, have not prevented the Council and the Commission from repeatedly taking GATT-inconsistent measures. This is evidenced in part by several decisions of the GATT Contracting Parties, formally establishing a breach of GATT obligations by the European Community and its Member States.[171] Other EEC and national measures, the legality of which under the GATT is at least dubious, were not put to the test in the GATT forum (notably, restrictions on Japanese imports).

Furthermore, although the Community's institutions and particularly the Commission are required to ensure that Member States comply with GATT obligations, they have not done so and are unlikely to do so. There is no evidence, for example, that the Council or the Commission ever challenged the Member States about the consistency with GATT of their national country-specific quotas on Japanese imports which are included in the 'negative list' appended to the common import régime. As one noted authority observed

---

168. *E.g.*, Council Reg. (EEC) 2176/84, OJ 1984, L201/1 (incorporating various GATT provisions on antidumping and countervailing duties).

169. *E.g.*, Art. 15 of Reg. 288/82 (the safeguard clause of the common import régime).

170. Ehlermann, *op. cit.* n. 158, at 137–138; Hilf, *id.*, at 183–184. But see on the latter point Maresceau, *id.*, at 126 (who suggests the Court should be consistent, and that if it denies 'direct effect' to GATT provisions it should not use them at all in preliminary rulings).

171. For a survey of GATT dispute settlement proceedings in which the European Community was involved as a defendant see Petersmann, *id.*, at 67–71.

rather pointedly: 'Clearly, (the Commission) dislikes the idea of using specifically Community provisions to do non-member countries' business for them'.[172]

There is, finally, little indication that the Court is predisposed to seek consistency between Community or national law and GATT rules via 'indirect' interpretations. In one case dealing with the interpretation of the Common Customs Tariff, the Court considered that since agreements regarding the Common Customs Tariff were reached between the Community and its partners in GATT, the principles underlying those agreements might be of assistance in interpreting the rules of classification applicable to it.[173] In another case the Court took cognizance of a GATT decision condemning a trade restriction of the Community. Unfortunately, the Court followed the Commission's erroneous interpretation of the GATT decision and trivialized the officially established inconsistencies between the Community's trade restriction and the relevant GATT rules.[174]

These rare decisions do not show that the Court is inclined to draw on GATT principles for guidance whenever they come into play. In any event, these decisions are only of marginal importance compared with several judgments of the Court, upholding discriminatory trade restrictions of the Community on the grounds that 'the (EEC) Treaty contains no general principle which may be relied upon by traders, compelling the Community in its external relations to accord equal treatment in all respects to non-member countries'.[175] These judgments contrast sharply with the non-discrimination principle which is fundamental to the GATT. Admittedly, some of these cases involved imports from non-GATT contracting parties.[176] Yet it is significant that the Court made no distinction between their position and the treatment to be accorded to imports from GATT contracting parties.[177] One is left with the awkward result that, whereas the Court has held that the Community is bound by the GATT, the Court does not oblige the Community institutions to observe the GATT's basic principle of non-discrimination – not even by way of 'indirect' interpretations of EEC law.

In short, binding though the GATT may be on the EEC and its Member

---

172. Ehlermann, *id.*, at 139.
173. Case 92/71, *Interfood* v. *Hauptzollamt Hamburg*, (1972) ECR, 242 (para. 6). But see, *e.g.*, the *SIOT* Case, *supra* n. 27, where the Court refused to review a national (!) measure against the GATT's principles on goods in transit, even though neither the EEC Treaty nor the applicable transit agreement (with Austria) contained specific commitments in relation to the disputed issue. Austria is a GATT contracting party.
174. Case 112/80, *Dürbeck* v. *Hauptzollamt Frankfurt/Main*, *supra* n. 50 (paras. 45–46). *Cf.* the GATT panel report on apples from Chile cited, *supra*, at n. 137.
175. Case 55/75, *Balkan-Import Export GmbH* v. *Hauptzollamt Berlin-Packhof*, (1976) ECR, 19 (para. 14); Case 245/81, *Edeka Zentrale AG* v. *Germany*, (1982) ECR, 2745 (para. 19); Case 52/81, *Faust* v. *Commission*, (1982) ECR, 3745 (para. 25).
176. The *Balkan-Import* case concerned restrictions on cheese imports from Bulgaria; the *Faust* case concerned restrictions on imports of preserved mushrooms from Taiwan. Both Bulgaria and Taiwan are not party to the GATT.
177. The *Edeka* case concerned restrictions on imports of preserved mushrooms from Taiwan and South Korea. South Korea is a GATT contracting party.

States as a matter of Community law,[178] the Community's legal order effectively permits the EEC institutions and national governments to ignore GATT rules. This situation threatens to reduce all GATT principles to diplomatic declarations of 'best efforts'. It is submitted that if and to the extent the European Community still subscribes to the method of welfare improvement outlined in the GATT, GATT rules should have domestic law effect within the Community's legal order.[179]

2. CREATING DOMESTIC LAW EFFECT OF GATT PRINCIPLES

Put in very basic terms, the GATT's principles oblige the contracting parties to use the most efficient policy instruments for whatever policy goals they have chosen to pursue. For instance, the GATT rules on non-discrimination envisage that trade policies must permit exporters to sell in the best market and consumers to buy from the cheapest source (see above, Part III.A). Hence, assuming that the Community still aims for efficiency in its external trade policies, it would be in the Community's interest to introduce and observe the non-discrimination principle regarding import restrictions in its domestic legal order, *even if this were to be done unilaterally* without awaiting similar actions from other GATT countries.

There are several ways to create domestic law effect of GATT principles in the Community's legal order. Some rudimentary proposals may further the discussion on this important issue.

GATT principles could be implemented in the secondary trade legislation of the Community. Experience shows that mere references to 'existing international obligations' in EEC trade legislation fail to give sufficient guidance and do not prevent inconsistent decisions. Accordingly, it will be necessary to spell out GATT principles in the Community's secondary trade legislation. This will, among others, facilitate judicial review at the request of private parties of specific trade measures issued by EEC institutions and Member States.

Secondly, though this may appear paradoxical at first sight, it ought to be accepted that the EEC legal order allows Community *legislation* to deviate from GATT obligations. This could weaken the resistance to direct review by the Court of national or Community trade *measures* against GATT principles. Such a review by the Court is, next to legislative implementation, another way to confer domestic legal effect on GATT rules. Court interpretations could be especially useful in filling the gaps left by the Community's secondary legislation that implements GATT principles.

It seems that much of the current opposition to 'direct effect' of GATT rules,

178. This is apart from the Member States' obligation under international law to observe the GATT by virtue of their individual accession and formal membership.
179. See generally Tumlir's contribution to the collection of essays cited, *supra*, in n. 158.

as well as opposition to any consideration of GATT rules by the Court, stems from the perceived supremacy of GATT (c.q. international legal) obligations over secondary Community legislation.[180] Supremacy has created concerns that the Community could only redress an unwelcome Court interpretation of a GATT rule by going to the GATT, and by persuading the other contracting parties to formally interpret the disputed GATT obligation in such a manner so as not to bind the Community to the Court's holding. If Court judgments were thus to force the Community to request concessions from the other GATT contracting parties, this might severely handicap the Community's bargaining position in GATT.

Such concerns could be dispelled if the Court's interpretations of GATT were amenable to legislative correction by the Council. At the same time it would have to be accepted that the Court cannot review corrective legislation against GATT rules, even in actions where the GATT's lack of 'direct effect' does not play a part (e.g., in actions based on Articles 169, 173 and 215 of the EEC Treaty).[181] This would discard possibilities to review Community legislation against the GATT which are presently still open, because they have not been ruled out by the Court. Yet discarding these possibilities, which have never been tried anyway, would seem a price worth payng to:

(a) allow private parties to request judicial review of administrative Community decisions or national measures against GATT rules in the absence of implementing secondary EEC legislation, and thereby

(b) encourage the Community authorities in individual cases and national authorities in general to act consistently with GATT rules, or while deviating from the GATT to act at least consistently with general principles established in secondary EEC trade legislation.

This construction recognizes that the decision whether or not to comply with the GATT ultimately is a political one. At the same time it ensures that GATT principles cannot be conveniently ignored by administrative decisions in individual cases.[182] If this construction cannot prevent GATT inconsistent legislation, in any case it would curb arbitrary decision-making. Finally, it

---

180. Hilf, *id.*, at 162. See also Bourgeois, 'Effects of International Agreements in European Community Law: Are the Dice Cast?', 82 *Michigan Law Review*, 1984, 2201 *et seq.* at 2221–2224 (who argues that the supremacy of international agreements over inconsistent Community law is still an open question).

181. The status of corrective legislation in relation to GATT principles cannot depend on and vary with the type of legal challenge that is brought against it. To hold otherwise would not remove all concerns about Court interpretations of the GATT, engendered by the latter's alleged supremacy over the Community's secondary legislation. It would also create legal uncertainties.

182. It is also acknowledged that an administrative decision of the Community authorities in a particular case, albeit issued in the form of a regulation, is incapable of amending secondary EEC trade legislation. Though no differentiation between classes of regulations can be found in the EEC Treaty (notably in Art. 189), there is ample precedent in the Court's case law for the proposition that implementing regulations cannot derogate from basic regulations. *E.g.* Case 113/77, *NTN Toyo Bearing Company* v. *Council*, 1979 ECR, 1185 (para. 21). Advocate-General Warner referred to the Latin adage *legem patere quam fecisti* on this point. *Id.*, at 1249–1250.

leaves open the possibility that the GATT Contracting Parties may oblige the Community, as a matter of international law, to redress a Court interpretation or to withdraw a legislative correction to such judgments. It does not affect the existing remedies of GATT contracting parties to challenge inconsistent Community or national measures of any kind in the GATT forum.

These proposals are unlikely to satisfy the ideals of international law. Yet they may be the best one can hope for at a time when international commitments do not inspire complete confidence. They seem preferable to the present situation where international commitments such as the GATT's enjoy no or very little effect in the Community's domestic legal order.

V. COMMUNITY ACTION AGAINST JAPANESE TRADE RESTRICTIONS IN GATT

Parallel to concerns about Japanese import penetration into the Common Market, complaints about barriers to EEC imports in the Japanese market multiply. Allegations of 'unfair' Japanese trade restrictions often serve to justify demands for Community restrictions on Japanese imports. The GATT's dispute settlement mechanism makes provision for retaliatory import restrictions, in the event the respondent country has been found to 'nullify or impair' GATT benefits accruing to the complaining country and does not voluntarily withdraw the offensive measure (Article XXIII GATT).

European industries that are injured by illicit Japanese trade practices, violative of GATT, can request the Community to take action and if necessary to retaliate against Japanese imports. This relatively novel remedy was introduced by the Community's new trade policy instrument in 1984 (discussed by Völker in Chapter Two of this book).[183] So far, no complaints have been filed that concern Japanese trade practices.[184] That is somewhat surprising in view of the many grievances nursed by European industries against Japan.

Of course, the Community can also take action against Japanese trade restrictions on its own initiative. It can open negotiations with Japan in GATT and request the abolition of restrictions, without calling into question their legality. In these negotiations Japan may demand a *quid pro quo* from the EEC in the form of reductions of Community restrictions on Japanese imports (although in recent years Japan has unilaterally implemented certain import promotion measures, in an attempt to ward off trade conflicts).[185] The

---

183. Council Reg. (EEC) 2641/84, OJ 1984, L252/1. *See generally* Bronckers, 'Private Response to Foreign Unfair Trade Practices – United States and EEC Complaint Procedures', 6 *Northwestern Journal of International Law & Business* 1984, 651 *et seq.*, at 714–750.

184. The first complaint (lodged by the Dutch chemical company Akzo) that was formally admitted by the Commission concerned a United States import ban on aramid fibres. See OJ 1986, C25/2.

185. *E.g.*, the three-year action programme announced by the Japanese Government in July 1985. Bull of the EC 1985, No. 7/8, 2.3.17.

Community can also initiate GATT dispute settlement proceedings, challenging the consistency of Japanese trade restrictions with GATT principles. If such a challenge is successful, Japan will be obliged to withdraw the disputed measures without being able to claim compensatory concessions from the EEC. Should Japan not meet this obligation, it may face retaliation from the Community.

These actions fit in the GATT framework. Yet from the Community's perspective they seem no match for the escalating tensions in its trade relations with Japan. As a result, EEC institutions have taken or are contemplating actions that could upset the GATT system.

A. THE 1982 GATT DISPUTE BETWEEN THE EEC AND JAPAN

On 22 and 23 March 1982 the EEC Council of Ministers decided on a remarkable course of action. Dissatisfied with the results of successive GATT negotiations with Japan, the Council announced that the Community would invoke the GATT's dispute settlement procedure 'to address the cause of economic friction at its root – Japan's low import propensity as regards manufactured products.'[186] Indeed, on 7 April 1982 the Commission delivered a 14-page document to the Japanese mission to GATT in Geneva, starting the procedure of Article XXIII GATT.[187] The document revealed that the Community had opted for a two-pronged attack.

Rather than challenging the GATT-consistency of specific Japanese measures, the EEC mainly objected to the Japanese trading and economic policies as a whole which it considered to have 'nullified or impaired' the benefits it expected from the various concessions negotiated with Japan. According to Sir Roy Denman, then the Commission's Director-General for External Affairs:

'(W)e have emphasized that the essential argument concerns the need for Japan to open up its market. This relates to the effect of Japanese trading and economic policies as a whole and the need to achieve a more balanced integration – commensurate with Japan's responsibilities – of the Japanese economy with that of its main industrialized partners and notably with the European Community.'[188]

In addition, the EEC reiterated its request to the Japanese authorities for

---

186. Para. 2 of the Council's communiqué reproduced in press release 5779/82 (Presse 33), distributed by its Secretariat-General. See also the *Staatscourant* of 29 March 1982, No. 61, 3.
187. See the article on p. 8 of the *Financial Times* of 8 April 1982, 'EEC calls for export pledge from Japan'.
188. Address on 'Trade Relations between Industrial Countries in Times of Crisis' before the Houston Chamber of Commerce (18 May 1982); transcript at p. 5.

export moderation towards the Community, notably in the sectors of cars, colour television sets and tubes, and certain machine tools.

The Commission was pleased with this decision, which it considered to be the Council's first substantive contribution to solving the 'Japanese problem'.[189] Yet the Community's remarkable initiative immediately raised critical questions. Thus it was rather striking that the Community requested 'export moderation undertakings' from Japan in a formal GATT action, given the dubious status of VERs in GATT (discussed above, in Part III.B.2).

The following sections concentrate on the Community's fundamental objection to Japan's economic policies. We will inquire whether this complaint meets the conditions to bring an action under Article XXIII and whether the Community can expect any relief should Japan fail to satisfy its demand for adjustments. A sketch of the procedure of Article XXIII precedes the discussion of these substantive issues.

1. THE PROCEDURE OF ARTICLE XXIII GATT[190]

When a dispute arises between contracting parties, they first have to consult with each other to try and find a mutually acceptable solution to their differences (Article XXII). If no satisfactory adjustment is effected between the parties, the complaining country may take its case to the entire GATT membership. The GATT Contracting Parties will often establish a panel, which is to prepare a report analyzing the relevant issues and which will propose resolutions. Panels operate as independent adjudicatory bodies, traditionally consisting of officials of governments who are not parties to the particular dispute. Many disagreements are settled by the disputing parties during the panel proceedings or on the basis of the panel report, before the GATT membership has even considered its findings. Panel reports acquire legal force once they are adopted by the GATT Contracting Parties.

Supposing that the Contracting Parties confirm a panel finding in favour of the complaining country, they may authorize the complainant to retaliate against the respondent country if the latter fails to withdraw the contested

---

189. See the front page article 'EEC resorts to GATT on Japanese trade surplus' of the *Financial Times* of 23 March 1982.
190. See generally Draft Understanding Regarding Notification, Consultation, Dispute Settlement and Surveillance, GATT, 26th Supp. BISD 231 (1980); Agreed Description of the Customary Practice of the GATT in the Field of Dispute Settlement (Art. XXIII.2), *id.*, at 236. For a perceptive analysis see McGovern's contribution to the collection of essays cited, in n. 158.
Note that the GATT contains a whole gamut of dispute settlement procedures, which has led one author to reflect that '(t)here is no single, sharply defined dispute-settlement procedure in GATT that can be readily distinguished from the remainder of GATT activity. Or, in the alternative, one can say that there are over 30 such procedures'. Jackson, *op. cit.* n. 117, at 164. Yet, for all practical purposes, Art. XXIII (in combination with the general obligation of Art. XXII to engage in consultations whenever so requested) constitutes the GATT's central dispute settlement procedure.

measure or does not reach a settlement with the complainant (*i.e.*, does not pay compensation to the complainant). Yet the authorization of retaliation is such an unusual step that it occurred only once in GATT history, when in the 1950s the Netherlands was authorized to restrict wheat flour imports from the United States in response to US restrictions on dairy products.[191] In most cases the respondent country has accepted and acted upon the recommendations of the GATT Contracting Parties.

Although the GATT's dispute settlement procedures have operated fairly successfully, there is still room for considerable improvement.[192] Revisions to the GATT's dispute settlement mechanism are likely to constitute a priority issue in the upcoming Uruguay-round of trade negotiations.

2. THE CONCEPT OF 'NULLIFICATION OR IMPAIRMENT'

The GATT's key provision on dispute settlement permits contracting parties to bring complaints against each other's trading practices, without having to establish a violation of one of the Agreement's rules. Article XXIII stipulates that not only

> '(a) the failure of another contracting party to carry out its obligations under this Agreement',

but also

> '(b) the application by another contracting party of any measure, whether or not it conflicts with the provisions of this Agreement',

or even

> '(c) the existence of any other situation'

is actionable if a contracting party should consider that:

> 'any benefit accruing to it directly or indirectly under this Agreement is being nullified or impaired'[193]

In its complaint against Japan, the Community argued *inter alia* that the Japanese economy and policies display a number of features that constitute a situation within the meaning of sub-paragraph (c).

---

191. GATT, 1st Supp. BISD 62 (1953).
192. See generally US International Trade Commission, *Review of the Effectiveness of Trade Dispute Settlement under the GATT and the Tokyo Round Agreements* (USITC Publ. No. 1793, December 1985).
193. Under the same circumstances action may also be taken if a contracting party considers that 'the attainment of any objective of the Agreement is being impeded'. This extension really does not add anything to the 'benefits' formula. Hudec, 'Retaliation against "Unreasonable" Foreign Trade Practices: The New Section 301 and GATT Nullification and Impairment', 59 *Minnesota Law Review* 1975, 461, 480.

The language 'any benefit accruing . . .' is rich in potential. It has been described as a grant of common law jurisdiction to enable a case-by-case definition of nullification or impairment.[194] In many, if not most, instances the determination of nullification has turned on the question whether the complaining party could have anticipated the offending conduct. To express this differently, the critical issue has been whether the defendant can be held responsible for frustration of reasonable expectations.[195] Making these 'non-violation' determinations is a delicate exercise, certainly for a political body like the GATT Contracting Parties. Indeed, there have been relatively few complaints of unfair trade practices under Article XXIII which could not be reduced to a violation of one of the Agreement's obligations.[196]

The widest-ranging 'non-violation' complaint in GATT history (until the EEC's attack on Japan) was brought by Uruguay in the early 1960s against fifteen developed countries. For the first time a nullification claim was not just connected with particular tariff concessions. Uruguay took objection to almost 600 trade restrictions which together, regardless of their legality, disrupted in its view the overall balance of Uruguay's GATT obligations and benefits. A panel was charged with the task of evaluating Uruguay's complaint. In its reports, the panel advanced several interesting propositions, which are especially relevant to the Community's case against Japan.[197]

The panel reports regarding Uruguay's complaint under Article XXIII

Uruguay chose to attack the trade bariers its products encountered abroad along two lines. It raised objections against the existence of individual measures which allegedly affected the volume and price of its exports, while at the same time complaining of an overall impalance of its rights and obligations in relation to the contracting parties concerned. Although it was repeatedly asked to elaborate on its complaint, Uruguay refused to pass judgment on the legality of the measures complained of or to specify the benefits accruing to it under the GATT which it deemed nullified or impaired.[198]

The panel did not agree with Uruguay's argument that any significant restriction on the exports of a contracting party as such constitutes nullification or impairment under Article XXIII. Its report said:

194. Hudec, *ibid.*
195. McGovern, *op. cit.* n. 117, at 39.
196. Petersmann, *op. cit.* n. 133, at 471 indicates that since 1948 more than 90% of the formal complaints under Article XXIII have been 'violation' complaints. He also points out some important procedural and substantive legal differences between 'violation' and 'non-violation' complaints. *Id.*, at 471–472.
197. The panel issued lengthy reports on several occasions, reproduced in GATT, 11th Supp. BISD 95 (1963) and 13th Supp. BISD 35 and 45 (1965). These reports were adopted by the GATT Contracting Parties. GATT, 11th Supp. BISD 56 (1963), and 13th Supp. BISD 35 n. 1 (1965), respectively.
198. See para. 10 of the panel's 1964 report. GATT, 13th Supp. BISD 45, 47 (1965).

'In its view impairment and nullification in the sense of Article XXIII does not arise merely because of the existence of any measures; the nullification or impairment must relate to benefits accruing to the contracting party "under the Agreement".

* * *

While it is not precluded that a *prima facie* case of nullification or impairment could arise even if there is no infringement of GATT provisions, it would be in such cases incumbent on the country invoking Article XXIII to demonstrate the grounds and reasons for its invocation. Detailed submissions on the part of that contracting party on these points were therefore essential for a judgment to be made under this Article.'[199]

Through these considerations the panel did not merely impose a heavy burden of proof on the complainant. The report suggests that a contracting party can claim nullification only if benefits (expressly) conferred by the Agreement are denied to it. This interpretation of course undermines the basis for 'non-violation' claims, since denial of a conferred benefit comes close to a violation of the General Agreement.[200]

Furthermore, the report gave short shrift to the overall imbalance Uruguay perceived in its relations with developed trading partners. It summarily disposed of this argument with the observation:

'In invoking the provisions of Article XXIII the Uruguayan delegation repeatedly referred to the general difficulties created for Uruguay by the prevalence of restrictive measures affecting its exports and to the resulting inequality in the terms on which temperate zone primary producers participated in world trade. The Panel noted that it was not charged with the examination of broader issues falling outside the purview of Article XXIII.'[201]

In light of the GATT's negotiating history, the panel's contention that the broader issue of overall imbalance lay 'outside the purview of Article XXIII' seems out of place. The preparatory work of Article XXIII clearly reveals that its drafters intended to cover these issues. In their opinion, for instance, even general economic circumstances for which no government was responsible (such as a depression) could present an occasion for a contracting party to bring action under Article XXIII.[202]

The panel's position reflects the GATT's reluctance to deal with 'non-violation' nullification. Uruguay, of course, had weakened its case by not substantiating its complaints. The panel might have reached a different

---

199. Excerpts from paras. 13 and 14 of the panel's 1962 general report. GATT, 11th Supp. BISD 95 *et seq.*, at 99–100 (1963).
200. Dam, *op. cit.* n. 10, at 362. In the end, the panel did recommend that seven of the contracting parties involved withdraw certain measures for which no justification could be found in the General Agreement.
201. Excerpt from para. 22 of the panel's 1962 general report, *op. cit.* n. 199, at 102.
202. Hudec, *op. cit.* n. 193, at 471 and 497; Jackson, *op. cit.* n. 117, at p. 180.

conclusion if Uruguay had accused the contracting parties concerned of bad faith and had requested permission to suspend a number of its concessions *vis-à-vis* those countries, without asking them to adjust their policies. In this connection one limitation on the regulatory pressure an Article XXIII proceeding can bring to bear should be kept in mind. The preparatory work suggests that a contracting party cannot, through an Article XXIII-procedure, impose positive obligations on other GATT members that are not contained in the Agreement.[203]

This is not to say that a claim of nullification of 'larger' benefits derived from the Agreement is inconceivable. The GATT's negotiating history provides many references supporting such an action, while panel reports rejecting these claims have been confined to facts and arguments of particular cases. One has to appreciate, however, that every complaint of 'non-violation' nullification ultimately appeals to the GATT community's sense of fairness. And only if there is a strong *communis opinio* will an organization like the GATT feel comfortable enough to declare the actions of one of its members unjustifiable and 'unfair'.[204]

These considerations present a formidable obstacle to a 'non-violation' complaint against an overall imbalance of benefits between one contracting party and another. In trade negotiations it has proven to be virtually impossible for the GATT contracting parties to measure whether the concessions they negotiate with each other on balance are indeed 'reciprocal and mutually advantageous'.[205] Obviously, this problem is exacerbated in the context of a dispute settlement proceeding, because a more objective standard is required here to evaluate subjective expectations which have allegedly not been met. Consequently, the GATT membership will find it even more difficult to reach a consensus and exercise the necessary judgment in cases where the denial of 'larger' benefits is at stake.

Against this background, we now turn to the Community's complaint against Japan.

3. EVALUATING THE EEC COMPLAINT AGAINST JAPAN

In its central argument the Community expressed dissatisfaction with the organization of the Japanese economy, which in its view was primarily responsible for unbalanced trade flows in manufactured products (the EEC cited as relevant factors the vertical integration of manufacturing, distribution, service and trading sectors of Japanese industry, the close inter-relationship between industry and finance, the role of the government which actively

---

203. Jackson, *op. cit.* n. 117, at p. 181.
204. Hudec, *op. cit.* n. 193, at 502.
205. See the GATT's Preamble and Art. XXVIII *bis*, para. 1 (the latter being specifically concerned with tariff negotiations).

encourages and protects local industry, and the undervaluation of the yen). It requested that the Japanese government take affirmative action in the sphere of economic and trade policies to increase the level of imports of manufactured goods.

The EEC was never likely to gain much from this initiative. First of all, the Community's standard for measuring the imbalance of benefits in its trading relations with Japan left room for doubt. In support of its claim, the Community pointed out *inter alia* that Japanese exports to the EEC had grown more rapidly than EEC exports to Japan. Yet at the same time, during the 1970s the EEC's exports to Japan increased at about the same rate as its exports to the rest of the world.[206] This suggests that a relative lack of competitiveness is another viable explanation for the Community's trade deficit with Japan, and perhaps – as some would have it – the principal reason.[207]

Furthermore, the EEC did not maintain that the alleged overall imbalance in trading benefits was caused by unforeseen Japanese actions which ran counter to expectations Japan had previously raised. Experience with 'non-violation' cases should have indicated that the GATT Contracting Parties would be disinclined to venture an opinion on the thorny issue of 'global imbalance' in these circumstances.

In addition, the Community's request for adjustment of Japan's *economic policies* reached beyond the jurisdiction of the GATT. It is significant that the Community focused its complaint on structural elements of the Japanese economy, and not so much on particular trade restrictions. Indeed, the nature of the 'closed market' issue which dominated trade relations between Japan and its Western trading partners in the 1950s and 60s has changed. Though a number of non-tariff trade barriers still restrict access to the Japanese market,[208] cultural and business practices have come to be perceived as more important obstacles to imports and foreign investment. Some have argued that it would be counter-productive to pressure Japan to change these cultural phenomena.[209] One need not go that far to question the Community's action before GATT.

As we have seen, Article XXIII does not allow one contracting party to impose positive obligations on another party which are not contained in the Agreement. Clearly, the Agreement nowhere obliges a contracting party to

---

206. Wilkinson, *Misunderstanding: Europe v. Japan*, 248 (1981).

207. E.g., Wilkinson, *id.*, at 231–232. See also Parliamentary Resolution, *supra* n. 156 (citing, in para. J, the Community industry's lack of investments in new technology in the past and the resulting inability to compete with Japanese industry as a 'major and important reason' for the current trade imbalance).

208. For example, in August 1986 the United States requested the GATT Contracting Parties to establish a panel in order to review Japanese import restrictions in twelve agricultural products sectors. GATT Doc. L/6037 (1986). At about the same time the Community formally requested consultations about Japanese customs duties, taxes and labelling practices on imported wines and alcoholic beverages. GATT Doc. L/6031 (1986).

209. See generally Abbott & Totman, '"Black Ships" and Balance Sheets: The Japanese Market and U.S.–Japan Relations', 3 *Northwestern Journal of International Law & Business* 1981, 103.

change its economic structure in order to increase the share of imported manufactures, *even if* the complainant can demonstrate nullification of benefits to which it is entitled under the Agreement. Not surprisingly therefore, Japan resisted the Community's frontal attack on its economic policies, and was only prepared to discuss specific (trade) issues. Other GATT contracting parties appeared surprised as well as the attempts of the EEC to change the structure of the Japanese economy.[210]

The Community's initiative is also debatable from a strategic point of view. Perhaps the Community activated the GATT dispute settlement machinery only to strengthen its negotiating posture *vis-à-vis* Japan. Yet every complaint invites the opposing party to raise counterclaims. Japan took the opportunity with both hands and announced it would formally challenge before GATT 57 discriminatory import restrictions affecting Japanese imports in the Community if the EEC pressed its case.[211] That did not happen.

More than four years after its filing the Community's complaint against Japan has not made any progress. Although several consultations were held in 1982 and 1983, the Community shied away from requesting the GATT Contracting Parties to establish a panel that would formally investigate the matter. Gradually the complaint was transferred, in diplomatic parlance, from the fridge to the freezer. In March 1986, however, the Council instructed the Commission to 'study thoroughly the practical use of GATT Article XXIII.2'.[212] This was a guarded allusion to a possible revitalization of the complaint. At the time of writing (fall of 1986) the Commission had not finalized this study.

B. OUTLOOK FOR NEW TRADE NEGOTIATIONS BETWEEN THE EEC AND JAPAN IN GATT

The growing trade deficit with Japan continues to worry the Community institutions. It incites them to consider further measures that are difficult to reconcile with the GATT system. A resolution recently adopted by the European Parliament reflects this trend.[213] Among several of its proposals that are at odds with the GATT's principles and spirit of trade liberalization (such as calls for Japanese export moderation), two Parliamentary suggestions merit closer examination.

The European Parliament approved earlier requests of the Commission and the Council that Japan set verifiable import targets on either a global or a

---

210. 'Trade tensions between EEC and Japan worsen' of the *Financial Times* of 13 July 1982, on p. 4.
211. 'Sociaal-economische situatie hoofdthema Europese Raad' of the *Financieele Dagblad* of 27/29 March 1982, on p. 7.
212. Agence Europe, 12 March 1986, at p. 3.
213. Parliamentary resolution of 11 September 1986, *supra*, n. 156.

sectoral basis to help increase foreign penetration of the Japanese market.[214] So far Japan has rejected these requests. It has pointed out that in the GATT system import targets only have been established for state trading countries (with which it does not want to be compared, being a market economy), and even these have not worked well.[215] Japan's objections appear to be well-founded. They are shared by at least some EEC Member States like the Netherlands.[216]

Furthermore, the European Parliament strongly endorsed declarations by the Commission that the Community should not grant any new concessions to Japan in the course of the forthcoming GATT round so long as its import propensity for manufactured goods remains low.[217] If the Community were to adopt this proposal, the new GATT negotiations might grind to an early halt. Pursuant to the GATT's Most-Favoured-Nation obligation of Article I, any 'advantage, favour, privilege or immunity' granted by the Community to the products of one country would have to be accorded 'immediately and unconditionally' to all GATT contracting parties, including Japan. Accordingly, in the event the Community would not want to grant concessions to Japan, it could not grant any concession to other countries without violating Article I.[218]

Although these particular desiderata of the Community institutions may never come to fruition, that would not make Japan's position any more comfortable. Sustained dissatisfaction among Japan's trading partners with the benefits derived from free trade, however ill-conceived, is likely to erode the GATT framework. Being a major beneficiary of the liberal trading system, Japan may be forced to take the lead in seeking ways to ease current economic tensions. It may have to take domestic economic measures that are not prescribed or envisaged by the GATT in order to, paradoxically, salvage the GATT system.

---

214. *Id.*, at para. 35.
215. See notably para. 1 of Annex B to Poland's Protocol of Accession to GATT (providing for an initial 7% increase annually of Poland's imports from GATT contracting parties). GATT, 15th Supp. BISD 46 (1968).
216. See letter of the Netherlands Minister of Economic Affairs to the Dutch Parliament of 27 August 1986. Kamerstukken IIeK., 19550 no. 3, at 8–9 (1985–1986).
Note, however, that the 1986 agreement between the United States and Japan on trade in a particular product sector (semiconductors) does incorporate Japanese government guarantees of an increased share of the Japanese market for US producers. Tarullo, 'The Structure of U.S.–Japan Trade Relations', 27 *Harvard International Law Journal* 1986, 343, 355.
217. Parliamentary resolution, *supra* n. 156, at para. 8.
218. The GATT's unconditional MFN principle, however, has been put under pressure for some time now, particularly in the United States. See Bronckers, *op. cit.* n. 183 at 668–671. It is therefore conceivable that the Community with respect to certain areas of concessions might be able to push through deviations from the MFN principle in the Uruguay-round, so as to create leverage in its negotiations with Japan.

CHAPTER FOUR

THE EEC'S COMMERCIAL POLICY CONCERNING TEXTILES

By R.J.P.M. van Dartel*

I. INTRODUCTION

For many years now the EEC has applied protective commercial policy measures in the textile and clothing sectors.

The details of this policy depend upon the commercial relationship between the EEC and the third countries in question. The differences in these commercial relationships are reflected in the textile regimes operated by the EEC.

Thus, based on the Multifibre Arrangement (MFA), the EEC has concluded a number of bilateral textile agreements principally with Asian countries, but also with a number of State-trading and South American countries. In addition, the EEC has informal arrangements with a number of countries with which it concluded preferential arrangements in the past. An autonomous textile regime is applied to another group of countries (mainly State-trading countries). Lastly, with regard to industrialised countries, general import regulations representing an elaboration of GATT regulations are applied.

In this article a description will be given of the textile regime of the Community[1]). Particular attention will be paid to the third extension of the MFA and two other subjects of great importance for textile policy, namely, the internal management system for Outward Processing Traffic and the application of the safeguard measures contained in Article 115 EEC (including the recent Tezi decision).

---

* Ministry of Economic Affairs, The Hague. The ideas expressed in this article are the personal views of the author.
1. Tariff measure will not be discussed.

II. THE POLICY REGARDING COUNTRIES PARTY TO THE MFA

A. THE DRAFTING OF THE MULTIFIBRE ARRANGEMENT WITHIN THE FRAMEWORK OF GATT

1. HISTORY

By the 1950s the cotton industries of the industrialised countries were facing the problem of cheap imports from low-cost countries. At the insistence of the United States (following the election promises of President Kennedy) discussions on multilateral rules for trade in cotton products took place. These negotiations resulted in the first instance, in the Short Term Arrangement for Cotton Products (operative from 1 October 1961 until 30 September 1962) followed by the adoption of a long-term arrangment (operative from 1962 to 1967 and twice extended until 1973).[2] These cotton arrangements were devised as a temporary departure from the GATT rules to allow the participating industrialised countries to restructure their industry. In addition to the well-intended provisions relating to the further liberalisation of world trade found in the arrangement, Article 3 allows individual countries to take safeguard measures in cases of market disruption. These specific protective measures deviate from the general GATT rules (non-discrimination); Article 4 of the arrangement allows for the conclusion of mutually acceptable bilateral agreements which do not deviate from the arrangement.

Prior to agreement being reached on these rules a great number of restrictions were being applied by some of the large importers. During the operation of the short-term arrangement, the US instituted a considerable number of restrictions based upon Article 3. Later the US concluded arrangements mainly on the basis of Article 4, and was followed in this respect by several other importing countries.

The six Member States of the EEC, however, carried out, at least partly, the well-intended liberalisation of restrictions envisaged by the arrangement. This explains the difficult position the EEC found itself in later negotiations.[3]

After operating for some time, the structure of these cotton rules was found to be too narrow by the cotton importing countries. Moreover, difficulties arose in other sectors of the market (artificial fibres and wool) calling for a broader form of arrangement.

These factors were the motivation for negotiations on similar rules which took place within the GATT framework in 1973, resulting in the Multifibre Arrangement.

---

2. To give some idea of the participating countries, on 1 January 1963 the following countries participated: Australia, Austria, Canada, Denmark, the Six Member States of the EEC, India, Israel, Japan, Mexico, Norway, Pakistan, Portugal, Spain, Sweden, United Arab Republic, United Kingdom (also on behalf of Hong Kong) and the United States.

3. For more information on this: *A Study on Cotton Textiles* GATT 1966/4. For further information on the cotton agreements see Kroeze: *Het Multi-Vezel Accoord*.

2. THE MULTIFIBRE ARRANGEMENT AND THE FIRST AND SECOND EXTENSION

In 1974 agreement was reached within the framework of GATT on a broader arrangement: The Multifibre Arrangement.[4] By virtue of this arrangement it became possible once again to apply restrictive measures to protect the industry of the importing countries.

In comparison to the cotton arrangement this arrangement is broader with regard to the number of products covered and contains more specific provisions. In this arrangement, too, a number of commendable objectives are outlined (in Article 1): the expansion of trade, the reduction of barriers to trade and the progressive liberalisation of world trade and at the same time ensuring an orderly and equitable development of trade, whilst preventing disruption of the market and individual lines of production in both the importing and exporting countries.

Paragraph 3 of Article 1 indicates the importance attached to supporting the economic and social development of the developing countries, ensuring a substantial increase in income from the export of textiles, as well as aiming at a greater share of the world trade in textiles for these developing countries. To achieve these aims all import restrictions must be abolished forthwith unless they fall under a programme in which they are abolished in stages or by measures conforming to Articles 3 and 4. These two articles conform to provisions contained in former cotton arrangements, and have been adopted with a view to set up a procedure by which restrictions on trade in textiles can be agreed upon. In the event that market disruption is determined one at first consults with the countries from which the disrupting import originates. Annex A sets out the criteria by which market disruption is determined.[5]

If these consultations achieve no result then the importing country can introduce import restrictions (Annex B contains rules for the levels of these import restrictions, the minimum annual growth of the restrictions (6%) and flexibility).

In unusual or critical circumstances, the importing country can impose restrictions immediately after the first consultation. Besides the possibility of introducing restrictions when faced with market disruption (as in Article 3), Article 4 contains an alternative procedure by which bilateral agreements may be concluded with the objects of preventing market disruption and ensuring the expansion and orderly development of trade. In practice this means that, on the bases of Article 4, bilateral agreements may be concluded containing a

---

4. For the official text see Council Decision 74/214 EEC, OJ 1974, L118/1.
5. The determination of market disruption is based on the existence of serious damage to the national producers. The factors leading to market disruption are:
– a strong and important (threatening) increase in the import of certain products of a certain origin;
– the prices of these imports are considerably lower than the prices on the market in the importing country.
The interests of the exporting countries should be taken into account when the examination of market disruption is made.

number of restrictions, growth rates, flexibility provisions, etc. Agreements such as these have been concluded by the importing countries with all important suppliers.

Article 1, paragraph 6, is also of importance for the introduction of restrictions in the textile sector.

'The provisions of this Arrangement shall not affect the rights and obligations of the participating countries under the GATT.'

From this provision one can conclude that the signatories of the MFA can still apply the safeguard measures of Article XIX GATT to textile products. The interpretation is confirmed by the fact that Article 3 allows for an exception to the prohibition on imposing restrictions on trade as long as such restrictions are justified under the GATT.

In Article 6 of the MFA regard is paid to the special position of the developing countries (newcomers). By virtue of their special position these countries are to be treated more favourably (*e.g.* larger quotas, higher growth rates, and for small suppliers restrictions should be completely avoided). Cotton producers should also be treated with special consideration on the basis of this Article.

In Article 8 the participating countries agree to collaborate to prevent circumvention of the Arrangement (fraud). If the country suffering injury is not satisfied with the cooperation it receives it can bring the matter before the Textiles Committee.[6] In the text of the MFA there is no mention of reductions of quotas as a means of counterbalancing the fraudulently imported shipments. Besides handling the problem of circumvention, the Textiles Committee, consisting of representatives of the participating parties, deals with matters brought to it by the 'Textile Surveillance Body'. At the same time the Committee conducts studies and analyses, collects statistics and looks at opportunities for promoting trade. Once a year the working of the MFA is evaluated and the results are reported to the contracting parties. One year before the expiry of the MFA the Committee negotiates the extension, modification or abolition of the MFA. The Textile Surveillance Body is entrusted with daily affairs (TSB, Article 11). This Committee consists of eight members and a chairman and supervises the implementation of the arrangement. The committee meets as often as necessary.[7]

Finally, the MFA contains provisions relating to the products covered (Article 12), the duration (Article 16 – 4 years), date of entry into force (Article 14 – 1 January 1974) and the possibility of withdrawal from the arrangement (Article 15 – withdrawal being effective 60 days after the Director General of the GATT has been notified).

---

6. Established under Article 10.
7. See for further working methods and tasks: Article 11, paras. 2–12.

The first extension of the MFA

After some discussion in the Textiles committee it was decided on 14 December 1977 to extend the MFA for another 4 years (in accordance with the procedure of Article 10, paragraph 5, MFA). This extension left the text of the MFA unaltered, but the conclusions of the Textiles Committee included 10 paragraphs laying down further administrative provisions.[8] These provisions confirmed that the working of the arrangement was not fully satisfactory. Paragraph 5.3 of the conclusions contains a provision with important consequences.[9] This so-called 'reasonable departures' clause was adopted at the request of the EEC, because it was of the opinion that its starting position was so weak that not all the provisions of the MFA could be fully applied.

The weakness of this position was due to the liberal stance taken by the Community during the period of the cotton arrangement and the long delay before the adoption of restrictive measures during MFA I. As a result the Community negotiated on the basis of a relatively high import penetration during the second MFA. This 'reasonable departures' clause made it possible for the EEC to negotiate bilateral agreements based on Article 4 containing a lessening of the import penetration of a number of large suppliers, and a reduction of growth rates. The bilateral agreements of the EEC under the second MFA clearly had a more restrictive character than the agreements under MFA I.

The second extension of the MFA[10]

On 22 December 1981, just before the expiry of MFA II, agreement was reached on the extension of the MFA by 4 years and 7 months (*i.e.* until 31 July 1986). The length of this term is explained by the fact that the EEC wanted a period of 5 years whereas the supplying countries wanted no more than 4 years. The extension left the text of the MFA unchanged. However, once again rules to which the participants were obliged to adhere were laid down in a Protocol of 24 paragraphs. This second protocol was somewhat more precisely defined than the previous one because it no longer contained a general 'reasonable departures' clause. The absence of this clause was the result of the Community's decision to abandon it (the Commission and some of the Member

---

8. For the official text: S2152 (COMER 378).

9. The Committee has agreed that in the framework of the Multifibre Arrangement all discussions and negotiations should take place in a spirit of fairness and flexibility to reach a mutually acceptable solution in accordance with Art. 4, para. 3 or Art. 3, paras. 3 and 4, which allow deviation from particular factors in particular cases in a reasonable way and by mutual consent.

10. For the official text: OJ 1982, L83/8. The contents of the Protocol will be discussed taking into consideration the EEC's objectives in the discussions on extension.

States were against the clause) and because the provision was unacceptable to the supplying countries and the US.

As a result of the omission of this provision from the Protocol, more detailed provisions were included, which, however, as a result of compromises, are still rather vague. A more precise elaboration of these provisions took place within the framework of the bilateral negotiations between the EEC and the supplying countries. In this paragraph the most important alterations with regard to the previous protocol will be discussed, while the concrete form of these alterations, established at the initiative of the EEC in the bilateral agreements with the supplying countries, will be provided in the notes.

First of all the EEC wanted to limit once again the levels of entry of the dominant suppliers for the most sensitive products (this concerns Hong-Kong, South Korea, Macao and Taiwan).[11] Cut-backs similar to these were also negotiated in 1977 under the reasonable departures clause. As this clause was lacking in the second protocol extending the Arrangement, the following stipulation was inserted (paragraph 6). 'The Committee noted the important role of and the goodwill expressed by certain exporting participants now predominant in the exporting of textile products in all three fibres covered by the Arrangement in finding and contributing to mutually acceptable solutions to particular problems relative to particularly large restraint levels arising out of the application of the Arrangement as extended by the Protocol.'

The EEC has tried to specify this promise of the larger suppliers in an exchange of letters with these countries.[12]

At the same time the EEC introduced in these negotiations the so-called 'surge mechanism'. With this the EEC wanted, at the initiative of the United Kingdom, to prevent imports from increasing too drastically as a result of a sudden filling up of under-utilized quotas. When imports of products under these restraint levels increase too fast consultations were to take place.

In these consultations rules could be fixed providing for a more gradual growth in the utilisation of these quotas during the duration of the MFA. This mechanism meant that in a number of instances the supplying countries would lose the certainty that they would be allowed to use their allotted quotas freely and to the full. In exchange for such a loss the EEC was prepared to offer compensation.

As this mechanism met with a lot of opposition from all other countries it has been vaguely worded in the extension Protocol (paragraph 10):

'The view was expressed that real difficulties may be caused in importing

11. In the discussions within the EEC, the more liberal states (the Netherlands, Denmark, and the Federal Republic of Germany) agreed to the cutting back of the larger suppliers so as to create more room for the less-developed small suppliers, some of whom had only just begun exporting textiles and clothing. Such cut-backs were necessary because the Member States were not keen to increase imports across the board.
12. In the bilateral agreements that have since been concluded with the larger suppliers cut-backs of, on average, something more than 7% have been inserted. Despite the stipulation in para. 6 of the extentions protocol, the EEC met with great difficulties in agreeing on such a reduction with these countries.

countries by sharp and substantial increases in imports as a result of significant differences between larger restraint levels negotiated in accordance with Annex B on the one hand and actual imports on the other. Where such significant difficulties stem from consistently underutilized larger restraint levels and cause or threaten serious palpable damage to domestic industry, an exporting participant may agree to mutually satisfactory solutions or arrngements.

Such solutions or arrangements shall provide for equitable and quantifiable compensation to the exporting participant to be agreed by both parties concerned.'[13]

Due to the absence of the 'reasonable departures' clause the importing countries also were in need of a stipulation in the extension protocol which made possible a lower growth rate than the 6% stipulated in Annex B of the MFA. For, the very low consumption growth in these countries (1% within the EEC in 1981) made an import growth of 6% unacceptable. Paragraph 9 thus allowed parties to a bilateral agreement to agree, in exceptional circumstances, to a lower positive growth rate[14] for a particular product from a particular source.[15]

Under this paragraph it was also possible to agree to lower flexibility rates in exceptional circumstances. (The flexibility provisions allow, for example, transfers of quantities between quotas or carry forward of unused quotas to the following year).

In addition to the provisions aimed at the *prevention of circumvention* (fraud, article 8) and the rules on administrative co-operation contained in the MFA, the extension Protocol allowed the deduction of the quantity involved from the quota of the country of true origin. Such deduction could only take place following consultation between the countries concerned. If no agreement was reached, then the Textile Surveilance Body could be referred to for its opinion.[16]

13. In the bilateral agreements the EEC elaborated this 'surge mechanism' as follows.
 If the use of the quota of a group I product rose by more than 10%, consultations could take place on the suspension of flexibility, the adjustment of the quota and on the compensation to be given by the Community. The applicability of the mechanism was not only limited to the most sensitive products but also to large quotas (more than 1% of the total import of the product concerned) and these quotas must be utilized by more than 50%. The mechanism could also be used for a region of the Community. The Article in the bilateral agreements allowed the EEC to impose restrictions unilaterally in case of failure of the consultations.
 Whether such a unilateral action was possible, given the wording of the stipulation in the extension protocol, is very doubtful. Looking back on it the EEC could have saved itself much trouble because the mechanism has never been applied. At the time of its introduction it was already clear that the requirement of compensation would make agreement within the EEC on the use of the clause virtually impossible.
14. In the discussion within the EEC some of the Member States even wanted to start from a basis of negative growth.
15. Whether the EEC was allowed to negotiate lower growth rates for a large number of products with all the supplying countries is debatable. Nevertheless, in the bilateral negotiations the EEC negotiated growth rates of less than 6% for the majority of the quotas.
16. In the bilateral agreements the EEC reserved the right to lower quota unilaterally if agreement was not reached in the consultations.

As the negotiations in Geneva took place between both supplying and importing countries, one can see the interests of these two groups (whether balanced or not) reflected in the Protocol. At the request of the supplying countries, stipulations were included in the protocol about a more favourable treatment for developing countries which supply only small quantities or are entering the market for the first time and for cotton producers (paragraph 12).

A special committee was set up to monitor the adjustment measures aiming at restructuring the textile industry in the importing countries.

At the end of the negotiations in Geneva a majority of the Member States of the EEC were of the opinion that the extension protocol contained too few guarantees to satisfactorily round off the bilateral negotiations. In order to reduce this risk, the EEC wanted to sign the MFA only conditionally, but this procedure was not accepted by the other parties. In order to get enough certainty and to keep enough pressure on during the negotiations of the bilateral agreements, the EEC spokesman in Geneva declared the following:

'I am prepared to recommend to the authorities of the Community acceptance of this Protocol. As I stated in July in this Committee, the conclusion of satisfactory bilateral agreements is essential for the EEC. I am sure you will not misunderstand me when I say that for us, this second stage is at least as important as the first and that if it proves impossible to conclude satisfactory new bilateral agreements we shall be unable to continue to participate in the MFA. The Community will examine the situation and reassess its position *vis-à-vis* the MFA in early autumn next year.[17]

On February 1982 the Council of Ministers of the EEC elaborated the following procedure for a possible withdrawal from the MFA: the Commission had to report to the Council on the progress of the bilateral negotiations by 30 September at the latest.

On the basis of this report, the Council would decide whether or not to continue the Community's participation in the MFA. If the Council failed to take a positive decision, the EEC would withdraw at the end of that year. After the Commission succeeded to conclude satisfactory bilateral agreements with all supplying countries, the EEC Council of Ministers decided on 13 December 1982 to continue participation in the MFA.[18]

17. On the basis of Art. 15 MFA the EEC could withdraw from the MFA 60 days after giving notice.
18. Only with Argentina no agreement was concluded because Argentina could not accept the territorial clause. In the bilateral agreements the following stipulation concerning the territorial application was inserted: 'This Agreement shall apply to the territories within which the Treaty establishing the European Economic Community is applied and under the conditions, laid down in that treaty on the one hand, and to the territory (of Argentina) on the other hand'.

Under Art. 131 EEC a special association relationship is established with the countries and territories overseas and the EEC treaty applies to these countries and territories (art. 227 EEC). In Annex IV of the Treaty a list of these countries and territories is given in which the Falkland Islands are mentioned.

Under no circumstances could the Argentinians agree on the application of the textile agreement to the Falkland Islands, which had no significance in practice, but a change in the territorial

3. THE THIRD EXTENSION OF THE MFA

Before elaborating the text of the third extension protocol two factors which influenced these negotiations will be dwelt upon first.[19] First of all, the discussion in the US about unilateral import restricting measures have influenced the attitude of the American delegation as well as that of other parties. The Jenkins Bill provided for a limitation of textile imports to the US from Taiwan, South Korea and Hong Kong by a maximum of 30% while imports from eight other Asiatic countries and Brazil would be frozen at their 1984 level. The Jenkins Bill was adopted by a large majority in Congress on 3 December 1985, but was vetoed afterwards by President Reagan. This veto can only be overruled by a two-third majority in both houses of the American Parliament.

The voting was scheduled to take place after completion of the MFA negotiations, making the fate of the Bill largely dependent on the result of these negotiations. The American delegation tried to prevent the adoption of the Bill by negotiating an extension protocol which was as protectionist as possible, while the supplying countries knew what too great an opposition to this would bring about.[20]

Another factor in the negotiations was the preparation of the new GATT round. Several developing countries wanted to ensure that participation in this new round was dependent on a sufficient liberalisation in the textile sector. By this, these countries hoped to put pressure on the importing countries with an interest in the new GATT round.

The protectionist result of these negotiations (above all concerning the points important to the Americans, such as the extension of product coverage, the possibility of taking long term unilateral measures and the treatment of the larger suppliers) indicates which factor played the most important role.

During these negotiations the EEC was in a relatively comfortable position. The EEC was no longer the most restrictive party, and no difficult provisions were included in the Commissoin mandate, such as the inclusion of a 'reasonable departures' clause, cut-backs for larger suppliers or the introduction of a surge mechanism. As for the topics for which the EEC wanted

application was unacceptable to the EEC. All this made the conclusion of an agreement impossible. Following this the EEC instituted a suveillance on the import of textile products from Argentina. In case these imports would grow too big in size, measures would be taken on the basis of Art. 3 MFA.

19. It is regrettable that the GATT study on the trade in textile and clothing products (*Textiles and Clothing in the World Economy*, GATT secretariat, July 1984) cannot be counted as one of these factors. In this elaborate study undertaken at the instruction of the Contracting Parties, the careful conclusion reached is that all parties would be better off with a liberalisation of the world trade in this sector. A transition period is advised.

The result of these negotiations reveals that the GATT Secretariat has been unable to convince the importing countries.

20. Although the many representatives of the American textile industry present in Geneva were afterwards not at all satisfied about the new extension protocol, the Jenkins Bill failed to receive the required majority by a narrow margin at the voting in the House of Representatives on 6 August, which made certain the continuation of the American paticipation in the MFA.

new passages to be inserted in the extension protocol (such as the protection of trade marks and reciprocity in the opening up of markets) the EEC proved willing to accept weak texts during the negotiations.

Taking into account the diverging interests of the developing countries and the growing irritation on their part concerning the ever continuing 'temporary' exception to the GATT rules, it is not surprising that agreement on the third extension of the MFA was not reached until the date of termination of MFA III, 31 July 1986. In the new protocol, which consists of 28 paragraphs, more detailed rules were given on the operation of the MFA in the five years to come (until 31 July 1991).

The contents of the third extension protocol

The above mentioned attitude of the American delegation, on certain points had led to further-reaching possibilities of protecting the home market. In this respect the extension of *fibre coverage* in paragraph 24 can be called the most important point. This paragraph makes it possible to limit trade in textiles made of vegetable fibres combined with fibres falling under the original MFA and blends containing silk, which are directly competitive with the original MFA products (products of cotton, wool, and man-made fibres).

Article 3 and 4 MFA can be invoked with respect to directly competitive imports of such textiles, in which any or all of those fibres in combination represent either the chief value of the fibres or 50 per cent or more by weight of the products, which cause market disruption or a real risk thereof.[21] This new stipulation extends the MFA to linen, ramee, silk blends and jute. Some historically traded textiles which were internationally traded in commercially significant quantities prior to 1982 are exclude from this extension of the scope (para. 24, sub iii).[22]

Also at the request of the Americans the scope of Article 3 sub 5 MFA, which allows for unilateral import restrictions in a situation of market disruption and after consultations have failed, has been widened. The maximum time of operation of such unilateral measures has been extended from 1 to 2 years (para. 8 extension protocol).

As was already possible under the '81 protocol, paragraph 9 enables parties to a bilateral agreement to agree, in exceptional circumstances to a lower positive growth rate for a particular product from a particular source. Under this paragraph it is also possible to agree to lower flexibility provisions in exceptional circumstances.

21. In case the share of these 'new' products remain below this percentage there is a possibility that the remaining constituent fibres (cotton, wool and man-made fibres) also bring the product under the scope of the MFA after all.
22. At the conclusion of the negotiations China and India placed a reservation on the time of their acceptance of the extension protocol. The US officially objected to this reservation. At the moment of writing it was not known, if these two countries would maintain this reservation when accepting the extension protocol. If so, this could lead to the application of the general safeguard provision of the GATT (art. XIX) for products made of these fibres.

A provision concerning the reduction of imports from the larger supplying countries (the so-called cut-back clause) is lacking in the new extension protocol. According to paragraph 10 of the new protocol lower figures concerning growth and flexibility can be agreed on with these countries, provided they are positive.[23]

In paragraph 11 an adapted version of the *'surge clause'* introduced by the EEC in the previous negotiations (aimed at opposing a too rapid filling up of underutilized quotas) has been inserted. The clause in this protocol has taken the weaker form of a consultation procedure but the requirement of compensation by the country making use of the procedure has also been weakened (compensation has to be provided *where appropriate*).

The prevention of *fraud* (especially circumvention of restrictions by directing trade via a country not subject to restrictions) is a priority for the importing countries. The following provisions have been included for the prevention of this type of fraud.

– Collaboration in regard to instances of false declarations regarding the quantity and type of textile products presented for import by the exchange of available information and documents in accordance with the national laws concerned, with a view to establishing the relevant facts and enabling the government concerned to take appropriate action under national laws and procedures (para. 17).
– The provision to combat fraud contained in the previous protocol has been made more effective by the inclusion of a procedure for better cooperation between importing and exporting countries by an improved exchange of information. 'To this end, it is agreed that such co-operation will include such administrative co-operation and exchange of available information and documents in accordance with national laws and procedures, as are necessary to establish the relevant facts.'

If sufficient proof exists that such a circumvention took place the amount involved can be deducted from the quota of the actual country of origin, but only if this country of origin agrees. If agreement is not reached the case must be brought before the TSB (para. 16).
– The EEC as well as the US have insisted on a provision to prevent the infringement of trademarks and designs. Paragraph 27 contains a weak and non-operational compromise.

'Participants noted the concern expressed by a number of participants with respect to the problem of infringement of registered trademarks and designs in trade in textiles and clothing and noted that such problems could be dealt with in accordance with the relevant national laws and regulations.'

Finally, with regard to the provisions inserted at the request of the importing countries, it is worth mentioning that the reciprocity asked for by the EEC (the opening up of the market by the EEC must go hand in hand with the opening up

---

23. These countries insisted on a more generous provision (growth rates above 1%), to which the Americans in particular objected.

of the markets by all other participating countries each in accordance with its economic situation and level of economic development) is hardly mentioned in the protocol. The EEC had to be satisfied with a general phrase in paragraph 3:

> 'The participants in the arrangement stressed the importance of promoting liberalization of trade in textiles and clothing. In this connection they recognized the need *for co-operative efforts by all participants.*'

Naturally the exporting countries also put forward several proposals during the negotiations. A large group was in favour of abolishing the MFA as soon as possible, but this soon proved to be impossible. Similarly, the fixing of a definite termination date was unacceptable to the importing countries. Finally, it was stated in paragraph 3 that the final objective is the applicaiton of GATT rules to trade in textiles.

When abolition proved unacceptable, the exporting countries tried to insert more extensive guarantees that protectionist measures would only be applied in situations where there really is market disruption resulting from imports from the country in question. To that end, together with an explicit reference to the appropriate factors for the determination of a situation of market disruption as referred to in Annex A (paragraph 5) of the MFA, a further specification was given in paragraph 6 of the extension protocol of the necessary information that has to be supplied before protection of the market can be resorted to.

> '... requests for action under Articles 3 or 4 shall be accompanied by available, specific and relevant factual information as up-to-date as possible, particularly in respect of factors set out in Annex A. In respect of requests made under Article 3, the information should be related, as closely as possible, to identifiable segments of production and to the reference period set out in Annex B. The importing participants agreed that actions based on the existence of serious damage to domestic producers or actual threat thereof in terms of paragraph I of Annex A cannot be based solely upon the level of imports or growth thereof. Participants agreed that in determining a situation of market disruption, due consideration has to be given to the evolution of the state of the domestic industry in the importing country, including its export performance and the market share held by this industry.'

Over the years the supplying countries, too, have realised that abolition of the MFA is only possible if a situation exists in which the textile and clothing industry in the developed countries is competitive again. For this reason the supplying countries are interested in the adjustment policies and measures and the process of autonomous adjustment in the importing countries. According to the supplying countries supervision on this matter needs to be improved. Already during the previous negotiations it was decided to establish a Sub-Committee on Adjustment, which periodically reports on the developments occurring within this field. According to the provisions of the new protocol, the Sub-Committee, in drafting these reports will no longer be restricted to information supplied by the country under investigation.

'The Sub-Committee on Adjustment should continue to make a periodic review of developments in autonomous adjustment processes and in policies and measures to facilitate adjustment, as well as in production and trade in textiles, on the basis of material and information to be provided by participating countries as well as additional material and information obtained by the Secretariat from other sources, and with the help of any supporting analysis by the Secretariat. Attention was drawn to the impact of technological developments on comparative advantage and competitiveness in textile trade. Participating countries were urged to provide the Sub-Committee on Adjustment with all relevant and up-to-date information relating, inter alia, to production and trade, necessary for the Sub-Committee to discharge its function and to report periodically to the Textiles Committee.' (para. 19)

Not only the stipulations concerning the proper application of the safeguard procedures and the continuation of the restructuring of industry[24] have been strengthened, but also those pertaining to the *more favourable treatment of the weakest group of countries* (to this group belong, according to the original MFA text, the small suppliers, new entrants and the cotton producers). To this group are added the least developed countries, to which the most flexible treatment will be applied.

'If circumstances oblige the importing country to introduce restraints on exports from the least developed countries, the treatment accorded to these countries should be significantly more favourable than that accorded to the other group referred to in this paragraph, preferably in all its elements but, at least, on overall terms.' (para. 13b)

Experiences during the previous MFA period taught the supplying countries that guarantees are necessary for the proper application of a bilateral agreement once it has been concluded.[25] Thus, the following was inserted in paragraph 18:

'Introduction of changes (such as changes in practices, rules, procedures, categorization of textile products, including those changes relating to the Harmonized System) in the implementation or interpretation of bilateral textile agreements or of the Arrangement, which have the effect of upsetting the balance of rights and obligations between the parties concerned, or which affect the ability of a participant to use or benefit fully from a bilateral agreement, or which disrupt trade, shall be avoided as far as possible. Where

---

24. However, it is hardly likely that the importing countries will change their policy following these provisions. Even the European Commission has never succeeded in obtaining any significant influence on the process of restructuring the textile industry in the Member States.

25. The most important experience in this regard resulted from the new origin rules fixed unilaterally by the US in 1984, making import of textile and clothing extra difficult and hampering supplying countries in fully using the quota awarded to them. (Customs Regulations Amendments Relating to Textiles and Textile Products. Federal Register/Vo./49 no. 151/Friday, August 3, 1984).

such changes are necessary, participants agreed that the participant initiating any such changes shall, wherever possible, inform and initiate consultations with the affected participant prior to the time that such changes may affect the trade in question, with a view to reaching a mutually acceptable solution regarding appropriate and equitable adjustments. Participants further agreed that where consultation prior to implementation of any such changes is not feasible, the participant initiating such changes will consult, as early as possible, with the affected participant with a view to reaching a mutually satisfactory solution regarding appropriate and equitable adjustments. Any dispute under this provision may be referred to the TSB for recommendation.'

The paragraph on a stricter treatment of larger suppliers also contains a reference to the application of the bilateral agreements:

'Importing participants at the same time recognized the importance to predominant exporting participants of stability in the textile trade and the need to ensure that stability and certainty throughout the full life of their bilateral agreements, keeping in mind also the need for orderly development in trade in textiles.'

Lastly, the extension protocol contains a few *general provisions*. Thus, the importance is re-affirmed of the effective functioning of the Textiles Committee, the Sub-Committee on Adjustment and the Textiles Surveillance Body. The TSB is given the power to interpret the relevant provisions of the MFA when considering cases and concerning the application of bilateral agreements and measures taken on the basis of the MFA (para. 22). The possibility of increasing the number of members of the TSB will be investigated. The MFA will be extended for another 5 years (the longest period so far) and will enter into force on 1 August 1986 for those countries having accepted the protocol on that date (para. 28).

B. THE APPLICATION OF THE MFA BY THE EEC

The EEC has concluded agreements with the most important low costproducers on the basis of article 4 of the Multi Fibre Arrangement. During MFA III the EEC concluded agreements with 27 countries.[26] These agreements expire at the end of 1986.

---

26. Bangladesh, Brazil, Bulgaria, Czechoslovakia, Colombia, Egypt (for cotton yarns an informal arrangement was concluded), Guatemala, Haiti, Hong-Kong, Hungary, India, Indonesia, Macao, Malaysia, Mexico, Pakistan, Peru, the Philippines, Poland, Romania, Singapore, Sri Lanka, Thailand, Uruguay, Yugoslavia and South Korea. A so-called *sui generis* agreement was concluded with China, at the start of the bilateral negotiations not a party to the MFA (it joined in 1984), which formally is not based on the MFA. This last agreement runs from 1984 to 1988.

In this chapter besides a few comments on the negotiations between the EEC and the supplying countries on the new bilateral agreements, the aims of the EEC in these negotiations will be discussed first.

1. THE OBJECTIVES OF THE EEC IN THE BILATERAL NEGOTIATIONS

a. Quantitative Objectives

A distinction can be made between the quantitative objectives of the EEC and its objectives for the text of the bilateral agreements.

With respect to import quantities, the EEC operates a system by which total maxima are fixed for the imports of textiles and clothing originating from countries subject to restraints.[27] These ceilings are fixed for the eight most sensitive products, the so-called Group I products. This Group I has been divided into eight categories: cotton yarns, cotton fabrics, fabrics of synthetic fibres, T-shirts, pullovers, trousers and ladies' and men's shirts. For the supplying MFA countries this means that the EEC has fixed import quantities within these total maxima (the so-called global ceilings) which indicate the total quantity of these sensitive products which can be imported from all the MFA countries that are under restraint. The maximum import quantities are distributed among the Member States. The Council has also fixed average growth rates for this group of products, which are far below the 6% prescribed by Annex B of the MFA. The EEC has divided the remaining products covered by the MFA into another two groups according to their sensitivity (Groups II and III).[28] No global ceilings have been set for these groups; however, the Council has fixed indicative maximum growth rates for these products in the mandate.[29]

In setting the average growth rates consideration was given to the fact that the Commission is negotiating lower growth rates with dominant suppliers. Furthermore the flexibility allowed for these countries will have to be limited. All of this had to be accomplished before the council could decide that satisfactory agreements had been concluded. However, the European Community still had a number of further objectives for the text of bilateral agreements.

---

27. Which countries, apart from the participants in the MFA, fall under these ceilings will be set out below. Broadly, these ceilings can be divided into two parts: quantities for the MFA countries and for the countries subject to an autonomous regime and in the second section, quantities for the countries enjoying a preferential trade relationship.
28. These groups have also been split up into a great number of categories. A group IV exists (within the EEC), which did not fall under the MFA before the extension of fibre coverage, but which at present does fall under it.
29. Partly also under 6%.

b. The text of the bilateral agreements

The EEC aimed at including a large number of standard provisions in the bilateral agreements during the negotiations with the supplying countries. These provisions are based on the MFA text, on the expected contents of the extension protocol (as the bilateral negotiations had already started before completion of the discussion in Geneva) and on the provisions in the Commission's mandate. The following provisions are of importance. Article 1 contains a reference to the MFA text, an EEC promise not to switch over to safeguard measures based on Article 3 MFA and Article XIX GATT, and a prohibition of measures of equivalent effect.

In the agreement the Community comes to an understanding with the third country concerned over a number of restrictions. Other products falling within the scope of the agreement are not completely free from restrictions, but fall under the basket mechanism.

Under this mechanism the import of a product remains unrestricted, but only up to a certain level, the so-called threshold level.[30] Once this quantity is exceeded (within the EEC as a whole or within a region of the EEC) the EEC can ask for consultation with the third country concerned. Pending these consultations the supplying country has a duty to limit its exports to 25% of the threshold level or 25% of the actual imports of the previous year, whichever is the higher. Should no agreement be reached during this consultation, the EEC can then impose a restriction unilaterally (not lower than the threshold or 106% of the imports of the previous year). This possibility of unilateral measures has been especially criticised by the supplying countries.

Article 11 provides for the possibility of consultations once fraud has been established. In these consultations the adjustment of the restrictions with regard to which the fraud has taken place may be discussed. Once again, the EEC has reserved the right to lower quotas unilaterally if agreement is not reached in the consultations.

In addition to the provisions discussed above, the standard agreement also contains provisions concerning flexibility, the operation of outward processing traffic (a number of agreements also contain special quotas for this type of trade, based on co-operation between industries)[31] the free import of handloom and folklore products and co-operation in the management of ceilings. The management of the ceilings takes place on the basis of double checking; in practice this means that the utilization of these ceilings is controlled by both the exporting (through an export document) and the

---

30. This threshold is calculated on the basis of a certain percentage of the previous year's total imports for that product into the EEC; this threshold quantity has also been split up over the Member States. The threshold has been increased considerably in the new agreements, but within the EEC an agreement was reached to react more quickly to any surpassing of the threshold, making the contents of the concession of a restricted nature, which partly offsets the liberalizing effect of the increased thresholds.
31. Outward processing traffic will be dealt with in Part VII of this chapter.

importing country (through an import licence). A price clause has been inserted in the agreements with state trading countries.

The bilateral agreements also contain provisions on the distribution of Community quotas among the Member States (Art. 14).[32]

A novelty is the possibility for a supplying country to transfer, within certain units[33] and after 1 June of each year, unused quantities from the quota-share of one member state to that of another Member State without having to ask the EEC for permission.

The surge clause, of such importance to the EEC during the previous negotiations, has now been included in the general consultation clause (Art. 16) in the form of a short specific reference. The possibility of unilateral action no longer exists.

In the annexes of the agreements extra access is given to children's clothing (by means of a special recalculation key). Children's clothing has become rather scarce (and therefore expensive) in the EEC, since the producing countries prefer to use their quota for adult clothing, which has a higher added value.

With regard to certain points, the bilateral agreements concluded before the conclusion of the extension protocol take into account the result of the negotiations in Geneva. Thus in the article on product coverage the 'original' MFA products are mentioned (cotton, wool and man made fibres), but a possibility to extend this coverage is given in one of the annexes, in case the same happens with regard to the MFA extension protocol. In the text of the arrangement the duration of the bilateral agreements has been fixed from 1 January 1987 until 31 December 1990, but automatic extension of 1 year is granted in one of the protocols, if the Multifibre Arrangement is extended for a period going beyond 31 December 1990. In an agreed minute annexed to the agreements the exporting country in question takes note of the importance attached by the Community to its proposal, made in the framework of the negotiations of the renewal of the MFA, regarding an undertaking by all participating countries to contribute to the liberalisation of trade in textiles, according to their level of development and economic position, by making an effort to open their markets and ensure fair trading conditions. In another agreed minute the Community underlines the importance it attaches to its proposal, made in Geneva, regarding intellectual property rights.

The EEC proposed three different types of agreements in the bilateral negotiations. The most extensive agreement (as described above) was

---

32. Starting-point for this distribution is the so-called 'burden-sharing' key giving a percentage of the Community quota to each member state: BRD 25.5; UK 21; France 16.5; Italy 13.5; Benelux 9.5; Spain 7.5; Denmark 2.7; Greece 1.5; Portugal 1.5 and Ireland 0.8.

33. The quantities that can be transferred amount to the following percentages of the quota-share to which the transer is made: 2% in the first year of the application of the agreement, 4% in the second, 8% in the third, 12% in the fourth and 16% in the fifth year. For the so-called dominant suppliers these percentages will be lower.

offered to the majority of supplying countries. A similar agreement, but without quotas, was proposed to Bangladesh and Uruguay which hardly export any textiles to the EEC (a so-called 'flexible agreement'). Nevertheless, in case exports from these countries disrupt the EEC market during the lifespan of the agreement, quotas can be imposed by invoking the basket exit clause included in the agreement.

With Colombia, Guatemala, Haiti and Mexico the Community concluded an exchange of letters containing a consultation clause. Should exports from one of the countries disrupt the EEC market, the exchange of letters obliges the supplying country to consult within a month on a possible solution (which will usually be a type of agreement including quotas). Furthermore, the exchange of letters contains provisions on, *inter alia*, cooperation in the control of tradeflows and on the duration (until 31 December 1991). A simpler form of this exchange of letters is concluded with even more 'harmless' textile exporting countries, like Bolivia, who want to benefit from the more favourable tariffs for textile and clothing products within the framework of the Generalised System of Preferences (GSP) applied by the EEC.

2. THE PROGRESS IN THE BILATERAL NEGOTIATIONS[34]

Before definitely joining the new MFA, the EEC in 1981 wanted assurances that satisfactory bilateral agreements would be concluded. As previously mentioned, this led to a difficult discussion with the other MFA partners in Geneva. This time the EEC opted for other assurances. Parallel to the negotiations in Geneva a start was made on the bilateral agreements. A bilateral agreement had already been concluded with 15 countries before the conclusion of the extension protocol in Geneva.[35] Due to this course of action by the EEC the negotiations in Geneva and the role of the extension protocol as a framework for the bilateral agreements lost some of their importance (also the US held separate negotiations with individual supplying countries in Geneva).

After the negotiations in Geneva the EEC concluded an agreement with the remaining eleven countries.[36]

---

34. Status as of 24 November 1986.
35. An agreement was concluded with the following countries: Bangaldesh, Colombia, Bulgaria (although not a member of GATT or MFA the textile trade with the EEC is governed by a bilateral agreement), Hungary, Macao, Malaysia, The Philippines, Peru, Poland, Roumania, Singapore, Sri Lanka, Indonesia, Czechoslovakia and Thailand.
36. Argentina (this time Argentina could accept the usual territorial application clause), Brazil, Guatemala, Haiti, Hong Kong, India, Mexico, Pakistan, South Korea (with this dominant supplier it was agreed to decrease trade for one product and to increase the quotas of other products in exchange) Uruguay and Yugoslavia (agreement as a protocol connected to the cooperation agreement between the EEC and Yugoslavia with the provisions of the MFA agreement described above).

The agreement with China expires on 31 December 1988 and will be renewed at a later stage. One can assume that, unlike the present one, the new agreement with China will be based on the MFA.

In these bilateral negotiations the EEC was able to offer higher quota levels and higher growth and flexibility rates; it was able to weaken the surge mechanism; did not have to discuss cut-backs with dominant suppliers and could, with regard to the new provisions (protection of trade marks and reciprocity), agree to general declarations in the annexes of the agreements.

During these bilateral negotiations the EEC offered to abolish several hardly used quotas. The mandate spoke of an intention to abolish 25% of all quotas, a goal which was attained. In some cases, however, the EEC had great difficulty 'selling' the abolition of a quota to the negotiating partner in question. Two reasons can explain this somewhat surprising situation. In the first place these unused quantities can be used to export other products in accordance with the flexibility provisions. In the second place the EEC was unwilling to give absolute guarantee that a quota, after having been abolished, would only be reinstated (through the application of the basket exit mechanism) at the original restraint level (plus growth). The EEC did, however, agree to take this original restraint level into account.

On 24 November the EEC Council of Ministers accepted the result of the multilateral and bilateral negotiations.

3. THE INTERNAL APPLICATION OF THE MFA

Within the EEC the bilateral agreements are managed on the basis of the provisions of Regulation 3589/82 (relating to Community rules on the importation of certain textile products originating from third countries).[37] This Regulation provides rules for the supervision of quotas, the levels of various quotas, the internal procedure for withdrawal from the basket and for the use of the surge clause, more stringent rules for the prevention of fraud, the treatment of flexibility requests from third countries and also criteria for the division of the quotas between the Member States (the burden sharing key).

The Regulation also establishes a textiles committee which is responsible for the administration of the Regulation and is composed of representatives of the Member States, under the chairmanship of the Commission. This committee usually meets once a week. It deals with basket exit requests, requests to use the flexibility possibilities and other management problems. This regulation is at present being adapted to take account of the result of the recent cycle of bilateral negotiations (including alterations in the surge and basket procedures, adapted rules for the transfer of import possibilities between Member States and, of course, the new quotasystem). This is why this brief discussion of regulation 3589/82 is sufficient.

37. OJ 1982, L374.

To indicate the special status of the agreement with China (not based on the MFA) a separate management regulation is fixed for the textile trade with this country (running till 31 December 1988).[38]

III. THE POLICY REGARDING A NUMBER OF PREFERENTIAL COUNTRIES

A. THE MEDITERRANEAN COUNTRIES

We are concerned here with countries with which the EEC has concluded preferential trade agreements and which export considerable quantities of textiles to the EEC.

By virtue of these preferential agreements, imports of textiles from these countries into the EEC are unrestricted. However, in the event that the EEC experiences damage from the high level of imports from these countries, it can request safeguard measures, to be applied under very precisely defined conditions.[39] Since 1978 the EEC has concluded informal arrangements with these countries, without explicitly referring to these safeguard provisions.[40]

1. THE LEGAL FORM OF THESE ARRANGEMENTS

The informal arrangements with these countries are not official agreements and are therefore not published. To officially institute restrictions without referring to the safeguard provisions would conflict with the preferential agreements. As a result the EEC has entered into arrangements which take into account the contents of the preferential agreements as far as possible. These arrangements contain so-called indicative ceilings: figures described as the export objectives of the Mediterranean country concerned.[41]

Separate figures for Outward Processing Traffic are also included in these objectives.

In the event that these indicative ceilings are exceeded, consultations follow, allowing the parties to take any measure necessary only if these consultations do not produce results within 15 days. In practice these arrangements mean that the supplying country promises not to exceed the export objective and that

---

38. Reg. 2072/84, OJ 1984, L198.
39. *E.g.* Art. 60 of the additional protocol to the association agreement with Turkey. The procedure within the EEC is contained in Reg. No. 1842/71, OJ 1971, L192.
40. Imports from the following countries produce problems: Turkey, Malta, Morocco, Tunisia, Egypt and Yugoslavia.
41. These figures have also been split up over the Member States. This sub-division, however, is not very strict because the Commission until now refuses to apply Art. 115 of the EEC Treaty with regard to textile imports from the preferential Mediterranean partners.

THE EEC'S COMMERCIAL POLICY CONCERNING TEXTILES   141

below these levels the EEC will not have recourse to safeguard measures. The latter by the way, can only be done on the basis of the safeguard clauses in the formal preferential agreements.

In the arrangements with these countries the parties have agreed to administrative cooperation so that the flow of trade may be more easily observed by both parties. Partly as a result of the weak legal basis of this textile regime, imports of textiles into the EEC from these countries have increased noticeably in recent years. The restrictive effect of this part of the EEC's textile policy therefore should not be over-estimated. The importance of this regime has diminished, however, because important Mediterranean suppliers (Greece, Spain and Portugal) have joined the EEC.

2. THE PRESENT ARRANGEMENTS

The EEC has concluded arrangements with Malta, Morocco, Tunisia, Egypt,[42] Cyprus and Turkey. These arrangements only run until the end of 1986 or longer. Negotiations on new arrangements have not been initiated.

For a long time the EEC had troublesome relations in the area of trade in textile and clothing products with the number one textiles supplier of the EEC, Turkey. Turkey refused to accept an arrangement and wanted to stick to the rules of the association agreement (free access with the exception of safeguard measures). When imports of textiles from Turkey to the EEC increased even further, the EEC did indeed, from 1982 onwards, take safeguard measures frequently, and by the end of 1984 even instituted restrictions for the next year basing this measure on the safeguard clause of the association agreement.[43] After starting an anti-dumping procedure the European Commission managed in 1982 to conclude a two-year arrangement (1982–1983) on cotton yarn with the Turkish association of textile exporters (not the Turkish government), including a maximum quantity and a minimum price. This arrangement has been extended every year and is still operational. Not until 28 May 1986 did the EEC reach an agreement with the Turkish association on an arrangement concerning the eleven most important textile and clothing products. the arrangements runs until 31 December 1988. The safeguard measures have since then been withdrawn.[44]

As mentioned previously in the discussion on the bilateral MFA agreements, the EEC and Yugoslavia are negotiating on a textile protocol which will be annexed to the co-operation agreement, the text of which is strongly related to the MFA agreements, but contains higher figures (quotas, growth, flexibility).

42. Cotton yarns fall under the operation of the preferential agreement with Egypt. The remaining products have been excluded from the operation of the agreement. The EEC had a MFA agreement with Egypt for these products.
The EEC has decided to negotiate with Egypt a new informal arrangment covering all products.
43. Reg. 3639/84 OJ 1984, L335.
44. Reg. 1770/86 OJ L153 of 7 June 1986.

3. THE INTERNAL APPLICATION OF THE PREFERENTIAL ARRANGEMENTS

As we are dealing here with informal textile arrangements, there are no internal EEC Regulations by which these arrangements are formalized. This means that the formal relationship with these countries is based upon the contents of the preferential agreements (free access with the possibility of safeguard measures). Above it was described how this was taken into account when the arrangements were drafted. In practice, this does not give rise to difficulties as long as the management of the indicative ceilings does not lead to the refusal of import licences.[45] Rules have been established in order to give effect to the administrative co-operation provided for in the arrangements, with the result that the Member States must automatically issue a licence for the import of textile products from these countries. This surveillance procedure is laid down in Regulation 2819/79,[46] which itself is based upon the general Community Regulation on imports (926/79, later replaced by Regulation 288/82).

In the surveillance rules in the Turkey arrangement the EEC went a step further given the fact that the issue of an import licence was made dependent on the presentation of an export document furnished by the Turkish export association.[47]

B. THE COUNTRIES FALLING UNDER THE LOMÉ CONVENTION

The EEC Member States have concluded a convention with part of their former colonies (the so-called ACP countries, *i.e.* countries in Africa, the Caribbean and the Pacific) which, also, regulates trade. This means that imports from these countries into the EEC are unrestricted except by safeguard measures. Since textile imports from these states started cautiously (in 1980 1.8% of EEC textile imports originated in these countries) a number of Member States wanted additional rules for these countries,[48] but no agreements or informal arrangements were in fact concluded.

However, the EEC has established the so-called ACP facility for the eight most sensitive textile products (*i.e.* Group I). Within the EEC's global import

---

45. Part VII on the Outward Processing Traffic will show that the execution of the OPT Regulation does lead to problems.
46. OJ 1979, L320/9, extended for the last time by Regulation 3558 and 3559/85 OJ 1985, L339.
47. Regulation 1769/86 OJ 1986, L153. This provisional granting of an import licence is hard to reconcile with the association agreement, all the more so since the arrangement on which the European Commission bases these conditions, has not been concluded with the Turkish government.
48. However the ACP textile industry is partly set up with development aid from the EEC.

ceilings a certain quantity has been set aside for all these ACP countries combined.

After these levels have been attained the EEC will consider whether consultations with these countries are necessary. This working method was communicated to these countries in October 1980 in the 'ACP–EEC' commercial co-operation subcommittee. Consultations have taken place in the past with the Ivory Coast and Mauritius.

Summing up, the relationship with these countries in the field of textiles can be described as follows: in principle imports are unrestricted, barring possible safeguard measures at the indicative levels fixed by the EEC for the most sensitive products. These quantities will form the starting point for consultations.

During the discussions within the EEC on the Commission's mandate for the negotiations on the MFA and the preferential arrangements, the Lomé countries have not been mentioned. It remains to be seen, therefore, if this system will be continued.

IV. THE AUTONOMOUS TEXTILES POLICY

The EEC operates an autonomous import regime in respect of a number of third countries. Where textiles are concerned, this regime applies to a number of State-trading countries (with which no MFA agreement has been concluded) and Taiwan (which is not member of GATT).

A. RELATIONSHIP WITH A NUMBER OF STATE-TRADING COUNTRIES

The autonomous import regime is applicable to State-trading countries with which no MFA agreements have been concluded.[49] The following Regulations are of importance for the policy regarding these countries:
– The Regulation relating to the Community's rules for imports from State-trading countries contains the products that have been liberalised at EEC level.[50] The procedure for deliberalisation and surveillance of the products liberalised at EEC level can be found in this Regulation.
– In the Regulation relating to the import rules in respect of State-trading countries, the rules for the products which still come under the autonomous quota system of the Community are laid down.[51] This regulation deals with

49. This relates to the following countries: Soviet Union, the GDR, Albania, Vietnam, Mongolia and North Korea.
50. Reg. 1765/82, OJ 1982, L195. See for further discussion the contribution by Völker, Chapter Two.
51. Reg. 3420/83, OJ 1983, L346. See for further discussion the contribution by Völker, Chapter Two.

national quotas and national liberalisations. The Regulation provides for the adjustment of quotas (the independent competence of the Member State decreases as the sensitivity of the textile product increases).
– The levels of these quotas can be found in the yearly Quota Decision of the Council based on Regulation 3420/83.[52]

B. TAIWAN

The autonomous import limitations in respect of Taiwan for the years 1983 to 1986 inclusive (in conformity with the terms of the bilateral agreements based on MFA III) are found in Regulation 3587/82. The quantities referred to in this Regulation have been adjusted a few times.[54] This Regulation provides for a kind of internal basket exit procedure. In case imports from Taiwan rise above a certain level (which is also related to the total import for the product concerned), a quota can be established (for the whole of the EEC or for a Member State).

At the same time the Regulation provides that the Member State can apply flexibility between quotas.

Adjustments of the quotas referred to in this Taiwan Regulation are discussed in the textiles committee instituted by Regulation 3589/82.

V. THE POLICY REGARDING THE INDUSTRIALISED COUNTRIES

The EEC has concluded neither agreements nor arrangements with these countries (here one can think of the US, Australia, Japan and the EFTA countries). By virtue of the fact that these countries possess production processes and wage levels which are similar to those of the EEC, no special difficulties arise with imports from these sources; as a result no quantitative limits have been set for these imports. This may be one reason why the EEC has not concluded agreements with these countries within the framework of the MFA.[55] Similarly, when imports from these countries increase, it will be difficult to satisfy the conditions for market disruption set out in Annex A of the MFA (in the event that their prices are markedly lower, it will be mostly a question of subsidies or dumping). Should one, without appealing to the MFA,

---

52. Decision 87/60, OJ 1987, L31.
54. For example in Reg. 3787/85, OJ 1985, L366, which contains the adjustments made in the light of the accession of Spain and Portugal.
55. At the most, only informal arrangements could be concluded with the EFTA countries because of the special (preferential) relationship.

wish to take measures against these countries, then such measures will have to be based on Article XIX GATT.[56]

This means that the measure has to be applicable to all third countries with which no limitations have been agreed upon. An internal Decision by the EEC on such a safeguard measure must be made on the basis of the procedures in the general import Regulations (Regulation 288/82 and Regulation 1765/82).[57] In 1980 the Community used this procedure to limit the import of synthetic yarns. Due to the low oil prices (*i.e.* raw material) in the US, imports of these yarns squeezed the local producers out of the market in the UK.

Through two Regulations based on the general import Regulation, the import of these yarns from all countries on to the UK market was restricted.[58] These measures were not extended after 1980.

VI. THE POLICY REGARDING THE NEW EEC MEMBER STATES

Before their accession to the EEC, Spain and Portugal belonged to the Mediterranean countries with which an informal agreement was concluded. (As described in paragraph IIIA). Yet even after their entry in January 1986 restrictions on textiles remained.

In protocols of the Act of Accession these countries promise to control their export of certain textile and clothing products in accordance with quantities stipulated in the protocols.[59] Protocol 3 contains rules for the textile trade between both countries. The previously informal arrangements have thus been formalized with a more strict management by the other Member States (the importing Member State will only issue an import licence if an export document issued by Spain or Portugal can be presented).

In the event that the quantities mentioned in the protocols are exceeded, the Commission will, should it consider it necessary, institute safeguard measures at the request of the Member State involved (in accordance with Art. 379, para. 2 Act of Accession).

The Spain protocol expires on 31 December 1989. The Portugal protocol will run until 31 December 1988 with an extension possibility of 1 year.

Spain can maintain strict quotas for a number of textile products during this period in relation to the other member states.[60]

In the Council discussion on the Commission's mandate for the negotiations on the MFA and the bilateral agreements Portugal was afraid that an increase

---

56. On the basis of Art. 1, para. 6, MFA, one can still apply the general GATT rules against signatories of the MFA. In the bilateral agreements the EEC has waived this right.
57. OJ 1982, L35 and OJ 1982, L195.
58. Reg. 387/80 and Reg. 388/80, OJ 1980, L95.
59. For Spain Protocol 9 based on Art. 49 of the Act of Accession, OJ 1985, L302/425. For Portugal Protocol 17 based on Art. 206 of the Act of Accession OJ 1985, L302/446.
60. In accordance with Article 43 of the Act of Accession.

of imports from third countries, following an easing up of the EEC import regime, would lead to a decrease in Portuguese textile exports to other Member States. At the request of Portugal nine Member States promised to treat Portuguese textiles in a flexible manner. Spain proclaimed to be unable to renounce the possibility of applying safeguard measures, while the UK, which buys half of the Portuguese textile exports to the EEC, showed consideration for the Portuguese arguments without, however, committing itself to anything.

VII. THE POLICY FOR OUTWARD PROCESSING TRAFFIC

A. GENERAL

A significant part of EEC textile imports takes place within the framework of Outward Processing Traffic (OPT).

This is a system whereby raw materials produced in the EEC are processed in a third country and then reimported into the EEC as finished goods (*e.g.* the raw fabrics are exported, made into trousers abroad, which are then imported into the EEC). The importer must first request an OPT licence, which guarantees that he can bring these goods back into the Community.[61] The EEC has opened up possibilities for OPT with a number of countries (State-trading[62] Mediterranean and MFA countries). Until 1982 the management of these quotas had taken place only at a national level. However, the EEC Council of Ministers reached agreement on 25 February 1982 on a Regulation containing Community rules for the management of these quotas. This Regulation has been negotiated for years at EEC level. A number of Member States have a great economic interest in this OPT traffic (the Federal Republic of Germany and the Benelux countries in particular carry out many OPT transactions), whilst other Member States see these transactions mainly as competition for their own industry and thus feel they should be limited as much as possible. As a result of these divergent views it took many years before agreement was reached on this Regulation. However, this deadlock had to come to an end, because the Commission saw OPT as an important negotiating point within the MFA, resulting finally in agreement within the Council of Ministers.[63] Under the Regulation the Commission wanted to reserve OPT transactions to those persons who felt the competition, namely the *producers* in the EEC. At first,

61. On the basis of the tariff rules for OPT (Directive 76/119/EEC) the importers should only pay import duties on the added value.
62. All OPT quotas for the State-trading countries are included in the authonomous regime, regardless of whether or not an MFA agreement has been concluded with the State-trading country concerned.
63. In the bilateral negotiations in 1982 for the first time OPT quotas were given to a few Asiatic MFA suppliers. In the new bilateral negotiations these special import possibilities are granted to more MFA partners.

the Commission even wanted to set a maximum number of OPT transactions for these producers, based on their own production. The Member States which by then already had experience with OPT, found this approach to be going too far. Such a rule would mean that trading companies would be totally excluded from this type of transaction and also that OPT transactions for industrial companies would be limited. This would have enormous implications for countries such as the Federal Republic Germany and the Netherlands.[64] In response to the objections of these Member States (and Denmark) the Commission watered down the proposal in order to get it accepted. However, one still cannot deny that the effect of this Regulation is to place industry in a more advantageous position than trade. The restoration of the competitive ability of the Community's industry is stated as the central objective of the Regulation; this of course has consequences for the position of trade.

B. THE CONTENTS OF THE OPT REGULATION[65]

1. TERRITORIAL SCOPE

Article 1 describes the scope of the Regulation. Apart from indicating the textile and clothing products which fall under the Regulation, this Article also contains the condition that the processing operations should take place in a third country for which rules on the surveillance or restriction of the import of textiles and clothing products[66] are in force and for which specific measures exist for OPT.

On the basis of these provisions, the Regulation applies to OPT transactions with State-trading countries (direct imports are subject to the restraint levels or surveillance provided for in the bilateral agreement in question; for OPT, on the other hand, separate autonomous quotas exist). Also the possibilities for OPT transactions provided for in the agreements with MFA countries fall under this Regulation.

In the informal arrangements with the Mediterranean countries, separate OPT objectives have been included. These countries have also agreed that this Regulation should be applicable. However, as long as these arrangements containing the specific measures for OPT have not been formalised, then, formally speaking, the rules of the preferential agreement are applicable. In this situation it must be accepted that the conditions for the application of this Regulation are not fulfilled. Because of the difficulties with the publication of these objectives, one may conclude that the application of this Regulation to

---

64. In the Netherlands a considerable part of the OPT is conducted by trading companies.
65. Reg. 636/82, OJ 1982, L76/1.
66. Textile and clothing products which are referred to in chapters 50 to 62 inclusive of the Community's customs tariff.

transactions with the Mediterranean countries rests on a strained footing with the preferential agreements.[67]

2. RECOURSE TO THE REGULATION

Article 2 of the Regulation sets out which persons shall have recourse to these rules:

'The person who, for his own account, manufactures similar products in a factory situated within the Community which are at the same stage of manufacturing as the compensating products to which the regulation is applied'.

The raw materials used should originate in the EEC (a limited exception to this is possible). The Annex to the Regulation fixes limits for the up-grading (making of yarns into a completed suit is considered production and not up-grading).

The result of this restriction is that without a specific derogation trade would be excluded and the freedom of industry would be limited. The term 'manufacturer of identical products' could imply that a manufacturer of jackets can no longer, by means of OPT transactions, produce trousers in order to offer complete suits. The Netherlands wanted to accept this limitation only if the traditional rights of trade and industry were respected. Following a lengthy discussion of these rights, the following derogation provision was included in Article 2, paragraph 3. The Member States can, by virtue of paragraph 2, sub-paragraph 1, deviate from the rule for persons who do not comply with the conditions of the paragraph. The derogation, however, does contain a number of limitations:

– the quantity for which the Member State can deviate is limited to historical trade in one of the previous two years;

67. However, the Council decided on 25 February 1982 that the Regulation is applicable to the Mediterranean countries without the formalisation of the OPT objectives. To comply with the application provisions in this field as well, the Commission developed the following line of reasoning. A surveillance system is instituted for direct imports, to the extent this has not been done yet (e.g. Reg. 2417/821 OJ 1982, L258), while OPT imports do not come under this type of surveillance. The absence of this kind of surveillance with respect to OPT constitutes, according to the Commission, the 'specific measures existing for OPT' which make the regulation applicable.

The non-formalisation of the OPT objectives also leads to problems with the execution of another provision of the Regulation. Member States are only allowed to issue licences within the trade policy limits. However, the refusal of licences which exceed the OPT objectives is not possible (because these objectives are not formalised). Once these objectives are exceeded one can only establish a strict import limitation on the basis of the safeguard clause in the preferential agreement.

The Commission tried to solve this problem by letting the supplying countries refuse an export licence. An exchange of letters with these countries has been agreed on, in which the Mediterranean countries promise to issue export licences for these products only, after the OPT licence issued by the EEC has been received (issued by the EEC before the export of the primary products).

- only raw materials manufactured within the EEC may be used, and Member States must also stay within the trade policy limits;
- the deviations are applied with priority for the benefit of those persons who have previously conducted these activities. If these persons do not use the quantity to the full, then the remainder can be awarded to other persons.

Summarizing, it can be said that access to outward processing traffic is primarily restricted to industrial companies (which must satisfy additional rules) but an exception has been made for traditional rights (with a possibility of a redistribution among trading companies within the total traditional quantities).

3. THE MANAGEMENT SYSTEM FOR OUTWARD PROCESSING TRAFFIC

Articles 3 to 12 inclusive regulate the management of the system. It is striking that the execution of the rules is for the greater part left to the Member States.

When granting OPT licences, the Member States can take into account the development of employment in the companies (on the basis of Article 3 and Article 5, paragraph 4). A licence can be refused when a company replaces national manufacturing by OPT and supervision of transactions. Also, a committee has been set up concerned with problems arising from the execution of the Regulation. The committee is chaired by the Commission and is composed of representatives of the Member States (no further reference to the authority of this committee is made in the Regulation). This Regulation came into effect on 1 September 1982.

VIII. THE APPLICATION OF THE SAFEGUARD CLAUSE OF ARTICLE 115 OF THE EEC TREATY

As appears from the above description of the textiles regime, almost 30 years after the setting up of the EEC, the internal borders of the EEC are still of great importance in areas where the EEC carries out a commercial policy. In textiles, the quotas are still divided over the Member States.[68] The application of the MFA within the EEC has even included a fixed key for this splitting up over the Member States (the so-called burden sharing key). In the discussions in the Council of Ministers on the extension of the MFA, it was stressed once again how much importance most Member States attach to this sub-division. Proposals to weaken this division by giving the supplying countries the possibility of exporting unused export quantities to other Member States were accepted with great difficulty and only to a certain extent. On the basis of the

---

68. The transitional measures accompanying the accession of Spain and Portugal (para. VI) have also led to extra barriers within the EEC.

present situation it can be ascertained that the sub-division of quotas among Member States is a given fact.

However, this division is not enough for the Member States. Textile products originating in third countries can be conveyed from one Member State to another because of the principle of free movement of goods. To prevent this, very frequent appeals are made to the safeguard clause contained in Article 115 of the EEC Treaty.[69] The *Tezi* Case, to be dealt with further on in this paragraph leads to the conclusion that in this field, too, little will change in the near future.

A. THE CONTENTS OF ARTICLE 115 EEC

Article 115 contains a safeguard clause which may be invoked in national commercial policy measures are being obstructed by a deflection of trade or if economic difficulties arise due to differences in the various national commercial policies. This situation arises because of the incompleteness of the common commercial policy.

Article 115 allows protective measures to be taken as long as the Member States get prior authorisation from the Commission. In practice such an authorisation from the Commission means that the Member State can refuse the import of a certain third country product which was put into free circulation in one of the Member States, for a limited period of time (in practice, until the end of the calendar year at most).

B. THE IMPLEMENTING DECISION[70]

In a Decision of 1980 the Commission laid down further rules for the application of Article 115 of the Treaty. A previous Decision was withdrawn after its rules of application were subjected to criticism by the European Court of Justice. The new Decision considerably limits the possibility of operating an import licence in intra-Community traffic (the almost unlimited authorisation for the operation of these licences in the previous Decision was rejected by the Court of Justice in the *Donckerwolcke* Case).[71] Under the new system two kinds of authorisation may be granted by the Commission on the basis of Article 115 of the EEC Treaty: authorisation for intra-Community surveillance and authorisation for further reaching protective measures (in practice the

---

69. From the figures in the annexes to this chapter on the application of Art. 115 in the years 1976–1985 (see IX), it appears that the largest shares of the protective measures are applied in the textile sector.
70. Decision 80/47 EEC, OJ 1980, L16.
71. Case 41/76, *Donckerwolcke* v. *Procureur de la Republique* (1976) ECR 1921 *et seq.*

latter means an import ban on third country products in free circulation). Thus a specific authorisation from the Commission is required in order to establish surveillance of products in free circulation.

C. INTRA-COMMUNITY SURVEILLANCE

When imports of a certain product into a Member State give rise to a risk of economic difficulties (1) imports of that product can, after authorisation by the Commission (2), be made dependent on the granting of an import licence (3) for a period of time to be determined by the Commission.

1. ECONOMIC DIFFICULTIES

It is worth noting that the Commission has dropped the first criterion of Article 115 of the Treaty and relies now only on the second (*i.e.* economic difficulties). One no longer speaks about 'obstruction of national commercial policy measures'.

2. THE AUTHORISATION FROM THE COMMISSION

As described above, for each application of intra-Community surveillance the Member State must request an authorisation from the Commission. Until now, the Commission has published several Decisions, under which a large number of authorisations were given to the Member States.[72]

In these Decisions the requests are tested for a number of criteria: divergent national commercial policies, threatening economic difficulties, whether there has been trade deflection in the past, and in the last Decisions the quotas have to be larger than 1% of the amount of the total restrictions for that product.

Because of this last criterion the number of surveillances of the second Decision has decreased marginally.

The present authorisations remain effective until 31 December 1986.

---

72. Decision 80/605/EEC, OJ 1980, L164, Decision 82/205/EEC, OJ 1982, L97/1, and Decision 85/340/EEC, OJ 1985, L178. For the principle discussion of this subject see the contribution by Timmermans, Chapter Five.

3. THE GRANTING OF THE LICENCE

The Decision sets out briefly the information which an importer must supply in its request for a licence.[73] The Member State must issue the import document within 5 days at no cost. Only if very large imports are envisaged the request may be held up for a maximum of a further 5 days pending the appeal under Article 115 of the EEC Treaty (therefore, a total of 10 days). Small shipments must be admitted whilst the appeal is being handled by the Commission. Even when the Member State is allowed to hold up a licence on the basis of this provision, the Commission mostly gives an authorisation to refuse the import only for the future on the basis of which the held-up shipment must be allowed in after all.[74]

On the basis of Article 4 of the Decision, Member States can request particulars of origin on the customs declaration or on the application for an import licence. With serious or established doubt, supplementary evidence may be requested, without impeding the entrance of the goods. This regulation does not allow asking systematically for a certificate of origin.

D. FURTHER REACHING PROTECTIVE MEASURES

When imports of a restricted good into a Member State produce economic difficulties, the Member State can take protective measures, following prior authorisation by the Commission. The authorisation sets out the conditions and manner of application of the protective measure. To get this authorisation, the Member State has to file a request providing a great deal of details to the Commission. By virtue of the large amount of information that an appeal to Article 115 must contain, it has become more difficult for the Member States to appeal.

Under the previous Decision the Commission made considerably fewer demands. From the beginning of 1981 this stringent system has been rigidly applied. This may be an explanation for the decrease in the number of appeals since 1981.[75]

From the figures in the annexes it is apparent that it is not the number of rejections by the Commission that has increased; the declining figures are to be attributed to the decrease in the number of appeals. From the figures attached to this article one can also see how large a role the textile sector plays in the

---

73. The identity of the importer and exporter, country of origin and Member State of provenance, description of the product, value and quantity, delivery data and the information to substantiate its being brought into free circulation within the Community.

74. In the *Ilford* Case a retroactive effect of an Art. 115 Decision was not refused, but the Court of Justice did consider it necessary that such a decision clearly indicates the justification for such a retroactive effect (Case 1/84 R, *Ilford SpA* v. *Commission* (1984) ECR, 423 et seq.).

75. In the annexes A, B and C to this chapter figures have been included on the number of appeals in 1976 until 1985.

application of Article 115 of the EEC Treaty. About 70% of the appeals made relate to textile products.

E. THE *TEZI* CASE[76]

In the discussion on the application of Article 115 of the EEC Treaty the question is frequently asked whether this safeguard clause is applicable to trade governed by the Multifibre Arrangement.

According to the opponents of such an application, there is no question of commercial measures taken by the Member States, a condition mentioned in Article 115 of the EEC Treaty.

In the *Tezi* Case the Court of Justice has ruled on this matter. In this case the Court had to judge a refusal by the Dutch government to issue an import licence to a Dutch textile trader wanting to import products produced in Macao into The Netherlands via the BRD. The refusal was based on a decision by the European Commission, authorizing the Dutch government to exclude these products from the free circulation in accordance with article 115 of the EEC Treaty.

The Dutch judge, to whom Tezi appealed, put two preliminary questions to the Court:

1. Do the articles 113 and 115 of the Treaty, taking into account the connection between them, have to be explained in such a way, that the Commission can still apply Article 115 to the field of international trade in textiles after the conclusion of the Arrangement concerning international trade in textiles (the Multifibre Arrangement) and the adoption of Council Regulation 3589/82?

2. In case question 1 is answered in the affirmative, does Article 115 of the Treaty have to be explained in such a way, that 'commercial measures taken by a Member State in accordance with this Treaty' can also mean a division per Member State of the Community's quantitative restrictions as laid down in annex IV to Council Regulation No. 3589/82?[77] Tezi's argument can be

---

76. Cases 59/84 and 242/84, not yet published. See, for an extensive treatment of these cases, the contribution by Timmermans, Chapter Five.

77. Only these two questions will be treated, the other arguments put forward by Tezi are irrelevant to this article.

The Facts: On 29 April 1983 Tezi requested five licences from the Dutch government for importing trousers produced in Macao and already imported into Germany. For these trousers the Benelux was allowed to operate a licence in the intra-EEC trade. The import licences were refused to Tezi on the basis of a decision by the Commission of 12 April 1983 (OJ 1983, C102) in which the Benelux was authorized to put a stop to imports of trousers from Macao via other Member States from 2 April until 30 November 1983. Against this refusal by the Dutch government Tezi appealed to the Dutch judge, who put two preliminary questions to the European Court of Justice on 2 October 1984. Both questions were answered by the Court in Case 242/84. However, after the expiry of the Commission's authorisation to refuse imports of trousers from Macao via other Member States, Tezi again applied for an import licence on 1 December 1983, following which the

summarized as follows. The EEC Treaty offers no scope to apply Article 115 to textile products coming under the MFA, because in this sector a Common Commercial Policy regulation (laid down in Regulation No. 3589/82) has been instituted. The way in which the Community makes use of this commercial policy competence is irrelevant. Tezi also argued that the Community Regulation (Regulation No. 3589/82) contains sufficient remedies for a possible trade deflection that occurs (by adapting the national or Community quota), making the application of Article 115 unnecessary.

The decision by the Court gives rise to the following remarks. Before arriving at this decision the Court of Justice had to avoid a difficult obstacle. Article 115 of the EEC Treaty does, after all, speak of measures of commercial policy taken in accordance with this Treaty by a Member State. Also in the *Donckerwolcke* Case[78] amply quoted by the Court, the latter remarks 'that it should be stressed with regard to the scope of such provisions, that under Article 115 limitations may only be placed on the free movement within the Community of goods enjoying the right to free circulation by virtue of measures of commercial policy adopted by the importing Member State in accordance with the Treaty'.

The Court overcomes the obstacle by concluding that the disparities resulting from the sub-division of the quotas are the consequence of initiatives autonomously taken by the Member States, but in accordance with the relevant Community provisions. Regulation No. 3589/82 only maintains the existing disparities to a certain degree, but with the intention of reducing them gradually and even abolishing them.

However, if one considers that in the course of operation of the Multifibre Arrangements the import restrictions applied by the Community have spread tremendously, and that these new restrictions (including sub-divisions) have been based on the Article 113 procedure, the observation that these new disparities are the result of initiatives taken autonomously by Member States but in accordance with the relevant Community provisions and that they involve an ending process becomes questionable.[79]

This decision, published at a sensitive moment, namely during the negotiations on the new MFA, allowed the Community to continue negotiations on the new MFA, internally as well as externally, along the same lines, but a price must clearly be paid for this in the field of the further development of the internal market.[80]

Dutch government again requested a 115-authorisation from the Commission, which it obtained. Tezi consequently went directly to the Court of Justice with a request to annul the Commission decision and a claim for compensation of damages (Case 59/84). On both accounts the Court of Justice delivered a decision on 5 March 1986.
 78. See n. 71.
 79. Tezi stated that the Benelux restriction with respect to Macao, has been instituted making use of Community procedures and did not exist during the time the Benelux commercial policy was still regulated nationally.
 80. Outside the textile sector, too, this Court decision can be of importance. The fact is that the Commission is of the opinion that after taking regional safeguard measures by the Community,

IX. CONCLUSION

In the previous version of this article the observation was made that it appeared that the temporary restrictions aimed at producing a breathing space for the industry have spread like an oil stain. To illustrate this the extension of the group of countries, to which restrictions were being applied, the increase in restrictions in the existing bilateral agreements of the EEC by the frequent application of the basket mechanism and the growth in intensity of the restrictions (*e.g.* through the introduction of the surge mechanism casting uncertainty on previously secured import opportunities), were pointed out.

Even after 1981 this development continued, extending the protection in this sector even further. Particularly the extension of product coverage in the new MFA means another step in this direction.

Abolishing the MFA still seems to be unfeasible in the near future.

The request by the supplying countries in the last negotiations on the MFA to agree on a definite date for the expiration of this arrangement, was completely ignored. Abolishing the MFA at this moment would, taking into account the position of the large importing countries, not lead to further liberalisation. Frequent application of the general safeguard clause contained in article XIX GATT and a flood of grey zone measures would be the result. This would create a very insecure situation for the exporting countries, the traders and the consumers. Therefore, the GATT secretariat pleaded in its study for a transitional period. However, the importing countries in Geneva did not want to consider even this moderate position.

The *Tezi* Case discussed in this article and the transitional measures for the textile trade with the new Member States indicate that the protection of Community industry also maintains its disruptive influence on trade within the EEC. Experience during the past decades has clearly shown that an increased external protection has led to more barriers to the free movement of goods inside the EEC (Proponents of a protectionist commercial policy sometimes suggest the contrary).

Also the attempts made by liberal Member States to create more flexibility in bilateral agreements at EEC level had very little effect. (The difficult abolition of unused and therefore useless quotas and the low growth rates for the important supplying countries show that the EEC is also not really willing to grow towards complete liberalisation).

Also in the future this high price for the protection of the European industry will have to be paid, in the form of numerous obstructions to internal and external trade, the negative effects in the relations between the EEC and the

deviating from a situation of complete liberalisation at community level, Article 115 of the EEC Treaty can also be applied to the product in question. The Commission has already applied Article 115 several times after the taking of such safeguard measures. This decision of the Court seems to confirm this opinion of the Commission. Apart from the doubts already expressed with regard to such an application of Article 115, the observation can be made that this article is not being used to realise a further unification of the import conditions but on the contrary, to move the EEC further away from a uniform commercial policy.

developing countries, and the burden of a considerable management apparatus that had to be set up for the execution of this policy, both nationally and in Brussels.

In consequence of this, the textile regime keeps showing what protectionism can bring about, namely a longlasting and ever further extending system, becoming more expensive on all accounts, with hardly any positive influence on the restructuring process of the protected industry. For the agenda of the new GATT round an old point will in any case be available next to several new topics. The results of the recent MFA negotiations make one fear, however, that even in these wider negotiations not much will change in the field of textiles.

X. ANNEXES

ANNEX A: APPLICATION OF ART 115 IN THE YEARS 1976–1983

Year	1976	1977	1978	1979	1980	1981	1982	1983
Products Textiles	72	75	258	269	273	184	156	176
Others (Agriculture + industrial)	38	46	59	78	83	71	85	77
Total	110	121	317	347	356	255	241	253
Gr	74	79	197	260	222	166	174	188
Ref	36	42	120	87	134	89	67	65

Gr: Granted
Ref: Refused

ANNEX B: APPLICATION OF ART. 115 IN 1984 (WITH DIVISION BETWEEN MEMBER STATES)

Products	Total	Benelux	Denmark	France	Greece	Ireland	Italy	FRG	UK
Textiles	155 (120 Gr) (35 Ref)	12 (12 Gr)	—	38 (26 Gr) (12 Ref)	—	68 (57 Gr) (11 Ref)	18 (11 Gr) (7 Ref)	—	19 (14 Gr) (5 Ref)
Others	48 (37 Gr) (11 Ref)	1 (1 Gr)	—	16 (12 Gr) (4 Ref)	—	2 (2 Gr)	27 (21 Gr) (6 Ref)	—	2 (1 Gr) (1 Ref)
Agriculture	12 (8 Gr) (4 Ref)	1 (1 Gr)	—	3 (1 Gr) (2 Ref)	—	—	4 (2 Gr) (2 Ref)	—	4 (4 Gr)
Total	215 (165 Gr) (50 Ref)	14 (14 Gr)	—	57 (39 Gr) (18 Ref)	—	70 (59 Gr) (11 Ref)	49 (34 Gr) (15 Ref)	—	25 (19 Gr) (6 Ref)

Gr: Granted
Ref: Refused

ANNEX C: APPLICATION OF ART. 115 IN 1985 (WITH DIVISION BETWEEN MEMBER STATES)

Products	Total	Benelux	Denmark	France	Greece	Ireland	Italy	FRG	UK
Textiles	143 (119 Gr) (24 Ref)	2 (2 Gr)	—	57 (43 Gr) (14 Ref)	—	61 (55 Gr) (6 Ref)	8 (7 Gr) (1 Ref)	—	15 (12 Gr) (3 Ref)
Others	53 (45 Gr) (8 Ref)	1 (1 Gr)	—	20 (19 Gr) (1 Ref)	—	2 (2 Gr)	23 (19 Gr) (4 Ref)	—	7 (4 Gr) (3 Ref)
Agriculture	15 (12 Gr) (3 Ref)	1 (1 Gr)	—	6 (4 Gr) (2 Ref)	—	1 (1 Ref)	4 (4 Gr)	—	3 (3 Gr)
Total	211 (176 Gr) (35 Ref)	4 (4 Gr)	—	83 (66 Gr) (17 Ref)	—	64 (57 Gr) (7 Ref)	35 (30 Gr) (15 Ref)	—	25 (19 Gr) (6 Ref)

Gr: Granted
Ref: Refused

CHAPTER FIVE

COMMUNITY COMMERCIAL POLICY ON TEXTILES: A LEGAL IMBROGLIO

By C.W.A. Timmermans*

INTRODUCTION

1. The legal régime on the external and internal Community trade in textiles, a mixture of Community and national régimes of a dazzling complexity, is a lawyer's paradise. At least, one would expect it to be so due to the numerous legal problems in this field that remain unsolved and the doubtful legality under Community law of various elements of this régime. However, the implementation of the highly protectionist textile régime over the last several years has not given rise, as far as I can see, to much litigation either in the national courts or in the Community Court.[1]

This is all the more amazing considering that the legal remedies under the EEC Treaty, together with the doctrine of direct effect of Community law provide adequate possibilities for legal protection.

Why, then, are importers so hesitant to go to the Courts? Is it because they fear that attacking the national Customs authorities in the Courts would be counter-productive? That might be so. However, this lack of litigation could also be due to ignorance of the legal intricacies of the import régimes and the possible remedies granted under the Community legal system. For these reasons, one can welcome the introduction in 1982 by the then revised common Community rules for imports, of an investigation procedure which precedes the enactment of surveillance or protective measures, and provides for disclosure in the Official Journal of the EC, as well as providing a right for interested (legal) persons to be heard.[2] These revised rules will make the

---

* Professor of Law, State University of Groningen, the Netherlands. The revision of this article for the 2nd edition of this book was completed in September 1986.

1. Recently the Court has given two important judgments in the *Tezi* Cases 242/84 and 59/84 (Decisions of 5 March 1986, not yet published), see hereafter nr. 15.

2. See Council Reg. No. 288/82 on common rules for imports, OJ 1982, L35, Arts. 6 and 7; Council Reg. Nos 1765/82 (State-trading countries) and 1766/82 (China) OJ 1982, L195, Arts. 6 and 7. Recent case-law of the Court of Justice seems to warrant the conclusion that under certain conditions interested persons who have intervened in the investigation procedure can attack procedural decisions of the Commission, *e.g.* not to enact protective measures, directly before the

management of the import régimes more transparent for the parties concerned. This investigation procedure should therefore also be incorporated in the Community régime for textiles covered by the Multifibre Arrangement (MFA). This régime must be reconsidered at any rate as from 1987.[3]

2. In his contribution to this book Van Dartel has already given a detailed survey of the various régimes applying to imports of textile products into the EEC. Broadly speaking, three general régimes apply depending on the products and the countries in which they originate: the MFA régime (Regulation No. 3589/82 with its subsequent amendments), the preferential régimes for a number of Mediterranean countries and the partners in the association of Lomé, and finally the autonomous Community régime on imports which applies to textile products not covered by the MFA régime or a preferential régime. This autonomous régime by the way, is certainly not a uniform one. It is in fact a collection of separate régimes of common Community rules differentiated according to countries or groups of countries on the one hand, and of national régimes which have received in varying degrees a Community 'dressing', on the other hand. I refer to the article by Van Dartel.

3. My contribution will first focus on three legal questions regarding the application of Article 113 of the EEC Treaty: To what extent are Member States still free to enact national protective measures for textile products? Is a protective system of Community quota split up into national quota compatible with Article 113 of the EEC Treaty and finally does this same article allow the Community to decide on a regional protection, *i.e.* protective measures limited to one or more Member States only? These questions do not relate to any of the just mentioned import régimes for textile products in particular. They arise with regard to almost all of them. To some extent therefore my remarks will inevitably overlap the contribution of Bourgeois. Subsequently, the implementation of the safeguard clause of Article 115 of the EEC Treaty will be discussed. Finally, attention will be paid to the remedies for legal protection.

I. LEGAL QUESTIONS RELATING TO ARTICLE 113 OF THE EEC TREATY

A. DIVISION OF POWERS BETWEEN EEC AND MEMBER STATES

4. The judgment of the Court of Justice in the *Donckerwolcke* Case has made two things perfectly clear. First, the power of the Community on matters of

---

Court by an Art. 173 action for annulment (*cf.* Case 264/82, *Timex Corporation* v. *Council and Commission*, 20 March 1985 and Case 169/84, *Cofaz* v. *Commission*, 28 January 1986, both decisions not yet published).
3. Reg. No. 3589/82 on common rules for imports of certain textile products originating in third countries (OJ 1982, L374) will expire on 31 December 1986.

external commercial policy, that is the power devolved upon Council and Commission under Article 113 EEC is of an exclusive nature.

Second, having lost all powers regarding commercial policy Member States can only lawfully enact measures in this field, either autonomously or by contracting international obligations, where they have been specifically authorised to do so by Community Decisions.[4] In my view a *specific* authorisation means that all relevant facts and circumstances of the case in question must be considered. A blank authorisation to Member States for the future would in fact result in a retransfer of powers by the Community to Member States and would therefore be incompatible with the exclusive nature of the Community's power. One could even go further and state as a general principle of Community constitutional law that powers attributed to the Treaties to the Community institutions have been so transferred on a permanent basis. They should be exercised by the Community institutions. In being so exercised, Member States can be allowed to enact the necessary implementary measures of a more technical or administrative nature but this cannot go so far as to grant Member States the power, or impose upon them an obligation, to draw up 'the basic rules'.[5] At any rate, in matters of commercial policy Member States can only lawfully act on the basis of a specific authorisation by the Community.

It must however be immediately added that in its recent *Bulk Oil* decision (Case 174/84 of 18 February 1986) the Court of Justice appears to allow an extremely generous interpretation of what can still be considered as a *specific* authorisation. The Court accepted a provision of the general régime on exports from 1969 which does no more than excluding a number of products listed in an annex from the principle of freedom of exportation (Regulation No. 2603/69, Article 10, OJ 1969, L324) as a sufficiently specific authorisation for a restrictive export régime relating to oil which the UK had applied only since 1979. This authorisation can merely be called specific in so far as the provision in question explicitly covers oil, not because it is based (how could it be?) on an evaluation of the situation of the year 1979 and later. Does this judgment imply that the practice of the Council to authorize regularly the prolongation of the still existing national trade-agreements, like it authorizes yearly the autonomous national quantitative import restrictions regarding State-trading countries (see nr. 5 hereafter), is too formalistic and unnecessary because an authorization needs not to be limited in time?

How this may be, at least one exception to this principle of a specific authorization, which the Court as such continues to insist upon in its *Bulk Oil* decision, can be derived from the Court's case law. In the absence of common Community rules, national measures introduced at a time in which the Community power on commercial policy was not yet an exclusive one, *i.e.*

---

4. Case 41/76, *Donckerwolcke* v. *Procureur* (1976) ECR 1937 (para. 32).
5. See Case 23/75, *Rey Soda* v. *Casa Conguaglio* (1975) ECR 1279 (para. 48).

before the end of the transitional period, can still be lawfully applied.[6] Any amendment of such measures by a Member State would, however, require a Community authorisation. I leave aside here the possibility, even the necessity, for Member States to act as trustees for the Community when Community action is urgently required but the Council is unable to reach a decision.[7]

5. Do the various import régimes on textile products satisfy these principles on the division of powers between Community and Member States? I doubt it. As far as the MFA régime applies, no problems seem to arise because this régime is entirely operated by the Community institutions, either the Council or the Commission. However, Member States still possess some powers to enact interim protective measures under the common import régime of Regulation No. 288/82. Until recently these powers were more substantial, but most of them expired on 31 December 1984 according to the relevant Regulations,[8] the Council not being able to find the necessary majority to amend the Regulations in time on this point. Actually, the Commission had proposed to relinquish these national powers, but the Council was neither able to adopt this proposal nor to amend it. So by its inaction the Council in fact endorsed the Commission's proposal, the relevant powers now being automatically relinquished by the mere application of the common import régimes themselves.[9] However, national powers to take interim protective measures still exist under Article 17, para. 5 of Regulation No. 288/82 with regard to products covered by a protective clause of a bilateral national trade-agreement as well as products which are liberalised in some Member States, but are subject to quota in others; with regard to the latter category the remaining national powers will expire on 31 December 1987.

The enactment of these national interim measures was and, in so far as they still can be taken, is without doubt embedded in a Community procedure: the Commission and other Member States must be informed; consultations must take place; a Member State's decision can be overruled either by the Commission or in last instance by the Council. All this does not take away the fact that a Member State may autonomously and without a specific authorisation by the Community, enact interim measures, albeit that where the Commission opposes these measures and the Council does not approve them, a Member State can continue to apply these measures for a limited period of time only (normally one month, but it may be extended to three months by Council

---

6. *Cf.* the *British Fishery* Cases, Case 804/79, *Commission* v. *U.K.* (1981) ECR 1045 *et seq.*; at 1073 (para. 21).

7. See British Fishery Cases, 32/79, *Commission* v. *U.K.* (1980) ECR 2403 *et seq.*, at 2434 (para. 15) and 804/79, *supra* n. 6, at 1075 (para. 30).

8. Art. 17 of Reg. No. 288/82, Art. 13 of Reg. No. 1765/82 (State-trading countries) and Art. 13 of No. 1766/82 (China). These national powers to enact interim protective measures relate to products covered by these regulations, the import of which into the Community is liberalised. However, the procedure of Art. 17 of Reg. No. 288/82 also covers products coming under the scope of this Regulation, which are subject to a régime of national liberalisation. See further the contribution by Völker, Chapter Two.

9. See Euromarktnieuws 1985 (38, 39).

decision).[10] This general authorisation for Member States to enact interim measures does not in my view conform to the *Donckerwolcke* doctrine. Moreover, these remaining national powers are quite unnecessary. Where protective measures are urgently required, the Commission is indeed empowered under the relevant Community regulations to take an immediate decision.[11] Normally, sensitive products will already be subject to a system of surveillance either on Community or on a national level. In both cases all relevant information has to be submitted to the Commission which can thus in full knowledge of the facts and on short notice decide on the necessary protection.

6. In quite a number of cases Member States still continue to apply national quantitative restrictions for specific products originating in specific countries. These cases are listed in Annex I of Regulation No. 288/82 and, with regard to State-trading countries, in Annex III of Regulation No. 3420/83 on import arrangements in respect of State-trading countries.[12] These national trade restrictions thus find a legal basis in Community law and to this extent the *Donckerwolcke* doctrine appears to be respected. The national quota regarding products originating in State-trading countries are even laid down each year or should be so, by Council Decision in virtue of Article 3 of Regulation No. 3420/83.[13]

The *Donckerwolcke* doctrine implies furthermore that each subsequent amendment of these national import régimes must be authorised by a Community decision. Indeed both the above mentioned Regulations provide for a Community procedure for these amendments. There are, however, some remarkable differences between these two procedures. Firstly, with regard to the situation where an amendment proposed by a Member State does not meet with an objection either from the Commission or another Member State. According to Article 9 of Regulation No. 3420/83 (State-trading countries) the amendment has then to be adopted by the Commission. Nothing could conform better to Community law. Under the régime of Article 20 of Regulation No. 288/82 (common rules for imports), however, no decision at all is required from the Commission, the Member State itself is entitled to enact the relevant measure. At best, the procedure of information and consultation laid down in Article 20 (2a to c and 3a) of this Regulation could be regarded as suggesting an implicit authorisation on the part of the Commission. Where objections are raised by the Commission or by another Member State, the matter will in all circumstances be settled by a Decision either of the Commission or the Council by virtue of Article 9 of Regulation 3420/83. Regulation 288/82, however, permits the Member State to enact the proposed

10. See *e.g.* Council Decision 83/125 and 83/215, OJ 1983, L86 and L121 regarding the introduction of protective measures applicable to tube and pipe fittings imported from Italy.
11. See *e.g.* Art. 15(1) of Reg. No. 288/82.
12. OJ 1983, L346.
13. The national quota for 1987 have been established by Council Decision No. 87/60, OJ 1987, L31.

amendment when, objections having been lodged, the Commission does not submit a proposal to the Council within a period of two weeks after the consultation has been opened (art. 20(3b)).[14]

More critical in the light of the *Dockerwolcke* doctrine are the autonomous powers still granted to Member States by Regulation No. 3420/83 (Article 10) to amend their national import arrangements in cases of extreme urgency, for instance by reducing existing import quota or banning all imports. Member States have been deprived of similar powers originally granted in virtue of Article 20 (para. 4.a.) of Regulation No. 288/82 by the amending Regulation No. 1243/86 (OJ 1986, L113). It is to be deplored that the Council did not enact at the same time a similar amendment (or the Commission did not propose such amendment!) with regard to Article 10 of Regulation No. 3420/83. These national powers can hardly be reconciled with *Donckerwolcke*. Moreover, as was said earlier: in cases of urgency the Commission, as an independent body, is the appropriate institution to act and it can do so swiftly.

7. In the meantime, the third renewal of the MFA arrangement has been approved by the EEC.[15] But what would have been the legal situation in the (unlikely) hypothesis that the Community will not adhere to MFA IV or would leave the MFA framework at a later stage? The question arises whether Member States could then fall back on their former national restrictive import policies with regard to textile products which have been replaced in the past by the MFA and related Community arrangements?

The question is pertinent because these former national quota systems still form part of Annex I of Regulation No. 288/82 (common rules on imports) in which the national quota systems have been listed. These former national quota for textile products, since replaced by the Community restrictions, now enacted by Regulation No. 3589/82, are slumbering for the moment and marked thereto in the said Annex with an asterisk. It is possible that when the Community leaves for one reason or another the MFA frame-work Member States, or at least some of them, would favour reviving these former national restrictive import arrangements and would try to obtain a Council Decision to that effect.

In my view, such a procedure would be unacceptable and in violation of the general principles of Community law regarding the division of powers between Community and Member States. The Commission should oppose such a solution energetically and refuse to submit any proposals to that effect to the Council. Once a Community régime has been enacted by virtue of Article 113 of the EEC Treaty, however imperfect it might be, the Community policy

---

14. As amended by Regulation 1243/86 (OJ 1986, L113). It should be noted that to some extent this amendment has increased the national powers instead of further unifying the common import régime as the recitals of this Regulation announce to be its objective: under Article 20(3b) Reg. No. 288/82 in its original version Member States had to wait three (now reduced to two) weeks before being authorised to amend their import restrictions.

15. See the contribution by Van Dartel.

cannot be re-nationalised. The common rules, now embodied in Regulation No. 3589/82 cannot be replaced by twelve different national régimes.[16] Of course, such a situation would at any rate require a Council Decision based on Article 113 of the EEC Treaty because of the exclusive nature of the Community's power on commerical policy. In my view, however, the Council cannot lawfully decide to authorise Member States to return to their national policies. That would be contrary to Article 113 of the EEC Treaty and in particular to the requirement that the common commercial policy has to be based on uniform principles. This process might go slowly and by stages; the Community policy need not be completely uniform from one day to the next, but once started, this process cannot be reversed. In other words, should the MFA arrangements be discontinued and Member States nevertheless still want to restrict imports of textile products from the supplier countries, a restrictive régime should be introduced based on common rules for the Community as a whole, preferably by applying the safeguard clauses of Regulation No. 288/82 or eventually the Regulations regarding State-trading countries (No. 1765/82 and No. 1766/82).[17]

This plea for a Community policy instead of a revival of national policies is not rooted in a doctrinarian view of the relationship between Community powers and national powers. It is based on the simple premise of a Customs Union, requiring as the EEC Treaty does, both the free circulation of goods originating in third countries, once they have been brought into the Community and as a necessary consequence, the achievement of a common commercial policy.

B. NATIONAL SUBQUOTA OR QUOTA LIMITED TO ONE OR MORE MEMBER STATES: COMPATIBLE WITH ARTICLE 113 OF THE EEC TREATY?

8. As has just been demonstrated, Article 113 of the EEC Treaty, by requiring that a common commercial policy of the Community be based on uniform principles, sets limits to the broad discretionary powers devolved upon the Council and the Commission under this Article. This common commercial policy is a necessary corollary to market integration. Without a common commercial policy deflections would inevitably occur within the Common Market, not only of trade but also of production and investment;[18] conditions for competition would inevitably become distorted between Member States.

---

16. *Cf.* Case 7/71, *Commission* v. *French Republic* (1971) ECR 1003 *et seq.*, paras. 10–20, at 1017 and the *Rey Soda* Case, *supra* n. 5; see too the fishery Cases, *supra* n. 7.
17. The Regs. No. 3019/77 of the Commission (OJ 1977, L357) and No. 256/78 of the Council (OJ 1978, L42) preceding Reg. No. 3059/78 were by the way based on the safeguard clauses of the general import regulations then applying: Reg. No. 109/70 (State-trading countries) and No. 1439/74.
18. See Bela Balassa, *The Theory of economic integration* (London, 1969), p. 70 *et seq.*

The realisation of a common commercial policy is therefore not a whim of European integrationists, but an economic imperative to prevent wastage of economic resources and to secure the economic benefits of a common market. This link between the Common Market and the common commercial policy explains and justifies why Article 113 of the EEC Treaty puts so much emphasis on the uniformity of principles which should govern the structuring of this common policy. It also follows that the requirement of uniformity is not a mere political statement, but a legal requirement.[19]

Now back to textiles. When measures are considered to protect the ailing textile industries against imports from low-cost-countries, both the existence of a common market and the imperative of a common commercial policy would seem to imply that this need for protection be assessed in terms of the Community's textile industry as a whole. And that is indeed what the drafting of the safeguard clauses in the Regulations on common rules for imports implies.[20] As far as textiles are concerned, the Community has indeed when elaborating its protective import arrangements, first assessed for the various groups of textile products the capacities for absorption of the Common Market as a whole and established global ceilings to that effect. Subsequently, these ceilings were divided over the MFA countries, the preferential countries etc.[21] However, once Community quota are introduced either in the context of the MFA or by virtue of one of the common import regulations these quota are not open for imports anywhere in the Community by any importer. These Community quota are subdivided in national subquota. Furthermore, all the relevant import regulations, including the MFA Regulation No. 3589/82, allow for the possibility of regional protection, that is establishing import quota which are limited to one or more Member States only. Are these practices of national subquota and regional protection compatible with the requirements of Article 113 of the EEC Treaty as to the uniformity of a common commercial policy?

9. I think that Community practice on the first issue is acceptable under Article 113. A sub-division of Community quota into national subquota can be justified as a technique for administering and implementing the import restrictions. But in principle only for those reasons. The national subquota should not reflect the need for protection of the twelve national markets separately and be operated accordingly. That, however, is much more a question regarding the scope of Article 115 of the EEC Treaty which will be discussed later on.

19. *Cf.* too the conclusion of Advocate-General VerLoren van Themaat in the *Tezi* Cases (59/84 and 242/84 of 5 March 1986), roneotyped version p. 30.
20. At least in the Dutch and the French version of these texts which require 'substantial injury to *the* Community producers' (emphasis added, CT). The English version, however, refers to 'Community producers', omitting the definite article. See Art. 15(1) and 16(1a) or Reg. No. 288/82 (common rules for import); Art. 11(1) and 12(1) of Reg. No. 1765/82 (State-trading countries) and No. 1766/82 (China).
21. See the contribution by Van Dartel, Chapter Four.

The normal régime for administering the Community quota, either decided autonomously or established by convention, is laid down in Regulation No. 1023/70.[22] This Regulation, by the way, contains flexible procedures to amend the subdivision of the quota over the Member States in order to adapt these to the flows of import trade. The régime of Regulation No. 1023/70 is, however, not applicable to the Community quota for MFA products, established by the Regulation No. 3589/82 and subsequent amending Regulations. Regulation No. 3589/82 contains its own régime for administering these Community quota for textile products and notably their subdivision into national subquota and the adaptation thereof.

It appears from the wording of Regulation No. 3589/82 itself that these import restrictions are more a coordination of national protective import policies than a real Community system of protection.[23] Particularly, the national subquota, characteristically called 'burden-sharing' in this context, are more than a mere administrative technique to organise a decentralised management system of Community quota. These national subquota obviously reflect the maxima which each individual Member State still considers an acceptable burden for its own national market, with particular regard, of course, to the situation of its own textile industry. In this respect these subquota are much more 'national' than under the normal régime of Regulation No. 1023/70. The Commission has, by the way, always stressed that the protective arrangements with regard to MFA products are not completely uniform.[24]

I do not think, however, that for these reasons these arrangements are to be condemned as incompatible with Article 113 of the EEC Treaty for lacking uniformity and being too nationalistic.[25] It is important to note in this respect that Regulation No. 3589/82 itself requires a better adaptation of the allocation of the national subquota to the patterns of trade and provides for the necessary procedures to that effect (Article 7). It should, however, be added immediately that MFA supplier countries in particular have complained about the lack of flexibility in the operation of the national subquota.[26] But this reproach is in fact not so much addressed to Regulation No. 3589/82 as to the ineffective or even incorrect application of some of the procedures laid down by this

---

22. OJ 1970, L124. See further the contribution by Völker, Chapter Two.
23. One reads in the tenth recital of Reg. No. 3489/82: 'whereas, however, the extent of the disparities existing in the conditions for importation of these products into the Member States and the particularly sensitive position of the Community textiles industry mean that the said conditions can be standardised only gradually; whereas for these reasons allocation of supplies cannot immediately be effected on the basis of requirements alone'. See too the explanations given by the Commission in the *Tezi*-cases (n. 1), as summed-up in the Conclusion of the Adv. Gen. (roneotyped version p. 13).
24. See answer to parliamentary question 772/78 of Patijn and Albers, OJ 1979, C45.
25. The Court has implicitly confirmed the compatibility of the national quota under Reg. No. 3589/82 with Article 113 in its *Tezi*-Decisions (n. 1).
26. See Commission Document E44/81 (Europe Information External Relations), p. 7. A rapid look at the number of Regulations enacted in application of Art. 7 of Reg. No. 3589/82, as listed in the TMC Asser Guide to EEC-Legislation, Supplement 1985, gives the impression that this adaptation procedure is increasingly applied in recent years.

Regulation. Moreover, this inflexibility is also due to the fact that the Commission has allowed the application of Article 115 of the EEC Treaty to shield the national markets from indirect imports through other Member States and in doing so has allowed the national subquota to become an effective instrument for protecting the national market. I shall develop this argument regarding Article 115 later on.

10. The second question of whether possibilities of regional protection are compatible with Article 113 of the EEC Treaty and the requirement of uniformity, is more delicate. Such a regional protection, that is the establishment by Community Decision of national quota for only one or some Member States, imports into the other Member States remaining unrestricted, can be enacted under Regulation No. 3589/82 (Article 5, 11(2) and (3)), as well as under the common import regulations.[27] Regional protection under Regulation No. 3589/82 has been granted frequently by the Commission in the past period.[28] At first sight regional protection is incompatible both with the existence of a common market and the requirements of a common commercial policy. Protective import arrangements under Article 113 of the EEC Treaty should be based, as has been said repeatedly, on an overall assessment of the situation of all Community producers and their need for protection. If the conditions for protective measures are fulfilled, imports should logically be restricted Community wide.[29] To limit such measures to one or more Member States in particular would at least require a special justification as is always necessary when a Community decision differentiates between Member States. One could think of a situation where the relevant market of the Community producers is geographically limited. In that case a regional protection might be suitable, easier to administer than a Community wide protection and therefore justifiable. However, the fact that the principle of free movement also applies to goods imported from third countries makes it impossible to shield the relevant regional market of the Community from indirect imports through other Member States where the regional protection does not apply.[30] A system of regional protection will therefore be only successful in exceptional circumstances (highly perishable goods, goods with high transport costs). This logic seems to be followed for the Custom Union of Benelux which is normally treated for the implementation of the restrictive import arrangements of the Community as one territory.

What then should one think of the frequent application of regional protection by the Community, particularly regarding textiles? One could leave this question unanswered because it is inextricably linked with the application

---

27. Art. 15(3a) and 16(2) of Reg. No. 288/82; Art. 11(3) and 12(3) of Reg. No. 1765/82 (State-trading countries) and No. 1766/82 (China).
28. See the Guide to EEC-legislation of the TMC Asser Institute, Supplement 1985.
29. The Court has accepted the possibility of a safeguard measure for the Community as a whole to combat difficulties that in fact mainly occurred in one Member State (Italy), in Case 40/72, *I. Schroeder* v. *Germany* (1973) ECR, 125 *et seq.*
30. See Adv. Gen. Roemer in his opinion on Case 40/72. See n. 29.

of the safeguard clause of Article 115 of the EEC Treaty. The Commission does indeed accept this application so that the national markets that are regionally protected, can be sealed off from the rest of the Common Market. Whether this application of Article 115 is lawful, will be discussed subsequently. At any rate, a system of regional protection which cannot be ensured through the application of Article 115, would be inadequate in most cases and should therefore, if protection is inevitable, be replaced by a Community wide protection.

My personal view on this question would be that Article 113 of the EEC Treaty puts certain limits to the power of Council or Commission to grant such a regional protection instead of enacting a Community wide protection. In all circumstances the need for protection can only be assessed Community wide. Secondly, regional protection must be justified in itself. The more so because it will automatically increase pressure by national producers on the national authorities to invoke Article 115 of the EEC Treaty and convince the Commission to grant the necessary authorisation to that effect. In view of the frequency and the apparently automatic granting of decisions allowing regional protection for textile products, one can only have serious doubts as to whether these conditions are respected in Community decision-making practice. I fear that the real explanation for this frequent phenomenon of regional protection is simply the fact that it is in this way that the two conflicting views held by Member States on the structuring of the common import policy for textiles can be reconciled: regional protection for the protagonists of protectionism; unrestricted import for those Member States defending a more market-oriented philosophy.[31]

II. THE APPLICATION OF ARTICLE 115 OF THE EEC TREATY ON TEXTILES

A. GENERAL[32]

11. The safeguard clause of Article 115 of the EEC Treaty remains applicable even after the end of the transitional period and has been frequently applied,

---

31. Vogelenzang defends an interpretation of Art. 113 of the EEC Treaty, and, related thereto, also of Art. 115 of the EEC Treaty, which acquiesces in these political realities. Vogelenzang, 'Two aspects of Article 115 EEC Treaty: its use to buttress Community-set sub-quotas, and the Commission's monitoring system', 18 *CMLRev.* 1981, 169. 'A common policy providing for protection of national markets within the Community is one of the options the EEC cannot do without politically', he writes on 175. My answer would be that political realities must of course weigh in the balance where Treaty provisions so vaguely drafted as Art. 113 are being interpreted, but that can only be done within the limits of what is still legally acceptable. Vogelenzang's interpretation is merely based on the political argument. He fails to justify it from a legal point of view.

32. For literature on Art. 115 of the EEC Treaty see: Ehbets, 'De beschermende maatregelen van art. 115 EEG-Verdag en het vrij verkeer van goederen', *SEW* 1978, 609; Lux, 'Ausschluss von der Gemeinschaftsbehandlung bei Umwegeinfuhren (Art. 115 EWGV)', *Europarecht* 1979, 382;

particularly with regard to textiles. This Article allows a Member State, after having obtained the necessary authorisation of the Commission, to protect its national market against imports of goods originating in third countries although these have been brought into free circulation in another Member State. The possibility of applying this safeguard clause, even after the end of the transitional period depends on the existence of a national régime of commercial policy, a common commercial policy not yet being finalised.[33] Article 115 covers two situations in this respect. First, the situation in which the execution of the national régime risks being obstructed by deflection of trade, for example because the relevant product, the direct import of which is restricted, is imported indirectly through other Member States. Second, Article 115 allows for protective measures when differences between still existing national régimes of commercial policy lead to economic difficulties in a Member State.

The possible application of Article 115 of the EEC Treaty after the transitional period is, it should be stressed, linked with the continued existence of a national commercial policy. This is of course an anomaly in itself, the Treaty requiring the common commercial policy to replace national policies before the end of the transitional period. As we know, there has been much delay in this respect, particularly with regard to the State-trading countries. It remains nevertheless that Article 115 is in essence a safeguard clause of a transitional nature. Once the still existing national régimes have been replaced by a common Community régime, it becomes obsolete. It should also be added that the *Donckerwolcke* judgment has definitely established that these national régimes, in order to qualify for a protection under Article 115, must first be specifically authorised by Community decision.[34] Article 115, indeed refers to national measures 'taken in accordance with this Treaty'. But even without this express reference, a Community authorisation would be required in view of the definite and exclusive transfer of powers in the field of commercial policy to the Community since the end of the transitional period.

A good example of national measures to which Article 115 could still be applied for that reason, are the still existing national import restrictions regarding State-trading countries, authorised by Regulation No. 3420/83 and subsequent implementing Decisions of the Council by virtue of Article 3 of this Regulation (above No. 6).

Timmermans, 'Troebel water ofwel de beschikkingenpraktijk ex Art. 115 EEG', *SEW* 1979, 636; Vogelenzang, see n. 31); Weber, 'Die Bedeutung des Art. 115 EWGV für die Freiheit des Warenverkehres', *Europarecht* 1979, 30.

33. See Case 41/76, *Donckerwolcke, supra* n. 4.
34. See *supra*, n. 33.

B. APPLICATION OF ARTICLE 115 OF THE EEC TREATY IN PRACTICE

12. The frequent applications of Article 115 in the past regard in a majority of cases textile products, most of them covered by the restrictive MFA import arrangements of Regulation No. 3059/78, as subsequently amended. The first boom occurred in 1978, the first year of operation of this scheme: 141 authorisations regarding textile products on a total of 197 authorisations. This figure increased in 1979 (199 authorisations for textile products on a total of 270).[35] It seems that the number of authorisations decreased in the following years, partly due to the fact that the Commission has tightened up the conditions for applying Article 115 (hereafter, no. 22). However, the figures listed in the TMC Asser Guide to EEC-legislation seem to indicate a reversal of this trend since 1983.[36]

C. SCOPE OF ARTICLE 115 OF THE EEC TREATY

13. Are these applications of Article 115 to textile products justified? That depends notably on the question whether the import restrictions applied by Member States can still be qualified as national measures, as 'measures of commercial policy taken in accordance with this Treaty by any Member State' within the meaning of Article 115. I shall now discuss this question for the three import régimes for textile products which can basically be distinguished: the MFA régime, the preferential régimes and the autonomous régimes of the common import regulations.

1. MFA REGIME OF REGULATION NO 3589/82

14. Most authorisations regarding textile products under Article 115 relate to MFA products. Member States invoke Article 115 in order to prevent the restrictions they apply on direct imports from an MFA supplier country being

---

35. These figures are given by Kretschmer, 'Beschränkungen des innergemeinschaftlichen Warenverkehrs nach der Kommissionsentscheidung 80/47/EWG', *Europarecht* 1981, 64.

36. A precise count cannot be made. Sometimes the Art. 115 Decisions of the Commission regard various categories of products, sometimes they relate (also) to various third Countries, in some cases not indicated by name. Unfortunately enough the Commission does not publish anymore – it did before 1982 – the full text of its Decisions. It only publishes a short notice in the C edition of the Official Journal of both every refusal of a Member State's request to apply Art. 115, which is a good thing, and of every authorisation of such a request. Only the Decisions allowing for intracommunity surveillance under Decision 80/47 are published in full in the L edition; Decisions authorising protective measures have ceased to be published since early 1982. This change of disclosure policy is to be regretted, the more so because it withholds information that is important for interested parties considering possibilities for legal action (see part III).

eluded by indirect imports through other Member States. These restrictions on direct imports are, however, not restrictions enacted by the national authorities themselves with the necessary blessing of the Community. They are part of a common Community import policy, laid down in Regulation No. 3589/82. In fact these direct import restrictions are the subquota into which Community quota have been subdivided (Articles 3 and 7 of Regulation No. 3589/82) or the national quota established by the Community when granting a regional protection (Article 11 of Regulation No. 3589/82). The Commission justifies the application of Article 115 to protect these national quota with the argument that the allocation of these quota is not yet fully adapted to the needs of the national markets.[37] Therefore, so the reasoning of the Commission goes, the common commercial policy has not yet been fully achieved and thus Article 115 remains available. Indeed, because of the failure to adapt the national quota to national demands, deflections of trade may occur which can cause economic difficulties or increase the already existing difficulties of the national textile producers.

15. In its recent *Tezi*-Decisions the Court of Justice, contrary to the conclusion of its Adv. Gen. VerLoren van Themaat, has fully endorsed this interpretation of Article 115 by the Commission. According to the Court application of Article 115 is only then excluded where a Community régime enacted under Article 113 implies 'a real common commercial policy', which means that 'uniform conditions for imports' apply for all Member States.[38] That condition is not fulfilled by the Community régime on import restrictions for textiles covered by the MFA because of the 'extent of the disparities existing in the conditions for importation of these products into the Member States (. . .)', which conditions 'can be standardized only gradually', so the Court explains referring to the recitals of Regulation No. 3589/82.

What exactly are these disparities? Do they result from the allocation of the Community quantitative limits into national quota which are insufficiently adapted to the needs of Member States as the Commission had stated in the *Tezi* procedures? Apparently not, because the Court adds that the disparities in question cannot be attributed to Regulation No. 3589/82 alone: the said disparities 'are rather caused by initiatives taken autonomously by the Member States, but according to the relevant Community rules' (para. 43, Case 242/84).[39] This (essential!) part of the argument of the Court is unclear. Does the Court refer to *other* national trade measures than the national quota? That cannot be true because Article 115 of the EEC Treaty has been applied in these cases to buttress these national quota. However, were the said reference by the

---

37. See the answer of the Commission to the parliamentary question of Patijn and Albers referred to in n. 24, above; see too the recitals of Decision 80/47 of the Commission regulating the application of Art. 115 of the EEC Treaty, OJ 1980, L16.
38. Para. 39, Case 242/84, my own translation, an official English translation not yet being available.
39. Again unofficial translation.

Court to relate to the national quota, these must be considered than as autonomous national trade policy measures, taken in conformity with Community law that is according to *Donckerwolcke* specifically authorised by the Council. The allocation by Regulation No. 3589/82 of the Community quantitative limits into national quota is then to be regarded as an authorisation by the Council of already existing national quantitative restrictions. Already a superficial reading of Regulation No. 3589/82 excludes this interpretation. Moreover, that interpretation, had it been possible, would certainly have been defended by the Commission and the Member States intervening in the *Tezi*-procedures, for existing case-law of the Court, and the *Donckerwolcke* Case more in particular, learn that Art. 115 remains undoubtedly available for this category of national measures duly authorised by a Community decision. Apart from its wording, also the history of Regulation No. 3589/82 proves that the measures in question are Community quantitative limits and do not imply an authorisation by the Community of autonomous national import restrictions.[40] Moreover such national restrictions did not exist at all in the Benelux countries (the *Tezi* procedures concerned imports of textiles from Macao into the Netherlands); what is more, as the Advocate-General points out, existing Dutch legislation on imports and exports does not provide any legal basis for such autonomous national measures of commercial policy.[41]

Actually, the Court accepts the justification laid-down in the recitals of Regulation No. 3589/82 without controlling its merits neither in fact nor in law. This justification, however, is far from clear. Advocate-General VerLoren van Themaat has probed during the oral hearing of the *Tezi*-Cases the Commission's representatives and elicited a statement, which was contrary by the way to the position defended by the Commission in the written procedure,[42] that the disparities referred to in the recitals of Regulation No. 3589/82 could only relate to already existing national measures, not therefore the national quota. The Advocate-General quite rightly argues that the need for only gradually standardizing national import conditions, invoked by the Council, can hardly be justified on the basis of a differentiation (national quota) called forth by the Regulation itself.

The overall impression is that the Court was more occupied by the result of this interpretation than by its justification. Perhaps the Court has shrunk away from the indeed considerable, political impact of the interpretation defended by its Advocate-General who pleaded non-application of Article 115 in this

---

40. Community quantitative limits for textiles covered by the MFA were enacted for the first time in 1977 as safeguard measures by virtue of the then applicable common import régime of Reg. Nos. 190/70 and 1439/74, see Reg. No. 3019/77 of the Commission OJ 1977, L357, confirmed by Reg. No. 256/78 of the Council, OJ 1978, L42. Moreover 'previous national restrictions' for textile products, are marked with an asterisk in Annex I of Regulation No. 288/82 (common rules on imports, 1982, L35). In this annex the asterisk is explained with the remark that these national restrictions were 'replaced by specific common rules'. One may assume that also Regulation No. 3589/82 is covered by this reference (see too nr. 7 of the text above).
41. Opinion of Adv.-Gen. VerLoren van Themaat, Cases 59/84 and 242/84, roneotyped text p. 36.
42. See Opinion of the Adv. Gen. (n. 41) p. 35.

context. The Dutch government particularly has laid emphasis in its submissions on the political consequences of such an interpretation. To bar access to Article 115 would considerably hamper the decision-making in the Council on the renewal of the MFA. The Commission has quite openly explained in the *Tezi*-proceedings that the Community quantitative limits under the MFA régime are no more than an addition of the quantities Member States are prepared to admit on their national markets ('burden-sharing'), on the understanding that Article 115 remains available to cut off the national markets from indirect imports. In doing so, the gulf could be bridged between protectionistic Member States and Member States like the Federal Republic of Germany more attached to principles of free trade. The arguments in favour of the continuing application of Article 115 in the MFA context thus come down to saying that the decision-making of the Council will be facilitated and its final outcome also be more favourable for the MFA supplier countries themselves, for the more protectionist Member States would certainly not accept the Community quantitative limits at the actual, high level when the road to Article 115 would be closed.[43]

16. In my view these arguments are not convincing.[44] One tends to forget that under this regime the protection of the national textile industry remains limited to markets of Member States with a restrictive national quota: on the markets of Member States with more 'liberal' quota they are in full competition with the low-priced MFA products. On the other hand, it is at least questionable whether this interpretation of Article 115 of the EEC Treaty is really more favourable for MFA-supplier countries. It might be that the Community quantitative limits are artificially high. If the quota of the more free-trade oriented Member States exceed the demands of their national markets, the surplus cannot be disposed of on the markets of the other Member States when these are sealed off by application of Article 115. In the long run the actual flow of imports will then adapt itself automatically to the real capacity for absorption of the protected and unprotected markets within the Community. The consequence could be that the Community quantitative limits will not be fully used.

Under these circumstances, the price to be paid for this interpretation of Article 115, accepted by the Court in the *Tezi*-Cases, seems too high. Market integration suffers because the free movement of products imported from third countries (Articles 9 and 10 of the EEC Treaty) is impeded, conditions for competition between companies in protected Member States and those in Member States with more open markets are distorted. What happens in fact in

43. *Cf.* paras. 48 and 49, Case 242/84, where the Court shows sympathy with this argumentation.
44. The Commission's interpretation of Art. 115 of the EEC Treaty is supported by Vogelenzang, mainly because there is no alternative that is politically acceptable (see n. 31 above) and by Kretschmer, *loc. cit.* (n. 35); Benke has, already in 1973, rejected the view that Art. 115 could be invoked to consolidate national subquota of a Community quota against indirect imports through other Member States, in Benke, 'Die Anwendung des Art. 115 EWG-Vertrag nach dem Ablauf der Ubergangszeit' (1973) *Neue Juristische Wochenschrift*, 2134.

these cases, is that the principles of the Customs Union are set aside. One tends to forget that there is meant to be no distinction in the Common Market between Community produced goods and goods originating in third countries, once they have been put into free circulation. Experience with the MFA régime shows, however, that if Member States are willing to accept the free movement of Community textile products, they do not accept free movement with regard to MFA products. The excuse of an uncompleted commercial policy is too obvious. Applying Article 115 to MFA products means that this article is being used for purposes for which at the time Article 226 of the EEC Treaty was available. But as we known, this time has passed. If neither a regional nor a Community wide protection of textile producers appears adequate to solve their problems, the remedies that remain under Community law are those of structural or regional policy.

Now it may be, as the Commission alleged in the *Tezi*-Cases that the allocation of the Community quantitative limits in national quota does not conform to the needs of the national markets. My answer to that would be, certainly not to apply Article 115, but to apply Regulation No. 3589/82 itself, which indeed requires a better allocation of the national quota (Article 7) and provides the necessary procedures to that effect. If for instance a quota allotted to the Federal Republic of Germany largely exceeded the needs of the German market, Article 115 should not be invoked to close the French or Benelux market to prevent the import of the German surplus. The Community should instead adapt the subdivision of the Community quota and divide the German surplus over the other Member States. If the protection of the textile producers within the Community still appears to be insufficient, the only solution would be to enhance Community protection; that is, by reducing the Community quota.

An additional argument to support this interpretation is to be found in Article 115 of the EEC Treaty itself. According to the wording of this Article the Commission must, before authorising protective national measures, first 'recommend the methods for the requisite cooperation between Member States'. The purport of these recommendations will be to achieve a better coordination of the national régimes of commercial policy and in doing so diminish the existing differences and eventually also economic difficulties caused thereby. However, as soon as the Community itself enacts a commercial régime, in this case by Regulation No. 3589/82, these recommendations become meaningless. The power to adapt the import régimes to the needs of the market is now devolved upon the Community. Instead of addressing recommendations to Member States, the Commission should now according to the procedures of Regulation No. 3589/82 amend the import régime itself or submit proposals to that effect to the Council.

At the same time the completion of the common commercial policy in this sector is put off indefinitely as a result of the now accepted interpretation of Article 115. One should not be led astray by the solemn statements of the Court on the necessity of a strict, time limited application of Article 115 and the prudent, cautious way in which this has to be done. Reality is different. Allowing Article 115 to be used as an instrument to ensure the feasibility of an incomplete, non-uniform, 'common' (in fact based on national needs and markets) commercial policy measure puts indeed a premium on continuing such a policy. By enacting a 'real' Community policy, Member States would deprive themselves of access to Article 115 and of the possibility therefore to determine themselves the level of protection of their national markets. Keeping the door to Article 115 wide open the Court hampers in my view the completion of the common commercial policy. The continuing story of the MFA (from 1974) itself furnishes the necessary proof: there are no signs at all that the third renewal of the MFA will terminate the still blooming practice of applying Article 115. The advantage of a more harmonious decision-making by the Council cannot offset these objections. Confronted with a failing decision-making process the Court has shown itself capable in the past of finding more adequate solutions than, as it has now done, acquiescing in the impotence of Member-States (and the Commission) to execute the Treaty.[45]

17. These arguments to deny application of Article 115 of the EEC Treaty with regard to the national quota into which Community quantitative limits have been divided under Regulation No. 3589/82 can also be invoked to deny application of this Article to cases of regional protection (*supra*, nr. 10). Here too, it should be repeated, the assessment of the need for protection is in principle Community wide and should be so in order to comply with Article 113 of the EEC Treaty. The risk of this regional protection being obstructed by indirect imports through other Member States where direct import has not been restricted, is of course considerable in the case of textile products. This, however, does not in itself justify the application of Article 115. If the regional protection is frustrated by indirect imports, the only solution compatible with the Treaty would be in my view to extend the protection to all Member States, that is to introduce a Community wide protection. Here too the question arises whether isolation of the national market through a regional quota enforced by virtue of Article 115 is indeed so favourable to the textile producers in that country: on the markets of the other Member States they are competing with the relevant MFA products without any protection at all.

Until now the Court has not ruled on the possible application of Article 115 to these cases of regional quota. The reasoning of the Court in the *Tezi* judgments not being all too clear, a definite answer cannot be derived from this case-law. Personally I fear, however, that would the Court continue the line of thinking of the *Tezi*-case-law, it will also acquiesce in the Commission's practice of applying Article 115 in order to buttress regional quota. These measures of regional protection (*supra*, nr. 10) are another fact of life in Community decision-making as the easiest way to reconcile the antagonists of protectionism and free trade.

45. *Cf. British Fishery* Cases, 804/79, *supra* n. 6.

Would the Court go so far, such an interpretation of Article 115 would again go against the interests of completing the common commercial policy. Worse, it will risk to jeopardise what has been so hard to achieve in the field of a common commercial policy. A snowball effect must be feared. Particularly, where regional quota have been enacted by virtue of one of the import regulations of the Community, pressure will inevitably be put on the Member State in question and the Commission to consolidate this regional protection by the application of Article 115. If the Commission allows this, and that is precisely what happens in practice (*infra*, Nos. 18 and 19), this will give a clear impetus to Member States to demand regional protection instead of a Community wide protection. If that happens the commercial policy of the Community will be common only in name, but will in fact be re-nationalised, at least as far as the operation of the safeguard clauses is concerned.

2. PREFERENTIAL RÉGIMES

18. One would expect that Article 115 of the EEC Treaty could no longer be applied to products originating in a third country which fall under one of the preferential régimes granted by the Community. The preferential countries are, generally speaking, and I refer here to the contribution by Van Dartel, the Mediterranean countries and the ACP (Lomé III) countries. The import into the Community of textile products originating in these preferential countries is liberalised unless a safeguard clause which is normally incorporated into these preferential agreements, is applied. This Community régime seems to exclude an application of Article 115. National policies have been relinquished: the common commercial policy is there.

Van Dartel has already referred to the informal arrangements concluded between the Community and the Mediterranean countries to regulate and limit import of sensitive textile products. It is clear that Article 115 cannot be applied to these products because from a legal point of view, their import into the Community remains liberalised and unrestricted, formal restrictions only being possible by the application of a safeguard clause.

Could this conclusion with regard to Article 115 be different in the event that such a safeguard clause is applied by the Community? The answer should apparently be no, because such application would occur within the normal context of a common commercial policy régime enacted by the Community in agreement with the third country or countries concerned. Nevertheless the Commission decided in July 1982 to apply Article 115 to textile products from Turkey, the import of which into the Community had previously been made subject to a regional restriction (France).[46] Application of Article 115 in this case is totally unwarranted in my view for the reasons already explained (*supra*,

---

46. Decision 82/577, OJ 1982, L243.

nr. 16).[47] The products in question are fully subject to a common comercial policy régime of the Community.

Could it not be argued that a system of regional protection is by its very nature a national commercial policy measure justifying the application of Article 115? The answer is no. I repeat: The Council or Commission can only allow for a regional protection after having assessed the need for protection of the Community as a whole; to limit this assessment to a particular national market is incompatible with Article 113 EEC. Moreover, to consider a regional protection decided upon under a common import régime of the Community as a revival of national commercial policy is also contrary to that basic principle of Community law that the Community cannot re-nationalise either its powers or the policies it enacts in exercising those powers (*supra*, nr. 4).

This generous interpretation by the Commission could produce precisely the effects that I mentioned earlier: Member States could now try to obtain a regional protection instead of a Community wide protection in order to gain access to Article 115. In this way the Commission has completely denatured Article 115. It has changed Article 115 from a safeguard clause that was clearly meant to be transitional to a permanent one. One can only hope, the recent *Tezi*-decisions notwithstanding, that the Court of Justice will be able to stop this process of disintegration in time.

3. AUTONOMOUS RÉGIMES

19. As Van Dartel has explained, the autonomous import régimes of the Community also apply to textile products originating in a number of third countries, mostly State-trading countries. After my earlier remarks I can be brief with regard to the possibility of applying Article 115 in this context. Where the import of these products is liberalised on a Community level, a subsequent enactment of import restrictions by virtue of one of the safeguard clauses embodied in these import regulations can by no means justify an application of article 115 to consolidate either the national subquota of a Community quota or a regional quota. The Commission has, however, admitted the latter in its Decision on the '*espadrilles chinoises*'.[48] This Decision meets with the same objections as were already made with regard to the Decision regarding the regional quota of textile products imported from Turkey into France (see No. 18).

Article 115 can, however, still be invoked as already mentioned with regard to the national quantitative restrictions covered by Regulation No. 3420/83.[49] The same can be said for the national import restrictions coming under the régime of Article 20 of Regulation No. 288/82.[50]

47. See for an opposite view Kretschmer, *loc. cit.*, *supra*, n. 35, at 70.
48. Decision 82/372, OJ 1982, L168.
49. OJ 1983, L346.
50. OJ 1982, L35.

D. THE NEW PROCEDURE FOR APPLYING ARTICLE 115 OF THE EEC TREATY (DECISION 80/47)[51]

20. The Commission has considerably tightened up the procedural constraints for the application of Article 115 by enacting Decision 80/47 of 20 December 1979[52] which replaced the Decision of 12 May 1971.[53] The Decision of 1971 gave a general authorisation to Member States to introduce (once certain conditions were fulfilled) a system of import licences for intracommunity trade and to delay issuing such an import licence whilst awaiting a Commission Decision under Article 115. After the *Donckerwolcke* judgment there remained little doubt that this procedure was incompatible with Community law.[54] Indeed, a departure from Article 30 of the EEC Treaty – and any system of import licences, even though automatically granted, must be so qualified – requires a *specific* authorisation under Article 115.

Decision 80/47 gives the Commission a bigger say in the procedure. Member States are only allowed to introduce a system of import documents, 'intracommunity surveillance' in the terms of the Decision, after having obtained the necessary authorisation from the Commission (Article 2). Intracommunity surveillance can only be so authorised where the import of the product in question risks causing economic difficulties in that Member State. An import document will have to be issued, apart from the two exceptions mentioned hereafter, within a maximum period of five working days after it has been requested. If the import of the relevant products does cause economic difficulties, the Member State can only enact protective measures after the Commission has given its authorisation. It is the Commission that establishes both the conditions and the method of implementation of these safeguard measures (Article 3). The mere introduction of a request to apply Article 115 does not allow the Member State to delay in issuing the import documents, as was admitted under the Decision of 1971. The new Decision 80/47 only allows such delay if the import, for which the documents have been requested, exceeds certain quantitative limits, *i.e.* 5% of the possible direct imports in that Member State or 1% of the total extra-EEC imports during the most recent period of 12 months for which statistical information is available. When these limits are exceeded, the maximum period for the issue of import documents is increased to ten working days. The import document can be refused only with the Commission's authorisation. If for one reason or another the procedure is delayed, the importer cannot be disadvantaged. He will always obtain the import document if after ten working days the Commission's decision has still not been made.

51. This Decision has been analysed by Kretschmer, *loc. cit.*, *supra*, n. 35, at 64; Timmermans, *SEW* 1981, 270 and Vogelenzang, *loc. cit.*, *supra*, n. 31, at 187.
52. OJ 1980, L16.
53. OJ 1971, L121, amended by Decision 73/55, OJ 1973, L80.
54. The Adv. Gen. Capotorti (Case 41/76, *Donckerwolcke* v. *Procureur*, *supra*, n. 4) and Warner (Case 52/77, *L. Cayrol* v. *Rivoira* (1977) ECR 2261 *et seq.*, at 2290), queried the lawfulness of the Decision of 1971.

Decision 80/47 lays down in much more detail the information which should accompany a request for the application of Article 115 than its predecessor. On the other hand, the information which the national authorities may require from an importer who requests an import document, is listed limitatively in Decision 80/47. Another improvement concerns the indication by the importer of the country of origin. Only in the case of serious and well-founded doubts, can further proof be required from the importer. However, this cannot prevent the import as such. Also in this respect Decision 80/47 demonstrates that the Commission has learnt from the *Donckerwolcke* judgment.[55]

By a Decision of 27 June 1980 the Commission has admitted an impressive number of requests by Member States for intracommunity surveillance, most of which relate to textile products.[56] These authorisations have been regularly renewed in the following years.

21. This new procedure can be welcomed. On the whole it satisfies the principles of the internal market, that is of the free movement of goods, much more adequately than the Decision of 1971.

The system of intracommunity surveillance, provided for by Article 2 of Decision 80/47, allows the national authorities to have at their disposal the necessary information concerning the development of indirect imports. So, the Member State can in due course ask for protective measures where these appear to be required. On the one hand, this surveillance also functions as an 'antichambre' for protective measures at a later stage. To be able to prevent a sizeable quantity of indirect imports, the national authorities must have first introduced intracommunity surveillance.[57] If an import document is requested for a quantity of goods exceeding the limits of Article 3, the Member State can ask the Commission to authorise protective measures under Article 115 of the EEC Treaty which also covers the imports in question. For that reason, the normal delay of five days for delivering the import document, is extended to ten days. If all other cases, however, the requested import documents will have to be granted unless of course the request has been made after a protective measure was already approved under Article 3.

This new system of Decision 80/47 reconciles in an ingenious manner both the requirement that an authorisation under Article 115 be granted *ad hoc*, and the imperative of legal certainty for the importers. However, Decision 80/47 authorises Member States to extend autonomously the delay for the issue of an import document by five days as soon as the quantitative limits of Article 3 of the Decision have been exceeded. Is this not a general authorisation contrary to the requirement that each national measure affecting the free movement of goods must be authorised previously by the Commission? I refer to the verdict

---

55. See para. 42 of Case 41/76, *Donckerwolcke*, n. 4.
56. OJ 1980, L164.
57. Could Art. 3 of Decision 80/47 also be applied with respect to indirect imports which are not yet subject to intracommunity surveillance granted under Art. 2 of that Decision? I would think so, but then of course the protection can only be admitted for the future; current indirect imports cannot be restricted.

in the *Donckerwolcke* judgment that refusing an import licence by way of an interim measure in view of a possible application of Article 115 is incompatible with Article 30 of the EEC Treaty.[58] In my view Decision 80/47 is in this respect compatible with *Donckerwolcke*. The possibility for Member States to extend the delay for the issue of an import document in fact forms an integral part of the system of intracommunity surveillance, and thus it is always covered by the Decision of the Commission authorising the setting up of such a surveillance.

Finally, with regard to the surveillance system, the question could be raised whether the requirement of an import document and the imposed delay of five days is really necessary if the document has at any rate to be issued after the delay has expired. Is this system not unnecessarily cumbersome for the importer and for that reason incompatible with the requirement of necessity under Article 115 and the underlying general principle of proportionality? Would it not be enough to require the importer to submit the necessary information? Requiring an import document within the framework of an intracommunity surveillance could then be limited to those cases where the intended imports exceed the quantitative limits of Article 3 of Decision 80/47. That, however, is exactly where the problem lies. The assessment of whether the intended import exceeds the said limits could as such be left to the importer. The limits in question are indeed of an objective nature and based on figures. That does not apply, however, where various import transactions are involved which not each on their own, but only taken together, exceed these limits. It is in view of these cases that a system of import documents which are to be issued within a short delay, can be justified as a necessary part of an intracommunity surveillance system.

III. JUDICIAL PROTECTION

22. In the foregoing I have expressed doubts as to the lawfulness in various respects, of both the Community import régimes applying to, or specifically enacted for, textile products, and also of the application by the Commission of Article 115 of the EEC Treaty on textiles. On the whole it is astonishing that on matters of such great practical importance – and indeed most of the legal questions raised, do not concern textiles alone but cover other sectors as well – so few cases have been brought before the Court of Justice. Therefore I want to finish my contribution with a few remarks on the possibilities for judicial review, particularly for private parties.

The normal way to get legal redress for private parties will be through the national Courts. The Community import régimes will be administered in an indirect way, that is through further implementatory measures taken at national level. Interested parties will normally be confronted with the Community rules

---

58. Paras. 39 and 40, see n. 4, at 1939.

through the intermediary of decisions taken by the national authorities, for instance on import documents. These national decisions should be challenged, of course, before the national Courts, but the preliminary procedure of Article 177 of the EEC Treaty enables the national judges to seek clarification of the validity of the Community Regulations or Decisions underlying the national measures. Consequently, the national Court can question the Court of Justice of the European Communities on the validity of a Community régime of regional protection or a Commission Decision granting an authorisation for safeguard measures under Article 115 of the EEC Treaty.[59]

It should also be stressed in this respect that questions relating to the division of powers between Community and Member States can be submitted to the Court of Justice provided that they are phrased as questions relating to the interpretation of Community law.[60] If, for instance, a national power to enact interim safeguard measures under a common import regulation seems to be incompatible with the exclusive nature of the Community power in the field of commercial policy, this question could certainly be put to the Court of Justice. If the Court denied such power to the Member State, the national measures would be *ultra vires* and should be treated as such by the national Court.

Direct access to the Court of Justice will remain the exception for private parties, but it is certainly not excluded. Apart from the possibility of an action for damages under Article 215 of the EEC Treaty, which can also be introduced in case of damage caused by unlawful legislative measures such as Regulations, an action for annulment under Article 173 of the EEC Treaty may be envisaged by a private party; but only with regard to a Decision taken by the Council or Commission and provided that the difficult hurdle of proving the necessary interest to sue ('direct and individual concern') can be overcome. The Court's case law demonstrates the practicability of this direct road to the Court, albeit a difficult and hazardous one. The Court has, in three cases in fact, heard appeals by importers against Decisions of the Commission granting the application of Article 115.[61] In these cases the importers were directly concerned by the Commission Decision because the national authorities had left no doubt that they would apply the safeguard measure once approved by the Commission. They were moreover individually concerned because the Commission had taken its Decision in full knowledge of the case of the importers in question and with explicit regard thereto. It follows that the direct action under Article 173 of the EEC Treaty against a Commission Decision applying Article 115 of the EEC Treaty will normally be available for those importers whose requests for an import document were refused by application of Article 3(4) of Decision

---

59. See for an example one of the *Tezi*-Cases: 242/84, *supra*, n. 1.
60. See for examples of earlier cases where questions on division of powers were raised by national Courts: Case 31/74, *Galli* (1975) ECR 47 *et seq.*, at 64, Case 77/76, *Cucchi* v. *Avez* (1977) ECR, 987 *et seq.*; Cases 3, 4 and 6/76, *Kramer* v. *Commission* (1976) ECR 1279 *et seq.*
61. Case 62/70, *Bock* v. *Commission* (1971) ECR, 897 *et seq.*, Case 29/75, *Kaufhof* v. *Commission* (1976) ECR, 431 *et seq.* and Case 59/84, *Tezi* v. *Commission* of 5 March 1986 (not yet published).

80/47, provided that these requests had been brought to the attention of the Commission according to Article 3(2) of the same Decision.

23. Legal remedies are therefore available to approach the Court in questions of legality of Community action relating to the common commercial policy. However, it is only fair to add that recent case-law in this field (*Bulk Oil/Tezi*) demonstrates an attitude of considerable judicial restraint on behalf of the Court. The Court appears to be fairly reticent – too reticent in the view of this writer – to intervene in the political compromises so laboriously agreed-upon within the Council. And no doubt, these issues of international trade policy are political hornets' nests. On the other hand, has not the firm stand of the Court in favour of integration and the intrinsic (legal) consequences of the integration process been in the past an essential condition for what European integration has actually achieved?

CHAPTER SIX

TRADE REGULATION SINCE THE TOKYO ROUND

By J. Steenbergen[*]

The Tokyo Round aimed not only at new tariff protocols, but also at a solution for a number of problems concerning the switch in emphasis from tariff to non-tariff trade barriers, the accommodation in the GATT of the emerging rules and views on North–South economic relations, the regulation of specific sectors such as agriculture, the organisation of settlement of disputes procedures, etc. This contribution sets out to give a brief survey of the implementation of the Tokyo Round agreements, the main problems raised by their application, and some problems that are not covered or solved by GATT rules developed in the Tokyo Round, at a time trading partners prepare for a new round of multilateral trade negotiations.

I. ISSUES ON WHICH NO AGREEMENT WAS REACHED IN THE TOKYO ROUND

First it might be useful to recall that some of the issues on the agenda of the Tokyo Round have not become the object of any code or arrangement as no agreement was reached among the Contracting Parties.

(i) The Tokyo Round did not establish a multilateral framework to integrate agricultural policies, although concrete results were obtained concerning some dairy products and bovine meat. The Contracting Parties also agreed on the necessity to improve international cooperation in agricultural matters, and to continue negotiations on a multilateral approach.[1]

---

[*] Partner with Braun Claeys Verbeke Sorel in Brussels and Associated senior lecturer at the Law School of the University of Leuven. The redaction was closed in September 1986.
1. GATT, *Les négociations commerciales multilatérales du Tokyo Round, Rapport additionnel* (Genève, 1980), pp. 13 and 21.

(ii) The Contracting Parties have not focused on problems concerning trade with State-trading countries or countries with a highly planned economy.
(iii) The Contracting Parties reached no final agreement on new general safeguard provisions. Although there was apparently a substantial agreement to allow for selective safeguard measures under Article XIX GATT, the parties could not agree on the question whether this would require a preliminary authorisation by a GATT Committee on Safeguards, or whether the parties who would take selective safeguard measures only would have to report to that Committee post factum.[2] The fact that no agreement was reached while it was considered necessary to negotiate a specific arrangement on selective safeguard measures, seems to confirm the traditional interpretation according to which safeguard measures have to apply to all imports of specific products, regardless of their origin.[3] The Contracting Parties also agreed on several exemptions granted to LDC's in the various new GATT codes.[4]
(iv) The Contracting Parties concluded no formal agreement on settlement of dispute procedures, but agreed on a *Memorandum of an agreement on the notification, consultation, and settlement of disputes*, and they organized consultation and settlement of disputes procedures in the various new GATT codes. In the Memorandum the parties confirm their intention (i) to comply with the various notification requirements and to notify as far as possible the adoption of every commercial measure which would affect the implementation of the GATT, (ii) to cooperate effectively in every consultation procedure asked for by their partners while giving a special attention to the interests of LDCs, (iii) to look for mediation when no agreement is reached by consultation, and (iv) while confirming the need to comply with the existing rules on settlement of disputes, they indicated a number of ameliorations that could improve the working of the special groups, and (v) finally they stated that they should act upon their recommendations.[5]

---

2. *Id.*, p. 16.
3. See further: M.C.E.J. Bronckers, *Selective safeguard measures in multilateral trade relations* (The Hague, 1985), 227 pp.
4. See GATT, *Rapport infra*, n. 5, p. 184, and see esp. Art. 14 of the Agreement on interpretation and application of Arts. VI, XVI and XXIII GATT. Art. 14 para. 2 extends the exemption explicitly to policies assisting industries in the export sector.
5. GATT, *Les négociations commerciales multilatérales du Tokyo Round, Rapport* (Genève, 1979), p. 184 and *Rapport additionnel*, p. 21.

II. THE IMPLEMENTATION IN THE EC[6] AND THE APPLICATION OF THE AGREEMENTS OF THE TOKYO ROUND

There have been to our knowledge no specific implementing measures in the Community concerning (i) the Arrangement regarding bovine meat; (ii) the International Dairy Arrangement; (iii) the Agreement on Civil aircraft, and (iv) the Agreement on import licensing procedures.[7]

They will not be discussed in any detail in this contribution. May it suffice to say that the meat and dairy agreements did little to alleviate criticism of the EC common agricultural policies. The agreements to some extent improved the exchange of information with regard to these sectors, but several provisions, such as the price provisions for dairy products, are difficult to enforce in the absence of a comprehensive dairy market regulation. The civil aviation agreement is, from the European side, mostly qualified as a tariff agreement and was as such a success as tariffs were reduced to a zero-level. The agreement on import licensing is generally considered to be a success.

A. AGREEMENT ON TECHNICAL BARRIERS TO TRADE

1. IMPLEMENTATION

The so-called standards code[8] has attracted considerable attention. It clarifies general GATT principles by formulating rules on national and most favoured nation treatment concerning the preparation, adoption and application of technical regulations and standards, or to a lesser extent, certification systems by central government bodies (Article 2, paragraph 1 and Article 7, paragraph 1).[9] It also contains a code of conduct on the choice or definition of technical standards or regulations.

It required as such no implementing measures of a general nature,[10] but it raised a number of delicate political and technical questions. Among the most

---

6. See further on EC, US and Japan: J.H. Jackson, J.V. Louis, M. Matsushita, *Implementing the Tokyo Round* (Ann Arbor, 1984) 223 pp.
7. All four Arrangements or Agreements have been published in OJ 1980, L71. The preamble to the Council Regulation (EEC) NO. 288/82 of 5 February 1982, on common rules for imports (OJ 1982, L35/1) refers to the Agreement on import licensing procedures but deals only with safeguard measures.
8. OJ 1980, L71/29. See for a general survey of this Agreement: Sweeney, 'Technical analysis of the technical barriers to trade Agreement', *Law & Pol'y Int'l Bus.*, 12 (1980), 179–217.
9. While Art. 2, para. 1 reads: '. . . products . . . shall be accorded . . .', Art. 7, paras. 1 and 2, on certification systems, stipulate that 'parties shall ensure . . .'.
10. See, however, the Commission's proposal for a Directive to the Council to organise consultations between the Community and the Member States on the application of certification systems organised under Community law to products imported from third countries, OJ 1980, C54/5.

important was the question whether rules on the free movement of goods and the application of standards such as developed in the *Cassis de Dijon* case law,[11] are to be applied towards all parties to the Agreement pursuant to its national treatment clause. The answers to these questions are complicated by a long standing dispute on the division of powers between the Community and the Member States in the field of technical standards.[12] It has led to the fact that the Agreement on technical barriers to trade is signed jointly by the Community and the Member States, which makes it very difficult to know whether the Community is to be considered as a single market or party for the purpose of the application of the Agreement, or whether each of the ten Member States are individually bound by the agreement in the same way as each of the other parties.

If the Community had signed alone, one could have argued that the Community signed both exercising its own external powers, conferred by Article 113 EEC or implied by its internal powers,[13] and as the agent for the Community of the Member States in so far as technical standards concern national powers. Third countries would probably have invoked the national treatment clause to benefit from rules applicable in intra-Community trade such as the *Cassis de Dijon* doctrine. But the Community and Member States might have been able to refer to the rules on local government regulations in so far as technical standards are not governed by Community law. While obligations contracted in the Agreement are strongly worded in case of central government regulations, the participants only agreed to 'take such reasonable measures as may be available to them to ensure that local government bodies within their territories comply with . . .' (Article 3, para. 1 and Article 8, para. 1). If Article 3, para. 1 and Article 8, para. 1 can be applied to the relations between the Community and its Member States, it would have remained possible to justify differences among the technical standards and certification systems of the Member States, even in cases where the differences result from national decisions that might as such be incompatible with the

---

11. *Cf.* Case 120/78, *Rewe* v. *Bundesmonopolverwaltung* (*Cassis de Dijon*), 20 Feb. 1979 (1979) ECR 649 *et seq.*; and *e.g.* Donner, 'Articles 30–36 EEC in general', Dutch Fide Report, 30 *SEW* 1982, 362–373; or Oliver, *Free movement of goods in the EEC* (London, 1982), 278.

12. The questions concerning the division of powers between the Community and the Member States cannot be discussed here. See Bourgeois, 'The Tokyo Round Agreements on technical barriers to trade and on government procurement in international and EEC perspective', 19 *CMLRev.* 1982, 21–22, and Timmermans, 'Division of external powers between Community and Member States in the field of harmonisation of national law', in Timmermans and Völker (Eds.), *Division of powers between the EC and their Member States* (Deventer, 1981), pp. 15–28. See concerning this agreement: Steenbergen, 'De Tokyo Ronde', *SEW* 28 1980, 762–766.

13. See for recent surveys: Barav, 'Division of external relations power between the EEC and the Member States in the case law of the Court of Justice' in Timmermans and Völker (Eds.), *op. cit.*, n. 12, pp. 29–64; Kovar, 'La contribution de la Cour de justice au développement de la condition internationale de la CE', *CDE* 1978, 527 *et seq.*; Louis and Brücker, in J. Mégret *et al.*, *Le droit de la CEE*, vol. 12 (Brussels, 1980), pp. 94–126; Pescatore, 'External relations in the case law of the Court of justice of the EC', 16 *CMLRev.* 1979, 615 *et seq.*; or Steenbergen, De Clercq and Foqué, *Change and adjustment: external relations and industrial policy of the EC* (Deventer 1983) paras. 79–89.

Agreement. And arguing along similar lines as the Court in the *Polydor* case,[14] one could have argued that specific rules, such as the *Cassis de Dijon* doctrine, can only apply within the Community because they are intrinsically linked to the integration process that characterises the evolving relations between the central and local centres of decision-making, and which justifies their exclusive application among the partners to that integration process.

Because the Member States also signed the Agreement individually, without specifying the scope of each signature, it is even easier to justify the existence of several certification systems applying different standards. But it is more difficult to justify a difference between rules applicable to intracommunity trade and rules applicable to trade with other parties to the GATT Agreement. Against such distinctions, third countries cannot only invoke the national treatment clause (*cf.* supra), but also the most favoured nation clauses embodied in Article 2, para. 1 and Article 7, para. 1. The signatures of the Member States make it virtually impossible to invoke the rules on local government regulations in order to justify a different treatment of intra- and extra-Community trade. Although the signatures of the Member States also suggest that they did not wish to invoke the rules on free trade areas in Article XIV GATT, these rules seem to remain the only legal basis in GATT to justify distinctions and policies which the Community has considered justified in its own legal order according to its Court's Decision in the *Polydor* case. Although the direct participation of the Member States may *prima facie* have strengthened the impact of the agreement, it is to be feared that the confusion concerning the degree to which the Community and its Member States have to extend their internal mechanisms to all Parties to the GATT Agreement, will mainly (i) slow down the efforts to strengthen the rules on the Community's internal market, and (ii) enhance the risk that Member States will define their standards and certification mechanisms according to the proposals by their most protectionist partners in order to safeguard that internal market.

According to Article 1 of a Council Decision of 15 January 1980,[15] the technical regulations, standards and certification and verification procedures laid down in the Directives for the removal of technical barriers to intracommunity trade shall apply, under any special conditions which may be laid down in those Directives, to all products on the Community market irrespective of their origin, save as otherwise provided in Title III of the Decision.

Article 1 also stipulates that the Member States shall take all appropriate action within their power to ensure that the technical regulations, standards and certification and verification procedures which are not harmonised at Community level, but are applied in these Member States and drawn up by official authorities or non-governmental bodies, are applied under any special

---

14. Case 270/80, *Polydor* v. *Harlequin* (1982) ECR 329; Case 17/81 *Pabst & Richarz* v. *Hauptzollamt Oldenburg*, (1982) ECR, 1331 *et seq.*; and Case 104/81, *Hauptzollamt* v. *Kupferberg*, (1982) ECR, 3641.
15. OJ 1980, L14/36. See on this decision also Bourgeois, *loc. cit.* n. 12, at 26–29.

conditions which may be laid down in the national texts to all products on the markets in question, irrespective of their origin, save as otherwise provided in the same Title III. In Title III, the Decision organises a consultation mechanism in case Member States consider that advantages resulting from the Agreement have been nullified or impaired, or that the attainment of its objectives has been impaired by any of the other parties, and that the reciprocity between the concessions made by the Community and those actually applied by the allegedly injuring party has consequently been nullified or impaired. In case the issue involves Community Directives, the Community shall decide, after consultations according to Articles 4–7, what appropriate measures should be taken in accordance to the Agreement (Article 5). In case no Community Directives have yet been adopted, such measures can be taken by the Member States (Article 6).

The Decision implies that, in the opinion of the Council, the GATT Agreement only applies to standards and certification systems as laid down in either Community Directives or the law of the Member States. It makes no reference to any rule or doctrine concerning the free movement of goods that might affect the interpretation or application of these standards. It also makes a distinction between Community standards and national standards, suggesting without actually saying so that the signatures of the Member States cover only the standards which are not yet harmonised at a Community level, and that those are covered by the respective Member States only. But it acknowledges at the same time that the Community participated as a single market or trade partner in the negotiations that led to the conclusion of the Agreement, because nullifications or impairments by third countries are partly appreciated in function of their impact on the reciprocity between the concessions made *by the Community* and those actually applied by the allegedly injuring party. Thus, the Decision seems to try to get around most of the problems mentioned in this paragraph, without giving many clear answers.

It should finally be mentioned that the Decision makes no distinction between products originating in third countries which are parties to the GATT Agreement, and other products. Moreover, Title III only applies to the parties to the Agreement. It organises the action *in the event of non-reciprocity* (title), in case Member States consider 'that an advantage directly or indirectly *resulting from the Agreement* has been nullified or impaired or that the attainment of one of the objectives of *the Agreement* has been impaired *by one or more of the other Parties* thereto, that their trading interests are significantly affected *and that reciprocity between the concessions made by the Community under the Agreement and those actually applied by the other Party or Parties* has consequently been nullified or impaired' (Article 3, our italics).

Thus, the Decision enables the Community to safeguard the reciprocity between the concessions made by parties to the Agreement, but it extends several of those concessions to third countries without requiring any kind of reciprocity, or organising any specific safeguards. In fact, it seems to imply that the main consequence of a participation to the Agreement for third countries, is not to benefit from Community concessions – which are largely extended to all trade partners by the Decision – but to become eligible for specific safeguard measures.

2. APPLICATION

Given the fairly limited scope of the standards code, one could not expect major achievements. The divergencies between standards and certification procedures remain substantial. It is nevertheless felt that most contracting parties tried to comply with the codes' guidelines when formulating new standards. The code stimulated efforts to formulate and implement internationally negotiated standards and the notification duty, duplicated on an intra-community level by a directive of 28 March 1983,[16] has significantly improved the transparency of domestic limitations or regulations applicable in signatory states.[17]

The main target for criticism remains Japan. These criticisms are concerned with the content of Japanese standards (often significantly different from US or EC standards) and with Japanese certification procedures (requiring the testing of many more samples than US or EC procedures), the way they are applied, and the general inertia and instransparency of the system. Only in 1983 Japan revised standards certification laws in order to comply with the national treatment clause.[18]

Four disputes brought to GATT, either under the code, or under the general GATT dispute settlement procedures, involved the EC: one case dealt with poultry processing and raised the issue whether the code applies to processing and production methods; a second case concerned a Canadian complaint that the EC imposed the use of US beef grading standards; a third case deals with EC standards for fertilisers allegedly benefiting to North American producers; and a fourth case with Spanish regulations on medical equipment. In the first and last cases, the parties came to a bilateral understanding. In the second case the GATT council adopted a panel report finding against the EC, and the third case is still pending. No major criticism has been formulated with regard to the working of the settlement of disputes or review mechanisms organized by the code.

---

16. OJ 1983, L109/8.
17. Thirty-four contracting parties accepted the standards code as of February 1986: McGovern, *International trade regulation*, 2nd ed. (London, 1986), p. 538. It should be noted, however, that the code only applies to mandatory regulations issued by central governments. See Annex 1 to code and applicable to products. The code does not apply to services, and neither does it according to the EC apply to processes or production methods.
18. Jackson *et al.*, *supra*, n. 6, at 110.

B. THE AGREEMENT ON GOVERNMENT PROCUREMENT

1. IMPLEMENTATION

The Agreement on government procurement[19] prompted a number of changes to the régime organised by Directive 77/62.[20] By Directive 80/767/EEC[21] the Council reduced the minimum value of contracts entering into its scope of application and extended the list of purchasing entities to which the Agreement applies.[22] The directive introduced a number of procedural changes, and stipulates in Article 7 that 'the Member States shall apply in their relations conditions as favourable as those which they grant to third countries in implementation of the Agreement.'

The Directive 80/767/EEC refers to the GATT Agreement in its preamble and in Article 7. But it only deals with intracommunity relations. This confirms that GATT Agreements entered into by the Community are directly binding the Member States to the extent that the parties to the Agreement are bound according to the law of GATT, in the extra-Community relations between EEC Member States and third parties to the GATT Agreement. It leaves the implementation of the Agreement to the Member States. But the Directive also implies that external obligations contracted by the Community can not be invoked in intra-Community relations as long as pre-existent Community law has not been brought into line with the new rules governing *extra* Community relations.[23]

In its Resolution of 22 July 1980[24] the Council also kept the management of *extra*-Community relations with third countries who are not parties to the GATT Agreement in line with the situation created among the parties to the Agreement, because it stated that the Member States can continue to apply in accordance with the Treaty existing commercial policy measures concerning government contracts to which the GATT Agreement does not apply. The Commission added in a statement that it intends to apply Article 115 EEC in order to safeguard the efficacy of national measures against the deflection of trade resulting from the free circulation within the Community of goods originating in third countries.[25]

The Agreement on government procurement introduced one of the most far-reaching amendments to international trade law. It may be recalled that the parties agreed according to Article II, para. 1 to grant 'immediately and unconditionally' national and most favoured nation treatment to products and

---

19. OJ 1980, L71/44.
20. OJ 1977, L13/1. See further Bourgeois, *loc. cit.*, *supra* n. 12, at 29–31.
21. Directive 80/767/EEC of 22 July 1980, OJ 1980, L215.
22. See Art. 3 and Annex I.
23. See further Steenbergen, 'The Status of GATT in Community law', 15 *JWTL* 1981, 340.
24. OJ 1980, C211/2.
25. OJ 1980, C211/1.

suppliers of other parties offering products originating within the custom territories of the parties.

The implementation and application of the government procurement code raised a number of questions.

Some follow from the scope of application as defined by the Agreement. The scope of the general exception to protect national security can, *e.g.*, be extremely large, because it is left to the parties to decide what *they* consider to be necessary for what they consider to be their (essential) security interests. Article VIII, para. 1, explicitly introduces the distinction between 'procurement indispensable for national security *or* for national defense purposes' (our italics). This brings to a large extent the various concepts of national (economic) security under the scope of the exception. And the virtual exclusion of several markets, such as those for telephone and telegraph, railways and power generating equipment, from the scope of the Agreement, has come in for severe criticism.[26] These questions can only be solved in further negotiations as scheduled by Article IX, para. 6.

Other questions concern the interpretation of the Agreement. It has *e.g.* been asked whether the Agreement covers leasing as well as more traditional purchase contracts. The consultation and settlement of disputes mechanism organised by the Agreement should help the parties to answer such questions. This also applies to the interpretation of the list of protectable interests enumerated in Article VIII, para. 2. It is not very different from Article 36 EEC, and the interpretation of what is to be considered necessary to protect these interests is not left to the parties which take such measures. The questions as to whether parties to the Agreement compiled with the publication requirements, can likewise be submitted to the parties according to the procedures organised under the Agreement.

2. APPLICATION

The application of the government procurement code is certainly not an unqualified success. Almost from the outset the new regime was criticized, primarily in the US, because of the exclusion of telecommunication, public transport and electricity generating equipment from the scope of application of the code in view of the lists of purchasing entities annexed to the Agreement. This criticism is, however, like other criticisms directed at the codes' scope of application, concerned with the code itself and not with the application of the code as agreed upon in the Tokyo Round. The review provided for under art. IX which was scheduled for 1983, was postponed.[27]

Other criticisms or problems are directly concerned with the implementation

---

26. See *e.g.* the contributions by Pomeranz, Anthony and Hagerty in *Law & Pol'y Int'l Bus.*, 11 (1979), 1295 and 1312 *et seq.*; or *The Economist*, 13/19 Mar. 1982, at 41–42.
27. Bens, 'Trade liberalisation and the global service economy', *JWTL* (1985) 11b.

and application of the code: *e.g.* with regard to the deadlines to participate in tenders, the issue whether leasing is covered by the code etc, the splitting of contracts into parts that do not exceed the code's 150,000 SDR threshold, the EC practice to deduct VAT when calculating the value of contracts, etc. Major criticisms have been addressed at Italy.

However, few issues have led to formal complaints under the code's settlement of disputes mechanism. As under domestic law, many hesitate to file a complaint in case of infringements of government procurement rules, often because of a fear for retaliation or because complaints seldom lead to a contract being transferred to the complainant, which makes the filing of a complaint financially unattractive to the injured undertakings.

The code did certainly not result in a major, or even a significant opening of world markets for government procurement. The criticism of the codes' scope of application are hardly surprising when realising that the percentage of government procurement in the EC covered by the code has been estimated at no more than 5%. Moreover, only 0.2% of government procurement by central authorities in the EC is contracted with suppliers in third countries.[28] We can therefore conclude that old habits die hard, and that foreign procurement remains virtually limited to cases where there is no domestic supplier or contract, passed in the framework of compensation or barter trade agreements.[29]

C. THE SUBSIDIES AND COUNTERVAILING DUTIES CODE

1. IMPLEMENTATION

The Agreement on interpretation and application of Articles VI, XVI and XXIII GATT[30] enabled the Community to organise countervailing duty procedures in accordance with the Agreement to protect the Common Market against imports that have been subsidised in infringement of the Agreement. It also required the Community to review its rules on sibsidies or its own subsidising policies according to the rules and guidelines set out in the Agreement.

---

28. *Europe*, 7–8 February 1985, 9.
29. See further Dejonghe, 'Het verbod van discriminatie bij overheidsopdrachten voor leveringen', 34 *SEW* (1986), 183.
30. OJ 1980, L71/72.

The Community's Countervailing Duty Procedures

As set out in other contributions to this publication, international trade law organises several legal remedies to safeguard international fair trading standards: (i) countervailing duty procedures to counteract (state) subsidies considered to be incompatible with international rules on subsidies; (ii) antidumping procedures to counteract dumping by exporting undertakings; and (iii) escape clause or safeguard procedures to safeguard the national interest of trade partners in specific circumstances. Although these three groups of remedies each serve, in theory, specific purposes, we see that in practice most countries or industries use whichever remedy is most conveniently developed in their legal system, whenever they consider to be injured by imports. Countervailing duty procedures traditionally received considerable attention in the US,[31] although countervailing duties have not all that often been imposed. But in Europe, the attention of private parties and governments usually concentrates almost exclusively on anti-dumping procedures (*cf. infra*) and escape or safeguard clauses.

The Community introduced nevertheless new rules on countervailing measures in the EEC Council Regulation and ECSC Commission Recommendation which also introduce new anti-dumping codes.[32] The EC implementation of the new GATT Code has raised no specific questions. The Community rules apply to all imports. Because they organise Community remedies *against* imports, there was no reason to restrict their applicability to parties to the GATT Agreement.

The Community's Rules on Subsidies

Articles 92–94 EEC, and the equivalent provisions in other Community treaties organise a much tighter control on subsidies than the new GATT provisions. And while the rules on State aid have not always been observed strictly by the Member States, recent developments illustrate that Community discipline becomes more real under difficult socio-economic circumstances, where the contrary might have been expected.[33] But this does not mean that the application of the EC rules on State aid or the Community aids[34] are always

---

31. See, with an analysis of the proposals: Rivers and Greenwald, 'The negotiation of a code on subsidies and countervailing measures: bridging fundamental policy differences', *Law & Pol'y Int'l Bus.*, 11 (1979), 1448 *et seq*.
32. Council Regulation (EEC) 3017/79 of 20 Dec. 1979 and Commission Recommendation 3018/79/ECSC of 21 Dec. 1979, OJ 1979, L339/1 and 15 as replaced by Reg. 2176/84 (OJ L201/1) and Dec. 2177/84 (OJ L201/17).
33. While between 1970 and 1976, the Commission dealt every year with 18–47 national measures, the Commission dealt between 1981 and 1985 yearly with 112 to 233 measures. See 14th Competition Report.
34. See *e.g.* the survey by Keur, 'Financiële instrumenten en coördinatie van het economisch beleid, 30 *SEW* (1982), 267–301.

compatible with the interpretation of the GATT Code by our trade partners. On the contrary, the development of trade relations after the Tokyo Round, and especially the Euro-American relations, clearly indicates that the new Agreement on subsidies and countervailing duties solved few, if any, outstanding problems apart from the acceptance of the injury test by the USA.[35] It gives no indications concerning the subsidies which might reduce imports and cause injury to the exporting country, although this harmful effect on trade and competition was confirmed to come under the scope of the Agreement[36] and it does not clarify at all the notion of 'subsidies other than export subsidies'. Even on export subsidies, which have been defined in more detail, the trade partners continue to disagree.[37] Moreover, the consultation mechanisms set up under the Agreement hardly have a conciliatory role: it is rather considered as an act of trade war to open negotiations within the GATT framework.[38]

2. APPLICATION

The subsidies code did not significantly reduce the number of scope of disputes involving subsidies. It has often been said that the code, while improving the rules governing countervailing duty procedures, hardly contributed to a more workable definition of legitimate and actionable subsidies, except for the annex giving an exemplary list of export subsidies. Under the code, the signatories relied on the settlement of disputes procedure to clarify the rules applicable to various forms of subsidies. However, for reasons some of which will be discussed later in this text, parties were either reluctant to bring cases under the code, or unable to decide the issues within the framework of the competent GATT bodies. It must be said that, since the Tokyo Round, almost all major trade disputes involved subsidies, the single most important exception being the Siberian pipeline issue which involved trade sanctions and general foreign policy considerations.

Agricultural subsidies remain the major cause of disputes. And although a significant number of complaints were filed, it is generally felt that the GATT Council or the Committee proved unable to obtain satisfactory results.[39]

35. Rivers and Greenwald, *loc. cit.* n. 31 at 1453. See, however, on the problems concerning the actual meaning of *material injury* the paragraph on the anti-dumping code. The subsidies code gives an additional indication *of the degree of injury* that can justify countervailing measures. Arts. 11, para. 2 and 13, para. 4 use not only the terms *injury*, *nullification* and *impairment*, but also *serious prejudice*.
36. Art. 8, para. 4.
37. See *e.g. Europe*, 21 July 1982, 5, and the Parliamentary Question by Fanton, No. 802/81, OJ 1981, C323/4 answered by Commissioner Haferkamp, on US (export) subsidies, or the speeches by Senator Helms, *Congressional Record-Senate*, 7 Oct. 1981, 11192–11195; or Mr. Hormats, *Official text*, ICA US Embassy in Brussels, 18 Dec. 1981, p. 9, on European export credits.
38. See not only the developments in the relations between the EEC and the USA, but also of the relations with Japan.
39. It can be said in general that with regard to the EC 14 out of the 17 complaints filed against the EC from 1975 to Sept. 1, 1985, were concerned with agricultural products (*i.e.* 33% of all

The other sector causing major trade conflicts, from the EC's point of view, has been steel. It can be argued that subsidies were one of the main causes for these disputes and that GATT did not (or was not allowed to) contribute to a settlement. On the contrary, the USA and the EC preferred to negotiate a series of bilateral settlements organising minimum prices.

D. THE NEW ANTI-DUMPING CODE

1. IMPLEMENTATION

The new anti-dumping code, or the Agreement on implementation of Article VI GATT,[40] clarified several notions used in the previous code that resulted from the Kennedy Round and strengthened its procedural matrix. Its required few changes to pre-existent Community law. But the Council and the Commission adopted nevertheless a new EC anti-dumping Regulation and a new ECSC Recommendation which have improved the Community procedures.[41] There are no indications that the EC implementation of the new Code raises specific problems.[42] As they are introduced by the same texts which implemented the subsidies code, the new anti-dumping rules also apply to all imports. Because the provisions on dumping organise Community remedies against damage caused by imports, there was no reason to restrict their applicability to parties to the GATT Agreement.

2. APPLICATION

It can be said that the Tokyo Round anti-dumping code has been a success. The implementation closely follows the (fairly detailed) provisions of the code, and the procedure as organised by the code organises a reasonably effective remedy while safeguarding the procedural rights of the defendant. With regard to the Tokyo Round's aim at imposing more strict time limits in order to avoid undue delays, it can *e.g.* be mentioned that notwithstanding a marked increase in the number of complaints, the average period required to obtain provisional duties was reduced between 1980 and 1983 from 7.5 to 5.7 months and the average period necessary to take definitive action from 9.6 to 7.8 months.[43]

complaints filed in that period). See US Senate Committee or Finance Report, USITC public No. 1793, table 2.
40. OJ 1980, L71/90.
41. See n. 26.
42. See on the problems that might have been caused by the way the Community signed the Agreement: Steenbergen, *loc. cit.*, n. 23, at 340–341.
43. First and Second Commission report on anti-dumping. See for an appreciation of the effectiveness of anti-dumping procedures further Steenbergen, 'Ondernemingen en handelspolitieke instrumenten (een) appreciatie', 33 *SEW* 1985.

The application of both the new GATT Code and the EC codes shows, however, that the new texts give no univocal answer to several questions. Among the economic most relevant ones is the question whether the Agreement offers protection against so-called imput or upstream dumping: the import of goods that are not dumped as such, but sold at an abnormally low price because they contain components that have been dumped at an earlier stage. The Agreement gives no specific indications to answer this question.

Both the US and the EC administrations maintain that it should not be possible to take anti-dumping measures in case of upstream dumping (except in case of circumvention of anti-dumping duties, which has led to a proposal to modify EEC anti-dumping rules not yet published when the redaction of this text was closed) but industry frequently lobbies in favour of such measures.

Two further problems are concerned with the terms of reference in anti-dumping proceedings: the concept of 'like products' and the transactions on the basis of which the normal value is established. Canadian (beef) and US (wine) proceedings suggest that both administrations consider that the concept of like products should include products upstream or downstream in the production cyclus in case there is no direct competition at a given stage of production. The EC is likely to refer both issues to GATT.

On the other hand, the EC when determining the normal value of Japanese products, considered that it should be determiend on the basis of the price practised at the first independant sale by the manufacturing (exporting) group, disregarding prices asked on the Japanese market when the manufacturing company sells to a related company organising distribution to independent customers on the Japanese market.[44] This issue is at present submitted to the Court of Justice.[45]

Europeans and Americans also still tend to disagree on the actual meaning of the term 'material injury' and on the question whether the dumping should be one of the relevant causes of the injury, the single most important cause, or the cause which is at least as important as the combined impact of the other causes. The term *material injury*, which is used in Article VI GATT, is repeated in a footnote to the Agreement, qualifying the concept of *injury* used in its text. Americans usually construct it as any degree of injury that is more substantial than what would be covered by a *de minimis*-rule.[46] The American interpretation might *in se* be compatible with the notion of *material injury* in English. But the fact that the parties still translate this concept by *préjudice important* in the equally authentic French text[47] shows that they intended to

44. Reg. (EEC) No. 1698/85, Electronic typewriters, OJ 1985, L163/1.
45. Case 56/85, *Brother*.
46. See Lorenzen, 'Technical analysis of the anti-dumping Agreement and the trade Agreements act', 11 *Law & Pol'y Int'l Bus.*, 1979, 1421.
47. See OJ 1980, L71/91. In Dutch it is translated by 'aanmerkelijke schade' (Pb EG. 1980, L71/91). It should perhaps be recalled that most US experts did not consider an injury test to be a condition for the imposition of anti-dumping duties until the Tokyo Round Agreement. The new Agreement did however not change the wording of Art. VI. Art. VI always provided that 'dumping . . . is to be condemned if it causes or threatens material injury . . .'. The new code merely introduced rules on the determination of injury (Art. 3).

adopt a more severe injury test. And while the new Agreement tends to confirm the European interpretation mainly by repeating the previous wording, it did throw new light on the issue of causation. According to Article 3, para. 4, of the new Agreement 'there may be other factors which at the time are injuring the industry, and injuries caused by other factors must not be attributed to dumped imports'. By stipulating that only the injuries caused by dumping can be taken into consideration, the provision suggests that dumping should be the *only* cause of the injury *taken into consideration*. In practice it will often be virtually impossible to distinguish the injury caused by dumping, from injury caused by other factors. But the new provisions at least indicate that dumping should be a 'material' cause of the injury.

Another problem is not raised by the GATT Code or its implementation, but by the specific rules on the determination of dumping in imports from non-market countries introduced by the new EC codes. According to Article 2 para. 5 of both the EEC and ECSC code, the normal value of goods imported from non-market countries shall be determined in an appropriate and not unreasonable manner on the basis of one of the following criteria:

(a) the price at which the like product of a market economy is actually sold:

   (i) for consumption on the domestic market of that country, or

   (ii) to other countries, including the Community; or

(b) the constructed value of the like product in a market economy third country; or

(c) if neither price nor constructed value as established under (a) or (b) above provides an adequate basis, the price actually paid or payable in the Community for the like product, duly adjusted, if necessary, to include a reasonable profit margin.

By allowing a comparison with the price of like products as sold by third countries with a market economy, the EC codes introduce criteria which are more related to what is to be considered normal on the EC market than to the characteristics of the exporting industry. In doing so it shifts the emphasis from the practice of dumping to the injury test, close to the point where countervailing measures can be taken in any case where injury has been established, regardless of the fact whether there has been dumping or not. This holds especially true when Art. 2, para. 5 and the adjustment provisions of Art. 2, para. 4 are applied cumulatively. As the traditional concept of dumping is almost impossible to apply in trade with non-market countries, the EC rules show the limits of what can be obtained by rules on dumping, and clearly indicate the need for a more specific approach to trade with State-trading countries.

It should finally be remarked that some circles would like to see more emphasis being given to the concept of social dumping when establishing normal value. They consider that products manufactured in circumstances which disregard specific minimum standards, such as ILO conventions, are not sold in the ordinary course of trade, and that in order to determine the normal value, the price charged in the country of origin should be adjusted accordingly.[48]

E. THE AGREEMENT ON CUSTOMS VALUATION

1. IMPLEMENTATION

The Agreement on implementation of Article VII GATT[49] has been implemented by Council Regulation (EEC) 1224/80 of 28 May 1980.[50] This Regulation closely follows the text of the Agreement. It has not raised any specific questions as to whether it ensures an adequate implementation of the Agreement, and applies to all imports. The Community always aimed at a uniformity of customs valuation rules, and made no major concessions. The Agreement's main purpose was to abolish the American customs evaluation according to the so-called *American Selling Price*. A restriction of the scope of application of Regulation 1224/80 to trade with parties to the Agreement would therefore have been counter-productive.

Regulation 1224/80 of the Council has in turn been implemented by a series of Commission Regulations.

2. APPLICATION

The agreement on customs valuation is generally considered to be an outstanding success.

III. COMMUNITY TRADE LAW BEYOND THE SCOPE OF THE TOKYO ROUND AGREEMENTS

As recalled before, no Agreement was reached in the Tokyo Round on safeguard measures. But the Community completed its review of trade law remedies discussed in the paragraph on the subsidies code, by introducing new safeguard procedures in Council Regulations (EEC) on common rules for imports, imports from State-trading countries, or from the People's Republic

---

48. See *e.g.* on views expressed in European Parliament, *Europe*, September 1986.
49. OJ 1980, L71/104.
50. OJ 1980, L134/1.

of China.[51] It also reviewed the application of Article 115 of the EEC Treaty concerning the measures Member States can take concerning the import of products originating from third countries and admitted in free circulation by another Member State.[52]

The new Regulation on common rules for imports mainly introduced rules with regard to a Community investigation procedure which are very similar to those required by the new GATT anti-dumping and subsidies Codes. They can be considered as a major improvement and go a long way to answer one of the main complaints formulated by US experts.

The Commission Decision on the application of Article 115 of the EEC Treaty deals with intra-Community trade, but strengthens substantially the Community's control over trade in imported products, by requiring a preliminary authorisation of the Commission for national surveillance or safeguard measures.[53]

The most significant development of EEC trade policy instruments since the implementation of the Tokyo Round agreements and related measures, was the adoption of the so-called New commercial policy instrument by Regulation 2641/84 in September 1984.[54] The instrument is often described as the EEC equivalent of US Trade Act Section 301. The aims are twofold: it provides (i) for complaints by a Community industry which considers that it has suffered injury as a result of practices attributable to third countries which are incompatible with international law or generally accepted rules; and (ii) procedures initiated by the Commission or at the request of a Member State in case commercial practices of third countries infringe upon the exercise of rights of which the Community may avail itself under international law or generally accepted rules. The instrument explicitly refers to rules of international law and international consultation or settlement of disputes mechanisms when defining the powers of the Community to take measures with regard to such practices. It can therefore not lead to conflicts with existent rules of international trade law. It can, however, as will be discussed below, change the profile of EC trade law practices by giving more emphasis to the management of international trade relations by litigation at the initiative of private parties.[55]

---

51. Council Regs. No. 288/82 of 5 Feb. 1982, OJ 1982, L35/1, No. 1765/82 and 1766/82 of 30 June 1982, OJ 1982, L195/1 and 21 and No. 3430/83 of 14 November 1983, OJ 1983, L313/1.

52. Commission Dec. 80/47/EEC of 20 Dec. 1979, OJ 1980, L16/14. In application of this Decision the Commission authorised Member States to organise intra-Community surveillance by Dec. 80/605/EEC, of 27 June 1980, OJ 1980, L164/20.

53. See further, with warnings about a Commission policy that could cause a re-nationalisation of the common commercial policy by a liberal use of Art. 115 of the EEC Treaty: Timmermans, 'Nieuwe procedure beschikking Art. 115 EEG', 29 *SEW* 1981, 270–278, and his contribution in Chapter Five.

54. OJ 1984, L252/1.

55. See on the new instrument further: Van Bael and Bellis, *op. cit.* or McGovern, *op. cit.* n. 17, or Bourgeois and Laurent, 'Le nouvel instrument de politique commerciale', 21 *RTDE* 1985, 41 or Steenbergen, The New Commercial policy instrument, 22 *CMLRev.* 1985, 421 and the contribution by Völker in Chapter Two.

IV. LEGAL REMEDIES AND SETTLEMENT OF DISPUTES

A. THE TOKYO ROUND

The legal remedies available to private parties are discussed in detail in the contributions on dumping and countervailing duty procedures. They will therefore not be discussed in this text. Suffice it to say that the Tokyo Round Agreements induced substantial improvements to the anti-dumping, countervailing duty and safeguard clause procedures.

Neither is it possible to discuss in this context in detail the settlement of disputes procedures organised under the new codes. The Bovine Meat Arrangement, the International Dairy Arrangement, the Agreement on Trade in Civil Aircraft, the Anti-Dumping Code, and the Agreement on Import Licensing Procedures, contain no specific settlement of disputes provisions and no sanctions, nor refer explicitly to the general provisions in Articles XXII and XXIII GATT in case no agreement is reached by consultation. This means that the basic jurisdiction remains with the Contracting Parties. As mentioned under I, they agreed to improve the working of these provisions in a Memorandum, but they did not change fundamentally the GATT dispute settlement machinery which has proven to be rather ineffective. The reference to the general provisions of the GATT, however, makes it possible to look for a potentially effective sanction as it is possible under Article XXIII GATT to suspend either concessions or other obligations according to what is considered to be an appropriate sanction.

The Agreements on technical barriers to trade, government procurement and customs valuation organise their own settlement of disputes machinery. They not only organise specific Committees consisting of representatives from each of the parties, but the parties agreed to a duty of consultation, whenever a party wants to discuss any matter affecting the implementation of the Agreement. There is no strict obligation to ask for consultation when a party considers the benefits it derives from the Agreement are in any way impaired by the actions of any other party. When no agreement is reached after consultation, the parties can bring the matter before the Committee if their interests are significantly affected. They have to complete the dispute settlement procedures organised under the Agreement before they can avail themselves in any other way of any right they have under GATT.

The Committee is to investigate the matter within 30 days, and if their investigation brings no solution, a technical expert group or a panel can be set up to investigate the matter further. When the investigation is completed and no Agreement has been reached yet, the report by the technical expert group or panel is considered by the Committee without delay. The Committee makes a statement on the facts, it can make recommendations to the parties, or any other ruling it deems appropriate. Parties which consider themselves unable to implement the recommendations made by the Committee have to furnish their reasons in writing. But if the Committee considers the circumstances serious enough to justify such action, it can only authorise a party to suspend the implementation of its own obligations under the Agreement towards other parties. This cannot always prove to be an effective remedy. It is, *e.g.*, often not a true sanction on the potential import, that a potential exporter whose offers have not been considered in a tendering procedure, does not have to take into consideration the offers of suppliers from the injuring State.

Only the Agreement on subsidies and countervailing duties both organises a dispute settlement procedure, and enables the Committee to authorise the injured party to take a wider range of appropriate counter-measures. It also requires parties to open consultation procedures before opening a formal investigation.

The potentially most satisfactory way to implement international trade rules is to set up an international authority empowered to decide on the interpretation of these rules, and eventually to impose sanctions that guarantee a reasonable degree of enforceability. In case the partners are not willing to accept a substantial transfer of sovereignty, the scope of the transfer can be limited by an Agreement on clearly and precisely formulated rules which do not require a high degree of potentially controversial interpretation. The new GATT Codes reflected the inability of the Contracting Parties, either to agree on such rules, or on the transfer of sovereignty, necessary to ensure an effective implementation of rules of a more general nature. The only remaining approach was to set rules which lay down a code of conduct for the governments which are willing to accept them, and which offer both a framework and standards to discuss domestic policies (both policies *vis-à-vis* the domestic industries, such as subsidies, and countervailing measures affecting imports) in intergovernmental negotiations. It is the approach chosen in the Tokyo Round, as is illustrated by the implementation and enforcement mechanisms organised in the new codes. The weaknesses of the provisions on enforcement and the unsatisfactory sanctions[56] are therefore not inconsistent with this option. They are rather the inevitable consequences of a political context that left no room for truly enforceable agreements, and forced the parties to emphasise the rules on consultation and conciliation.

The option for a more intergovernmental approach, virtually excluding direct actions by private parties on an international forum, did, however, not necessarily imply that the Contracting Parties preferred a power to a rule-oriented approach to international dispute settlement.[57] The new rules offered a more sophisticated framework for political negotiations. They have not only set up fora for consultations but the rules and standards they introduce helped to reduce substantially the discretionary character that is often

---

56. See *e.g. The Economist*, 31 July 1982, 18.
57. See on this distinction: Jackson, 'The Crumbling Institutions of the Liberal Trade System', 12 *JWTL* 1978, 98 *et seq.*

reproached to an intergovernmental approach to the management of international relations. The Agreements follow in this the pattern of multilateralisation which characterises many of the Agreements concluded by the European Communities such as the Lomé Convention: they frequently try to formulate standards of international behaviour by organising cooperation and consultation mechanisms. Legal rules are used in such Agreements often to make problems negotiable and to set trends in negotiations, rather than to make all of the proposed solutions enforceable.

B. APPLICATION

This approach was not without major risks, which were aggravated by the attitudes towards litigation as a way of regulating international trade referred to in the paragraph on the subsidies code.

Developments in Euro-American relations[58] illustrate that there is not only the risk that some countries will feel justified to countervail in almost every case where any *injury, nullification* or *impairment*[59] can be proved, but also that other countries might feel all too easily that they gave due consideration *to trade, normal competition and the legitimate interests of their partners.*[60] Both risks can lead to various forms of creeping protectionism. Countervailing procedures are more protectionistic than they appear to be from the US perspective[61] and they can lead to a reaction that may be too lenient towards subsidies. The inability to formulate adequate rules for some of the most sensitive issues, has therefore, if anything, accentuated the problems caused by the asymmetry in the approach of major trade partners to industrial policies, to the management of trade relations, and in their attitudes to litigation. There are few indications that the GATT Committees have been able to bring the most sensitive issues, such as the disputes on subsidies, any closer to a solution. On the contrary, it has been mentioned already that a mere reference to GATT is sometimes almost considered as an act of economic warfare.

Rather than settling disputes within the GATT framework, parties frequently preferred to negotiate bilateral arrangements. They feared that due to the political significance of the issues the GATT mechanisms would be unable to establish a consensus, or that the discussions might even bring the GATT mechanisms to a breaking point. US–EC steel arrangements[62] or the

58. See further on Euro-American relations: Steenbergen, 'De EG en de Verenigde Staten', *Internationale Spectator*, 1982, 354–359.
59. See the paragraphs on the subsidies and anti-dumping codes, and especially n. 30.
60. Art. 11, para. 2 of the subsidies code.
61. This is particularly true towards countries which depend for a comparatively high percentage of GNP on exports generated by comparatively small companies for whom the risk of being involved in costly procedures with regard to a significant percentage of their turnover can be most inhibiting. See on costs of procedures in US: Jackson, 'Perspectives on the jurisprudence of international trade', 82 *Michigan Law Rev.*, 1984, 1570.
62. See *e.g.* Dec. 2871–2873/82, OJ 1982, L307/11 and Dec. 3081/83, OJ 1983, L301/48.

US–Japan car and microprocessors dealings are two characteristic examples of the bilateralisation of the management of trade relations. We might add that the bilateral textile agreements concluded in the context of the Multifiber Arrangement, while formally taken in the framework of a multilateral arrangement concluded in accordance to GATT rules, are *de facto* also examples of the tendency to settle the more delicate issues bilaterally.[63] It can be said that the MFA merely covers the bilateral agreements. But it would be grossly exaggerated to say that the new consultation mechanisms, and therefore the new codes, have largely proven to be a failure. On less sensitive or spectacular issues, progress has been made, and several Committees work towards an effective clarification or improvement of international trade law.

The tables on pp. 206–208, taken from a report to the US Senate Finance Committee[64] give an idea of the quantitative significance of GATT procedures and their outcome.

It can further be added that one third of 84 complaints filed between 1948 and 1985 were filed after the Tokyo Round.

One of the abovementioned Reports' most significant findings is the conclusion, addressed at some of the GATT mechanisms' most ardent and frustrated critics,[65] that many of the persons interviewed in Geneva and academia expressed the view that the process works fairly well, except when GATT is asked to deal with issues of major domestic political significance to a large partner. Reference is usually made to the EC and its common agricultural policy. It can be deduced that unless a workable consensus can be achieved (with the EC) on rules governing such issues or their application to such sectors, or unless a balance of power can be achieved which forces consistent troublemakers (as they were called) to cooperate, parties bringing disputes on such measures can, regardless of procedural difficulties or improvements, not hope for an effective remedy. While the preceeding appreciation of settlement of disputes mechanisms in international trade is confirmed by the Reports' findings indicating that the system works best where the issues are narrowly focused or technical, it is, if not surprising, nevertheless disquieting that one can also conclude that the system only works well when parties are of comparable economic and political strength.[66]

We can furthermore point to a recent but increasing convergence in the attitudes of European and US private industry and administration towards litigation. The significant increase in anti-dumping proceedings brought in the EC and the introduction of the EC's new commercial policy instrument (even

---

63. The GATT textiles committee prepared the protocol extending the arrangement for a period of five years until 31 July 1991. This protocol is likely to re-affirm the commitment of the participating countries to Art. 6 of the Arrangement, and to grant, in case any import restrictions have to be imposed, differential and more favourable treatment to the least developed countries, small suppliers, and new entries. See further the contribution by Van Dartel, Chapter Four.

64. *Review of the effectiveness of trade disputes settlement under the GATT and the Tokyo Round agreements*, US ITC Publication 1793, Dec. 1985, tables 2 and 4.

65. See for a highly critical text distributed by the US Mission to the EC also USAT TRB doc. of 13 March, 1986.

66. See *Reports to US Senate*, Finance Committee, p. 83.

Table 1—Summary of cases by country or country grouping,[1] type of product, and type of trade measure, 1975 to Sept. 1, 1985

1975 to Sept. 1, 1985

Country	Total	Percent of total[2]	Type of Product			Type of Measures				
			Manu-factured[3]	Agri-cultural[4]	Other[5]	Tariff[6]	Subsidy	Quota[7]	Tax	Other NTM[8]	Other
Total cases	42	100	16	21	5	8	8	12	3	10	1
United States:											
Filed by	16	38	4	10	2	1	3	4	2	6	0
Filed against	8	19	4	3	1	3	0	3	0	2	0
Total	24	57									
European Community countries:[9]											
Filed by	7	17	4	0	3	3	0	0	0	3	1
Filed against	17	40	2	14	1	2	8	3	1	3	0
Total	24	57									
Canada:											
Filed by	6	14	3	3	0	1	0	4	0	1	0
Filed against	5	12	2	1	2	1	0	1	1	2	0
Total	11	26									
Japan:											
Filed by	0	0	0	0	0	0	0	0	0	0	0
Filed against	7	17	5	1	1	0	0	4	1	1	1
Total	7	17									
Australia:											
Filed by	2	5	0	2	0	0	2	0	0	0	0
Filed against	0	0	0	0	0	0	0	0	0	0	0
Total	2	5									
Other developed countries:[10]											
Filed by	2	4	2	0	0	1	0	0	1	0	0
Filed against	5	12	3	2	0	2	0	1	0	2	0
Total	7	17									

Developing countries:[11]										
Filed by	9	21	3	6	0	2	3	4	0	0
Filed against	0	0	0	0	0	0	0	0	0	0
Total	9	21	3	6	0	2	3	4	0	0

1. See app. I for listing of cases included in each country grouping. Country groupings were based on the definitions found in the World Bank's 1984 edition of the *World Development Report*. Gross National Product per capita is the criteria used by the Bank to classify countries by a stage of development.
2. Percentages do not always total due to rounding.
3. The manufactured product category does not include processed agricultural products.
4. The agricultural product category includes raw and processed agricultural and fisheries products.
5. The other category consists mostly of cases involving a general practice, rather than a specific product.
6. The tariff category also encompasses tariff-quotas.
7. Embargoes are included under quotas.
8. The 'Other NTM' (non-tariff measures) category includes, for example, import licensing, standards, and other domestic regulatory actions.
9. The European Community country grouping includes Belgium, Denmark, Federal Republic of Germany, France, Iceland, Italy, Luxembourg, Netherlands and the United Kingdom. Greece is not included here because all cases directly involving Greece took place prior to its accession to the EC in 1982.
10. Finland, New Zealand, South Africa, Spain and Norway.
11. Argentina, Brazil, Chile, Hong Kong, India and Nicaragua.

Table 2—Summary of outcome of dispute settlement cases,
1948 to Sept. 1, 1985[1]

Outcome	Overall, 1948–Sept. 1, 1985 Number	Overall, 1948–Sept. 1, 1985 Percent of total	1948 to 1974 Number	1948 to 1974 Percent of total	1975 to Sept. 1, 1985 Number	1975 to Sept. 1, 1985 Percent of total
Complaint not supported[2]	4	5.0	2	4.8	2	6.1
Implementation action taken:[4]						
Disputed practice terminated	25	33.3	19	45.2	6	18.2
Other action:						
Some practices terminated	6	8.0	3	7.1	3	9.1
Disputed practice adjusted	9	12.0	6	14.3	3	9.1
Other settlement	14	18.7	7	16.7	7	21.2
Subtotal	54	72.0	35	83.3	19	57.6
No implementation action taken:						
Decision not to adopt report[3]	1	1.3	0	—	1	3.0
Report adopted:[3]						
No action taken[4]	5	6.7	0	—	5	15.2
Retaliation authorized[3]	1	1.3	1	2.4	0	—
Subtotal	7	9.3	1	2.4	6	18.2
Complaint not pursued[5]	8	10.7	3	7.1	5	15.2
Outcome unknown	2	2.7	1	2.4	1	3.0
Total cases	75	100.0	42	100.0	33	100.0
Pending cases:[6]						
Report submitted, adoption pending	4	—	0	—	4	—
Report not yet submitted	5	—	0	—	5	—

1. For listing of cases included in each category, see app. I.
2. Contracting Parties determined that the allegations of the complainant were not supported by the evidence submitted.
3. By the Contracting Parties or NTM code signatories.
4. By the offending party following either adoption of a report and recommendations or resolution through bilateral settlement.
5. By the complaining party after having requested a panel.
6. Cases for which stages of the GATT process is still active, including the two subcategories, (1) adoption of the report submitted by the panel has not yet been formally rejected but is still outstanding, and (2) the panel has not yet submitted its report to the Contracting parties or NTM code signatories.

though experience with the instrument is still minimal as no measures have yet been taken on the basis of Reg. 2641/84) indicate an increased willingness to use litigation as a means to adjust trade relations. A similar tendency is shown by the number of trade disputes brought by the EC to GATT even though these actions are still to be qualified as a reaction of 'counterpending'.[67] They do not yet indicate a fundamental change in EC strategies. And it remains also as yet uncertain whether increased recourse to trade law litigation in the EC will mitigate the trend to settle major disputes by bilateral protectionist arrangements such as the US–EC steel arrangements.

V. CONCLUSIONS ON AN AGENDA FOR FURTHER NEGOTIATIONS

Based on the results of the Tokyo Round and recent events, we can distinguish in view of the preceding paragraphs, the following areas where additional agreements are needed in order to avoid or limit the risk and scope of trade conflicts:

(i) areas where no agreements or no substantial agreements were concluded in the Tokyo Round:

- agriculture
- safeguard clauses
- settlement of disputes procedures
- East–West trade.

(ii) areas where the Tokyo Round agreements proved insufficient:

- government procurement
- subsidies
- technical standards
- to which we can add the demands of the developing countries to give more attention to their needs in the management of world trade.

(iii) areas which have been added to the international trade agenda since the Tokyo Round:

- services
- industrial property law protection[68]
- to which we should add the increasing need to improve discipline with regard to multilateral (*e.g.* multifibre agreement) as well as bilateral

---

67. See also Hudec, 'Legal issues in US/EC trade policy: GATT litigation 1961–1965', CEPS/National Bureau of Economic Research Conference paper, 12 June, 1986.

68. Counterfeiting was discussed at the end of the Tokyo Round negotiations but no consensus was reached, and it can be argued that industrial property protection, as discussed at present, is a new issue to GATT.

(*e.g.* bilateral agreements concluded in the framework of the multifibre agreement, the US–EC steel arrangements, the US–Japan car and semi-conductor arrangements) agreements derogating substantially from GATT MFN principles.

A. THE URUGUAY ROUND

The Ministerial Declaration on the Uruguay Round[69] lists, apart from tariffs, the following subjects for negotiation; a general discussion of non-tariff measures and more specifically:

- tropical products
- natural resource products
- textiles and clothing
- agriculture
- safeguards
- dispute settlement
- trade related aspects of intellectual property rights
- trade related investment measures
- services
- as well as a general review of GATT articles and agreements (codes) and arrangements negotiated in the Tokyo Round.

When we compare the Uruguay Round agenda with the issues listed in the previous paragraph, we can see that, with the exception of East–West trade, all issues figure on the agenda, either explicitly, or under the heading 'review of MTN (Tokyo Round) agreements'. The Uruguay Round agenda is furthermore characterised by a greater emphasis on development policy related issues and by a prudent opening towards a discussion of international investment. The first aspect is hardly surprising given the need to reach consensus among a group of Contracting Parties, many of whom are developing countries.

The second aspect opens, together with the planned discussions on services, the way for a significant broadening of the scope of GATT rules. While the GATT dealt exclusively with trade in goods, some contracting parties, and especially the US, would like to develop GATT into the forum to discuss all aspects of international economic relations other than the monetary issues discussed in the IMF. It should be pointed out, however, that while the contracting parties agreed to discuss services in parallel to the multilateral negotiations on trade in goods and according to GATT procedures and practices, it was decided that these discussions would be between Ministers, representing their Governments, and not between GATT Contracting Parties. Only at the end of the round will it be decided whether arrangements with regard to services will be incorporated into the GATT legal framework or not.

69. GATT document Min (86)/W/19, 20 Sept. 1986.

When comparing the agenda with the Report of Eminent Persons[70] we can notice that the agenda provides, as suggested in the Report, for discussions on agriculture, subsidies and various non-tariff barriers (by providing for a review of MTN agreements), some surveillance of trade policy measures (at least with regard to the interesting paragraph on stand still and roll back of protectionist measures – declaring a trade policy 'cease-fire' during the negotiations), safeguards, developing countries, services and dispute settlement. The roll back agreement requires moreover the Contracting Parties to bring a wide range of trade restrictions in conformity with GATT. It is less clear to what extent that paragraph also implies a strengthening of the rules on customs unions and free trade areas, and the Ministerial Declaration is rather less ambitious than the Report with regard to textiles and clothing, the transparency of trade policy making and the world debt problem.

B. KEY ISSUES ON THE URUGUAY ROUND AGENDA

In view of the preparatory talks and developments in international trade relations since the Tokyo Round, we may assume that the Uruguay Round will be dominated, apart from issues concerned with non-tariff barriers to the Japanese market, by problems that are major issues in US–EC trade relations, or in North–South relations.

1. US–EC TRADE RELATIONS

An analysis of US–EC trade conflicts shows that, except for the dispute with regard to the Siberian Gas Pipeline and US export restrictions, major disputes almost invariably involved subsidies, mostly agricultural subsidies, and that one of the main frustrations of the US is concerned with the alleged inability of the GATT mechanisms to deal with such conflicts. We may therefore conclude that the key issue in US–EC trade relations is and remains agricultural subsidies. The other subsidy issues are less disruptive, and the GATT settlement of disputes issue will, if it has not been solved, at least have been contained significantly once an operational consensus has been reached with regard to trade in agricultural products.

It is, given the recurrent mood in the US Congress, probably not exaggerated to say that the stakes in the new round can be rather high. A failure to reach a consensus, on at least some of the issues of major interest to the US and particularly on areas where the US, rightly or wrongly, feel that EC attitudes threaten the effective management of a world trade system ensuring an equitable balance between free trade and fair trade, is likely to strengthen

70. *Trade policies for a better future*, Geneva 1985, 60 pp.

unilateralist and bilateralist tendencies in the US. The US–Japanese car discussions in the early 1980's, the US–Japanese microprocessor arrangement and the US–Japanese understanding on exchange rates and monetary matters of 1986 all indicate an increasing tendency to settle major issues between the US and Japan without any EC involvement, and potentially not only in disregard but against European interests. The EC, as a major exporter, can hardly afford a breakdown of the multilateral framework if that would effectively lead to a marginalisation of the EC in trade policy making. The choice between a continuation of EC strategy aiming at avoiding any substantial discussion of agricultural or other sensitive issues in a multilateral framework, at the risk of an increased isolation and perhaps even a marginalisation of the EC, and a new more constructive and on some issues perhaps also more aggressive negotiating stand, at the risk of major internal difficulties over agricultural reforms, is the major policy choice the EC has to face with regard to the new round.

Fortunately we can also add that while it has never been more difficult to avoid substantial negotiations on agricultural policies, it has at the same time become easier to discuss agricultural subsidies in view of the US Farm bill. The US agricultural lobby is likely to make it extremely difficult for the US administration to withdraw or reduce the present level of support. GATT negotiations can therefore hardly aim at an abolishment of agricultural subsidies and can concentrate on the determination of acceptable levels of support.

2. NORTH–SOUTH TRADE

With regard to North–South trade, we can expect that negotiations will concentrate on two issues: access for industrial and agricultural products originating in developing countries on the markets of industrialised countries, and reciprocity in trade relations between industrialised countries and NIC's.

Developing countries are likely to insist on easier access to the EC market for industrialised products in general, and for textiles and (processed or unprocessed) agricultural products in particular. The first apsect is concerned with tariff differentiation between raw materials/semi-finished/and finished products,[71] as well as with quantitative restrictions and other non-tariff

71. The weighted average tariffs for industrial products were, before and after the Tokyo Round, estimated by the GATT secretariat at (in %):

	before	after	reduction
primary products	1.1	0.5	60
semi-finished products	4.6	3.3	27
finished products	13.6	10.3	24
agricultural products	7.9	6.9	12

(Source: GATT, *Les négociations commerciales multilatérales du Tokyo Round*, Geneva 1979, p. 149.)

measures. On the tariff issue, the EC will have to look for balanced concessions, giving equitable access to industrial products originating from developing countries (which implies a treatment of finished or semi-finished products not significantly less favourable than primary products), while improving a tariff structure which makes it attractive to maintain at least part of the manufacturing processes in the EC (which implies a treatment of finished products less favourable than the treatment of semi-finished products). Textiles are dealt with in another contribution to this publication.

This leaves again agriculture as one of the major areas of conflict. It follows that the EC is increasingly isolated with regard to agricultural export subsidies and import levies, as it comes under pressure, not only from the US, Australia and New Zealand (traditional exporters), but also from a growing list of developing countries. The latter development makes it increasingly difficult for the EC to maintain credibility as a go-between between the US and the third world. It remains as yet difficult to predict the medium term consequences of such isolation with regard to the over-all outcome of the negotiations, but a number of recent reactions tend to indicate that it becomes gradually more difficult for the EC to maintain a constructive profile in respect of the GATT multilateral framework by compensating a rather defensive if not negative attitude with regard to some US claims with a more welcoming attitude towards the developing countries.

It should be added that it is likely to be more difficult for all industrialised countries, and not only for the EC, to win the support of the developing countries in the Uruguay Round. In the Tokyo Round, as in previous rounds, discussions with the developing countries largely concentrated on exemptions from general GATT principles or code provisions. But not much more can be gained by such exemptions. It can even be argued that some exemptions, such as those allowed for under the standards code, are even detrimental to LDC interests. The emphasis is therefore likely to switch further from exemptions with regard to rules applicable to domestic production and the protection of infant industries on LDC markets to improved access to the markets of industrialised countries.

Industrialised countries are on the other hand likely to claim more reciprocity in the access to NIC markets.[72] This raises inevitably the issue of graduation: until what stage of development can developing countries be allowed to protect infant industries while receiving, if not preferential, at least most favoured nation treatment on the markets of industrialised countries. Again, market protection is organised not only by quantitative and other non-tariff barriers, but also by tariff measures, often made possible by a comparatively low percentage of bindings, or tariff bindings at a level which is substantially higher than the CCT. The EC will therefore have to press for a further reduction of the disparity between high tariffs and low tariffs, and in increase of the number of binding concessions. Furthermore, a specific claim

72. See on this issue further: Pelkmans, 'The EC and the NICs', *Journal of European Integration*, 1981, 137 *et seq.*

on developing countries, which has become increasingly significant since the Tokyo Round, is concerned with the standard of industrial property protection and trade in counterfeited goods.

3. FACTUAL BACKGROUND

It may be useful to recall that both US–EC and North–South trade issues will be discussed against a factual background that has evolved considerably since the Tokyo Round. One of the more significant developments is that in 1984 the value of North American exports to the Pacific area reached the same order of magnitude as exports to Western Europe (imports had already surpassed imports from Europe in the seventies).[73]

When looking at the triangle North America–Japan–EC, we can see that North American exports to Europe are still more significant than to Japan, but North American–Japanese trade grows, in both directions, faster than North American–EC or EC–Japanese trade, and EC–Japanese trade represents to Japan only a fraction of North American–Japanese trade. While during the Tokyo Round (1973–1979) the expansion of the EC exports to the industrial areas, the developing areas and the Eastern trading area tended to grow faster in volume than both Japanese and North American exports, European exports showed hardly any growth between 1979 and 1984 (the world total went up from 262,050 to 277,515 million US dollar excluding intra-EC exports) at a time Japanese exports increased by 65% to 170,040 million US dollars and North American exports by 29% to 295,170 million US dollars. Another significant development is that North America succeeded to the EC as the world's largest exporter and, since 1983, also as the developing countries' largest export market.[74]

The relationship between trade and monetary policy is not a new phenomenon, as indeed the opening of the Tokyo Round almost coincided with the collapse of the Bretton Wood regime. The preliminary discussions on the Uruguay Round were held at a period of renewed awareness of the impact of monetary matters on trade flows, which has led to the New York Plaza meeting of September 1985 and the Tokyo economic summit communiqué of 1986. We should add, however, that while we saw since the New York Plaza meeting a significant depreciation of the dollar *vis-à-vis* the Ecu, and even more so *vis-à-vis* the yen, such developments failed, even 14 months later, to have a substantial impact on trade flows. We can therefore not rule out that the latent belief that trade policy measures should give way to monetary policy measures will erode, thus renewing the pressure for more protectionist trade policy measures.

And apart from monetary policy issues, the trade policy making

73. GATT press release 1374, 19 Sept. 1985, 15.
74. GATT, *International trade 1984/85*, Geneva 1985, table A40 (in million US dollars). (See Annex I.)

environment is at the opening of the Uruguay Round, perhaps even more than at the time of the Tokyo Round, influenced by balance of payment and debt-service problems in a significant number of developing countries, forcing a number of trade partners to use counter- or barter-trade techniques. The expansion of counter- and barter-trade is likely to increase the pressure on reasonably solvent trade partners to respect general GATT principles with regard to the limited number of trade flows for which open trade remains financially viable.

C. SOME SELECTED ISSUES

1. AGRICULTURE

For the reasons explained above, agriculture will at least from the EC point of view, be the most delicate issue. It is the key to a long term reduction of conflicts in US/EC trade as well as in trade of the EC with Australia, New Zealand and an increasing list of developing countries. This contribution cannot aim at formulating detailed suggestions. It merely tries to illustrate the complexity of the issues in case the Contracting Parties would decide to limit the impact of measures such as import levies, export restitutions and domestic price guarantees (for sake of convenience these measures will perhaps inappropriately be referred to as subsidies), *e.g.* along the lines suggested by the Report of Eminent persons.

It is not too difficult to formulate proposals with regard to an international compromise on export subsidies, when starting from the assumption that the contracting parties will be looking for an agreement reducing export subsidies rather than abolishing such subsidies. An equitable formula should take into account the domestic subsidies of both the exporting and the importing country. One idea could be to determine, by analogy to the OECD export subsidy code, a level of acceptable subsidies. The exporting country should however only be entitled to grant such subsidies provided it grants no substantial domestic subsidies to its agricultural producers. And it should on the other hand be entitled to add to its export subsidies a support equivalent to the subsidies granted in the importing country to the domestic producers of competing products. The formula could in other words be: domestic price in the exporting country − domestic subsidies in the exporting country + acceptable degree of export subsidies + compensation for domestic subsidies and unjustified import levies in the importing country. Such formula has the advantage of limiting the scope of international negotiations to the admittedly difficult issue of determining a ceiling for export subsidies. The appreciation of domestic subsidies would be left to *ad hoc* appreciations and litigation.[75]

---

75. It can be added that exporting subsidies, as well as domestic subsidies, of competitors on third markets cannot be countervailed under the proposed formula. Such measures would only be

It is more difficult to regulate the protectionist impact of domestic subsidies and import levies. The preceding formula only provides for a subsidy by the exporting country, thus putting a high burden on parties not responsible for any infringement of GATT principles in order to compensate for the questionable practices of others.[76] Moreover, domestic subsidies encourage as much as export subsidies investments in surplus capacity, and are therefore co-responsible for keeping world prices below the cost of production,[77] much to the detriment of the developing countries. One type of compromise might be a rule limiting the production volumes for which domestic price support can be offered at a price level above world prices to volumes roughly equivalent to the domestic consumption.

Such a rule can only contribute to an opening of markets protected by import levies bridging the gap between world prices and guaranteed domestic prices, if accompanied by an effective prohibition or reduction of import levies. But even if no compromise can be reached in respect of import levies, the suggested rule would, combined with the possibility to levy countervailing duties on subsidised imports and to grant compensatory export subsidies, contribute to a reduction of the disruptive effects of subsidised production on world markets.

Equally difficult is an adjustment of the common agricultural policy to any of the suggestions formulated in the preceding paragraphs, even if negotiations only result in rules on export subsidies. As long as the Community's intervention prices are substantially higher than world market prices, such rule implies a differentiation between prices guaranteed on the domestic market (price + export subsidy) and obtained in export transactions. In order to avoid an even more dramatic build-up of intervention stocks, such differentiation will in turn necessitate the determination of production levels that can be bought at the intervention prices applicable on the domestic market, thus requiring the establishment of a system distributing production quota for which price guarantees would be maintained. Agricultural production would then automatically be brought down to such volumes as can be exported profitably at world market prices plus the internationally acceptable export subsidies.

2. SUBSIDIES

A second issue, which is perhaps even more closely linked to national sociopolitical concepts, policies and traditions, is the regulation of non-agricultural subsidies. While the new code organised a framework that should

countervailable by measures such as those provided for under the EC new commercial policy instrument.
76. See *e.g.* Sarris, *EC–US agricultural trade confrontation* paper to CEPS–National Bureau of Economic Research Conference, Brussels, 12 June 1986.
77. See *e.g.* Hayes and Schmitz, *US–EC trade relations: can a price war in agricultural commodities be avoided.* Paper to the CEPS–NBER seminar referred to in previous note.

enable the parties to develop new and more operational Agreements, it is equally clear that the new rules of substantive law are insufficient to settle the disputes between major trade partners. Especially in Euro-American relations, it has become increasingly clear that the threat of anti-dumping, countervailing duties or safeguard measures will remain, unless the parties reach a more operational Agreement. Such an Agreement should aim at listing acceptable and actionable subsidies, and require a specific Agreement on the 'actionability' of subsidies by private parties in the domestic courts of the Contracting Parties. This would help to reduce the grey area of contested subsidies, that should only be discussed between governments, preferably on international fora such as those set up under the present GATT Code. In the efforts to list the more and the less objectionable subsidies, tentative conclusions can perhaps be drawn from the following classification of subsidies:[78]

(a) Subsidies to Competitive Industries

They can certainly be injurious, but they are frequently very difficult to define, and therefore politically difficult to regulate effectively, except in the case of general measures which affect specific transactions such as export subsidies, or measures to promote the development of specific regions, or that are easily identifiable as benefits that can – as subsidies – be deducted from the taxable profits under the legislation of the granting State. It is also dubious whether they represent a relevant volume, once we deduct the export subsidies, regional policy measures, or transfers of resources which can be dealt with under the government procurement code, etc. It may therefore be indicated that one should concentrate on these subsidies which can be defined with reasonable accuracy, rather than to risk a delicate analysis of general domestic economic policies.

(b) Aid to Infant Industries or Specific Regions

These subsidies are usually considered to be less objectionable, as equal treatment means that equals should be treated in the same way, and those who are unequal in a way proportional to their inequality. There are also indications that aid to infant industries has to be limited in time in order to obtain a gradual transition to maturity. They tend to become self-defeating if continued for too long. But as far as they help an economy to take off, they are probably more beneficial to global trade than harmful to the individual manufacturers who

---

78. See further Steenbergen, De Clercq and Foqué, *op. cit.*, n. 13, para. 298 *et seq.*

might occasionally feel injured, it may therefore remain more reasonable to provide exemptions for these forms of subsidies than to concentrate on fighting them, but this issue cannot be separated from the issue of graduation of developing countries.

(c) Aid to Ailing Industries

These subsidies attract usually the most attention. But if it is true that aid to ailing industries leads to general impoverishment, not only of the world economy, but especially of the subsidising State, they should be self-defeating, if we ensure that these industries and the subsidising countries face open world competition. It seems therefore more important to avoid further trade barriers by the granting States, than to fight the subsidies. It is from that perspective at least as harmful to the world trade system to maintain trigger-price mechanisms unless they are of a clearly transitionary nature and to agree with orderly marketing agreements and voluntary export controls, as to accept a subsidising policy. Because subsidies are so difficult and delicate to regulate in any circumstances, the acceptance of other trade barriers neutralises what might well be the only effective check on subsidising policies. The acceptance of substantial barriers to trade also annuls the prime objective which justifies the regulation of subsidies.

3. TECHNICAL STANDARDS

A further major challenge remains the regulation of technical standards. Both Community and international practice clearly show that even subtle differences in technical standards can turn into formidable barriers to trade while remaining easily justifiable under the existent international rules. An adequate reduction of technical trade barriers therefore requires the recognition of type approvals granted by trade partners, which in turn either requires a harmonisation of technical standards or the recognition of technical standards and certification procedures as introduced by trade partners. Harmonisation is likely to be a very lengthy process, and EC experience is not encouraging.

To limit the consequences of inadequate harmonisation, the Court of Justice of the EC rendered decisions introducing principles that became known as the *Cassis de Dijon* doctrine.[79] This doctrine was not intended to be applicable to trade with third countries. But the *Cassis de Dijon* approach can be chosen by trade partners in specific agreements on technical standards on homologation

---

79. See n. 11.

procedures. This approach seems, among countries with a similar socio-economic context, by far preferable to a compulsory preliminary harmonisation of technical standards.

It might therefore be useful to suggest a framework for the conclusion of bilateral agreements or limited multilateral codes by which parties recognize each other's standards and certification procedures. The EC has considerable experience in this field and could make a valuable contribution.

4. GOVERNMENT PROCUREMENT

Government procurement is concerned with an ever increasing percentage of purchasing power and world trade. Together with technical standards, rules on government procurement constitute some of the most significant trade barriers; although the present code is not a success, it is difficult to see how substantial progress can be made. In order to avoid in the future frustrating litigation as we see now under the subsidies rules, it might be useful to provide for realistic exemptions from the present code, *e.g.* with regard to research and development oriented purchases, while organising a brainstorming in order to improve the implementation of the present code. It should be added that it will prove difficult to enlarge the scope of application of the present code significantly without upsetting the reciprocity of concessions. While it can be argued that the present code favours small parties whose purchases will more easily pass under the threshold, some of the sectors the US would like to bring under the scope in the field of transport, telecommunications and energy production are concerned with services and utilities which are often organised by public authorities or companies in Europe, while being privately organised in the US.

5. SERVICES

Just as it would be irealistic to ignore non-tariff trade barriers in the regulation of the international trade in goods, one can no longer ignore the significance of the service sector. It has *e.g.* been estimated that services represented more than 43% of the final consumption of Belgian households in 1984, and that services represented in 1984 59.7% of the Belgian gross national product.[80] But it should also be recognised that services are an extremely heterogenious concept. In international trade, we have to make a distinction between the opening of foreign branches or subsidiaries (establishment) and the freedom to provide services to customers abroad. And a summary analysis of *e.g.* banking

---

80. NIS (Belgium), *Statistische studien*, 76, 1985, Nationale Rekeningen 1975–1984.

or insurance law will show that the nature of applicable regulations can vary to an extent which makes it virtually impossible to provide for any detailed regulation that would be equally applicable to the various service sectors.

It may therefore be more realistic to aim at an agreement listing the GATT provisions that can be applied to services and creating a framework in which sector agreements can be negotiated. The basic or horizontal agreement could *e.g.* refer to the GATT settlement of disputes mechanisms and other 'institutional' provisions and it can further be discussed whether the most favoured nations and national treatment principles could apply to services. One might further study the possibility to provide for specific anti-dumping or subsidy rules (as is already proposed by the EC Commission with regard to shipping).

D. CONCLUSIONS

The appreciation of the agenda for the Uruguay Round and the suggestions with regard to a negotiating strategy for the European Communities given in the preceding paragraphs, are formulated on the assumption that an open market policy remains in the Community's fundamental interest.

It is interesting to note in this respect that recent studies continue to confirm that a balanced growth of Community industry is more likely to be fostered by open market policies than by a protection of the Community market.[81] May it suffice to summarize the following two arguments in favour of this thesis:

(i) The development of a healthy industrial base and a competitive service industry in Europe is clearly stimulated by outside competition. Stimuli from outside should therefore never be ignored, even though there may occasionally be good reasons to take protectionist measures of limited scope in order to facilitate the adjustment of specific sectors (provided such trade policy measures are accompanied by effective industrial policy measures and only if it is guaranteed that protection will be lifted after a comparatively short period of time), and even though there are persuasive arguments in favour of some formal support (subsidies or government procurement) of research and development in Community industry.

(ii) The Community is a major exporter. It should remain so if it wants to maintain employment at a reasonable level and if it wishes to avoid excessive deficits on its trade balance. It becomes increasingly clear that the Community cannot hope to continue to enjoy relatively easy access to third markets unless it is willing to remain a major importer.

81. See *e.g.* Pelkmans, *Vrijhandel en protectionisme* (The Hague, 1985) 140 p. en Pearce, Sutton and Batchelor, *Protection and industrial policy in Europe* (London, 1985), 220 pp.

It is equally significant that the before-mentioned studies indicate that the further establishment of the internal market of the European Community do not offer a real alternative to an open trade policy. It can be argued convincingly that, while for certain products or activities it might be possible to concentrate on the Community market (which implies the abolishment of internal barriers and allows for increased external protection), most of the industrial sectors asking for protection are as likely to be hurt by intra-community trade as they are by external trade, and one can add that the exporting industries are likely to continue to need the world market as well as they need improved access to the Community's internal market. Without offering a remedy to Europe's more ailing industries, the substitution of national protectionism by Community protectionism would therefore put its more competitive industries at risk.

Moreover the preceding paragraphs indicate that the Community might become increasingly dependent on an effective framework for multilateral trade regulation in view of its continued dependance on export markets and the risk of an erosion of its bilateral negotiating power caused by a reduction of its relative share of world trade. The latter phenomenon is partly the inevitable of the emergence of new trade partners and as such the result of a positive development. But the figures also indicate a loss of market share to other industrialised countries. It would nevertheless be incorrect to lament Europe's decline, provided Europe faces the challenge not only by improving the competitiveness of its social economic structures, but also by adjusting its trade policy strategies to a changing environment.

ANNEX

ANNEX: GATT INTERNATIONAL TRADE 1984/5, TABLE A40

Destination		Industrial Areas						Developing Areas						
Origin		North America	Japan	Western Europe Total	EC	EFTA	Total	Australia, New Zealand, S. Africa	Central and South America	South and East Asia	West Asia	Africa	Total[a]	Eastern Trading Area	Unspec.	World
North Africa	1963	7,830	2,175	9,680	7,780	960	19,685	1,010	3,800	3,060	605	790	8,435	440	10	29,580
	1973	31,960	10,005	24,810	19,945	2,615	66,775	2,750	10,640	7,090	2,980	1,705	22,480	3,415	40	95,460
	1979	68,780	20,810	57,090	46,440	6,590	146,680	6,220	30,090	19,480	11,490	5,440	66,680	9,140	50	228,770
	1981	82,475	25,280	70,735	57,235	8,380	178,490	10,105	44,390	24,790	15,690	9,045	94,405	10,750	300	294,050
	1982	77,315	24,355	65,420	52,645	7,420	167,090	8,740	34,820	26,580	16,725	8,705	87,345	9,645	200	273,020
	1983	88,735	25,115	60,605	48,330	7,680	174,455	7,325	27,110	27,695	14,610	7,200	77,095	8,010	155	267,040
	1984	107,910	27,140	61,870	50,315	7,040	196,920	8,640	30,795	28,600	11,915	7,460	79,280	10,080	230	295,150
Japan	1963	1,645	—	725	520	115	2,370	280	315	1,475	180	260	2,255	250	165	5,320
	1973	10,550	—	6,605	4,630	1,320	17,155	2,060	2,180	8,930	1,535	905	13,690	1,960	2,065	36,930
	1979	28,340	—	16,630	13,445	2,450	44,970	4,195	5,830	26,100	9,640	3,140	45,030	7,385	1,380	102,960
	1981	42,305	—	23,940	18,885	3,960	66,245	7,920	8,510	34,370	15,675	5,950	64,945	9,515	3,275	151,900
	1982	39,475	—	21,670	16,955	3,585	61,145	7,175	6,245	31,815	15,840	4,105	58,395	8,400	3,465	138,580
	1983	46,925	—	23,250	18,480	3,705	70,175	6,990	4,005	34,485	15,800	3,505	58,285	8,930	2,420	146,800
	1984	64,875	—	24,115	19,405	3,700	88,990	8,200	4,815	36,720	12,685	3,560	58,430	10,600	2,820	170,040
Western Europe	1963	5,750	620	40,860	30,155	8,900	47,230	2,460	2,915	2,595	2,010	3,515	11,210	2,805	435	64,140
	1973	22,225	3,665	179,095	135,635	33,475	204,985	5,590	8,500	6,020	7,130	10,660	32,570	12,785	2,950	258,880
	1979	47,340	8,390	481,810	378,250	81,550	537,540	11,100	21,880	19,550	34,860	38,400	115,150	34,440	4,480	702,710
	1981	55,095	8,105	479,805	375,645	82,315	543,005	14,930	25,005	23,020	48,190	51,970	149,085	36,470	6,160	749,650
	1982	54,450	7,935	468,985	369,105	78,555	531,370	13,630	19,945	23,480	51,780	43,215	139,215	33,345	6,040	723,600
	1983	59,420	8,490	464,800	366,810	76,790	532,710	11,885	15,920	23,035	48,060	37,885	125,695	33,750	5,520	709,560
	1984	74,530	9,350	474,845	374,985	78,280	558,725	13,320	16,325	23,825	42,445	35,385	118,955	32,640	5,270	728,910
European Communities	1963	4,785	515	33,010	24,080	7,390	38,305	2,240	2,450	2,300	1,710	3,250	9,870	1,810	330	52,560
	1973	18,180	2,860	147,200	113,100	25,750	168,240	4,910	6,800	5,090	5,860	9,300	27,300	9,040	2,340	211,830
	1979	39,270	6,380	398,720	315,210	64,760	444,370	9,640	17,095	16,325	28,730	33,290	95,880	23,720	3,650	577,260
	1981	45,065	6,210	390,920	308,225	64,185	443,195	13,000	19,465	19,185	39,045	44,120	122,625	21,615	5,165	605,600
	1982	45,850	6,135	382,615	302,950	61,415	434,640	11,985	15,390	19,765	41,195	35,795	112,865	19,060	4,720	583,230
	1983	49,340	6,455	377,325	298,920	60,250	433,120	10,285	12,360	19,235	38,135	31,290	101,950	20,630	4,315	570,300
	1984	60,835	6,960	380,705	301,515	60,820	448,500	11,355	13,090	19,560	33,235	29,050	95,800	19,570	3,905	579,130
European Free Trade Association	1963	770	95	6,735	5,125	1,335	7,600	215	380	250	215	250	1,105	720	50	9,690
	1973	2,885	700	26,585	18,190	6,910	30,170	620	1,235	820	790	955	3,810	2,450	430	37,480
	1979	6,140	1,600	68,930	50,980	15,100	76,670	1,290	2,755	2,815	4,230	2,815	12,630	6,980	620	98,190
	1981	6,795	1,510	73,520	54,660	15,985	81,825	1,685	3,355	3,125	5,230	4,135	15,915	8,220	455	108,100
	1982	6,565	485	70,635	52,925	14,995	78,685	1,450	2,520	3,035	5,615	3,650	14,890	7,910	675	103,615
	1983	7,890	1,670	71,210	54,090	14,505	80,770	1,400	2,080	3,085	5,315	3,095	13,635	7,605	540	103,950
	1984	10,295	1,950	74,410	56,940	14,870	86,655	1,700	1,900	3,535	4,590	2,925	13,035	7,060	600	109,050

TRADE REGULATION SINCE THE TOKYO ROUND

ANNEX: GATT INTERNATIONAL TRADE, 1984/5, TABLE A40

Total Developing Areas[a]	1963	6,620	2,070	13,400	11,825	935	22,140	830	1,995	2,930	715	960	6,685	1,670	525	31,850
	1973	23,510	14,790	41,175	35,265	2,850	79,475	1,965	7,435	9,925	2,515	2,520	22,540	5,290	1,130	110,400
	1979	100,405	54,665	136,885	114,905	9,375	291,955	5,430	30,610	40,435	15,180	9,855	96,615	15,100	5,000	494,100
	1981	122,120	76,010	161,705	130,390	12,380	359,835	8,515	44,115	63,205	23,550	16,115	147,875	21,685	7,490	545,400
	1982	99,560	69,120	137,345	111,100	9,835	306,025	8,005	39,580	61,505	22,820	13,520	139,375	21,690	5,605	479,700
	1983	104,070	63,490	118,110	93,985	8,240	285,670	6,335	34,210	58,690	22,175	11,795	127,750	22,815	4,820	447,400
	1984	119,590	67,260	118,010	93,240	8,380	304,660	7,460	35,600	61,200	21,940	11,850	131,480	24,930	5,470	474,000
Eastern Trading Area	1963	120	235	3,150	2,010	790	3,505	35	745	1,025	230	465	2,465	12,375	340	18,720
	1973	180	1,980	12,610	8,400	2,630	15,370	145	1,410	2,290	1,295	1,550	6,545	32,390	2,750	57,200
	1979	2,170	4,720	38,975	24,570	8,200	46,365	300	4,890	6,910	5,725	4,230	21,780	78,800	4,755	152,000
	1981	5,105	6,375	46,615	30,275	9,545	56,395	400	6,085	11,035	9,230	5,305	21,655	89,530	6,020	184,000
	1982	3,080	6,330	47,960	31,435	9,790	57,370	375	7,055	10,785	10,095	5,765	33,830	94,370	7,055	193,000
	1983	3,450	6,150	48,380	31,280	9,700	57,980	285	7,190	11,425	9,225	5,675	33,530	102,930	7,475	202,200
	1984	4,530	6,900	50,170	33,000	9,300	61,600	340	7,480	13,190	9,030	5,670	35,390	106,420	6,950	210,700
World Total	1963	22,700	5,730	70,130	54,500	11,760	98,560	4,900	9,820	11,360	3,790	6,190	31,720	17,860	1,660	154,700
	1973	91,200	34,240	269,285	208,450	43,135	394,725	13,450	30,445	35,545	15,690	17,950	100,600	56,450	9,075	574,300
	1979	252,155	94,925	741,350	585,265	110,300	1,088,430	28,780	93,795	116,435	77,890	62,385	352,830	146,750	17,910	1,634,700
	1981	309,860	123,330	792,060	620,010	117,930	1,225,250	43,870	128,710	161,340	114,040	90,140	497,980	169,900	26,000	1,963,000
	1982	277,790	115,160	750,200	588,580	110,365	1,143,150	39,745	108,200	158,715	118,760	76,600	466,040	169,500	25,265	1,843,700
	1983	306,420	110,515	723,455	565,910	107,130	1,140,390	34,495	88,955	159,870	111,260	67,470	431,105	177,895	23,115	1,807,000
	1984	375,520	118,250	737,480	578,160	107,630	1,231,250	40,120	95,500	168,410	99,720	65,320	432,840	186,630	24,560	1,915,400

[a] Including developing countries and territories which do not belong to the four geographic areas shown.

Note: For sources and methods, see Appendix.

TABLES

I. CASES

Case 22/70, AETR	65
Case 62/70, Bock	182
Case 7/71, Commission v. France	165
Case 22/71, Béguelin	79
Case 92/71, Interfood	108
Joined Cases 21–24/72, Int'l Fruit Company (third)	63
Case 40/72, Schroeder	168
Case 5/73, Balkan Import/Export	42
Joined Cases 37, 38/73, Indiamex	24
Joined Cases 40–48, 50, 54, 56, 111, 113–114/73, Suiker Unie	81
Case 31/74, Galli	182
Case 71/74, Frubo	79
Case 23/75, Rey Soda	161, 165
Case 29/75, Kaufhof	182
Case 38/75, Douaneagent	63
Case 51/75, EMI	37, 52, 75, 79
Case 55/75, Balkan Import/Export	108
Case 87/75, Bresciani	49
Joined Cases 3, 4 and 6/76, Kramer	182
Case 41/76, Donckerwolcke	8, 9, 35, 52, 65, 73, 74, 75, 84, 85, 150, 154, 160, 161, 163, 170, 173, 179, 180, 181
Case 77/76, Cucchi v. Avez	182
Case 13/77, Inno/Atab	82
Case 52/77, Cayrol	179
Case 70/77, Simenthal	24
Case 113/77, NTN	110
Case 34/78, Yoshida Nederland	87
Case 114/78, Yoshida GmbH	87
Case 120/78, Cassis de Dijon	188, 189, 218
Joined Cases 209–215, 218/78, Fedetab	81
Case 225/78, Bouhelier (second)	37, 75
Case 804/79, British Fisheries	162, 165, 176
Case 812/79, A.G. v. Burgoa	12
Case 112/80, Dürbeck	70, 108
Case 270/80, Polydor	75, 189
Case 17/81, Pabst & Richarz	49
Case 52/81, Faust	108
Case 104/81, Kupferberg	49
Joined Cases 240–242, 261–262, 268–269/82, SSI	81
Case 245/81, Edeka	108
Case 246/81, Lord Bethel	15

226   TABLES

Case 266/81, SIOT 64, 108
Joined Cases 267–269/81, SPI/SAMI 63, 108
Case 218/82, Commission v. Council 84
Case 264/82, Timex 160
Case 1/84R, Ilford 85, 152
Case 59/84, Tezi v. Commission 10, 84, 150, *153–154*,
                                                                   155, 159, 166, 167,
                                                                   172–177, 182, 183
Case 169/84, Cofaz 160
Case 174/84, Bulk Oil 9, 51, 52, 65, 161, 183
Case 242/84, Tezi v. Min. EZ 84, 150, *153–154*,
                                                                   155, 159, 166, 167,
                                                                   172–177, 182, 183
Case 56/85, Brother 198
Case 45/86, Commission v. Council 5
Case 70/87, Fediol 106

II. OPINIONS

Opinion 1/75, Understanding on Local Cost Standard 7
Opinion 1/76 4
Opinion 1/78, Int'l Rubber Agreement 4, 5, 8

III. EEC TREATY

ARTICLES

Art. 3(b) 3	Art. 115 .... 10, 31, 36, 53, 54,
Art. 9 .... 24, 25, 174	70, *83–85*, 86, 87,
Art. 10 174	89, 140, *149–154*,
Art. 27 .... 6, 29	155, 160, 166,
Art. 28 .... 6, 23, 26	168, *169–181*, 182,
Art. 30 .... 37, 76, 179, 181	192, 200–201
Art. 36 193	Art. 131 128
Arts. 30–36 .... 75, 76, 83	Art. 133 .... 5, 7
Art. 43 .... 5, 6	Art. 149 88
Art. 75 .... 4, 5	Art. 155 31
Art. 85 .... 79, 80, 81, 82, 89	Art. 169 .... 75, 76, 89, 106
Art. 90 82	Art. 173 .... 15, 110, 160, 182
Arts. 92–94 195	Art. 175 15
Art. 111 .... 23, 31	Art. 177 .... 15, 49, 106, 182
Art. 112 6	Art. 189 .... 17, 110
Art. 113 .... 3, 4, 5, 6, 10, 13, 14,	Art. 215 .... 106, 110, 182
23, 29, 31, 35, 37, 48, 51	Art. 224 6
54, 64, *65–67*, 69,	Art. 226 175
74, 75, 76, 84, 88,	Art. 227 .... 31, 128
89, 90, 153, 154,	Art. 228 .... 4, 90, 106
160–169, 178, 188	Art. 232 24
Art. 114 .... 7, 69, 70	Art. 235 .... 10, 29, 31

REGULATIONS

Reg. No. 17/62	80
Reg. No. 802/68	31, 33, 86
Reg. No. 803/68	29
Reg. No. 950/68	23, 24, 26
Reg. No. 2041/68	51
Reg. No. 2603/69	50, 51, 52, 161
Reg. No. 109/70	165, 173
Reg. No. 1023/70	53, 167
Reg. No. 1842/71	36, 140
Reg. No. 2837/72	36
Reg. No. 1439/74	52, 165, 173
Reg. No. 1989/76	68
Reg. No. 2067/77	87
Reg. No. 2127/77	68
Reg. No. 3019/77	165, 173
Reg. No. 256/78	165, 173
Reg. No. 3059/78	165, 171
Reg. No. 926/79	142
Reg. No. 2819/79	142
Reg. No. 3017/79	195
Reg. No. 387/80	145
Reg. No. 388/80	145
Reg. No. 1224/80	29, 200
Reg. No. 1661/80	36
Reg. No. 348/81	10
Reg. No. 1533/81	17
Reg. No. 288/82	9, 10, 16, 32, 34, 36, 37, 39, 41, 42, 43, 44, 53, 68, 70, 73, 74, 75, 77, 78, 84, 88, 95, 142, 145, 159, 162–166, 168, 173, 178, 187, 200
Reg. No. 636/82	147
Reg. No. 1765/82	9, 10, 16, 36, 43, 44, 143, 145
Reg. No. 1766/82	34, 36, 159, 162, 165, 166, 168, 200
Reg. No. 1934/82	52
Reg. No. 2417/82	148
Reg. No. 2870/82	51
Reg. No. 3528/82	35, 41
Reg. No. 3587/82	144
Reg. No. 3589/82	139, 144, 153, 154, 160, 164, 165, 166, 167, 168, 172, 173, 175, 176
Reg. No. 873/83	39, 42
Reg. No. 2050/83	42
Reg. No. 3420/83	9, 36, 37, 143, 144, 163, 164, 170, 178, 200
Reg. No. 3506/83	104
Reg. No. 1087/84	35, 41, 95
Reg. No. 2072/84	190
Reg. No. 2176/84	16, 38, 39, 41, 47, 70, 107, 195
Reg. No. 2641/84	14, 16, 38, 39, *44–50*, 111, 201, 209
Reg. No. 3639/84	141
Reg. No. 1698/85	198
Reg. No. 3558/85	142
Reg. No. 3559/85	142
Reg. No. 3679/85	72, 103
Reg. No. 3787/85	144
Reg. No. 130/86	72
Reg. No. 1069/86	103
Reg. No. 1243/86	9, 35, 43, 74, 75, 88, 164
Reg. No. 1388/86	11
Reg. No. 1707/86	11
Reg. No. 1769/86	142
Reg. No. 1770/86	141
Reg. No. 3618/86	24
Reg. No. 3842/86	13
Reg. No. 3924/86	26
Reg. No. 3925/86	26
Reg. No. 3926/86	26

DECISIONS

Dec. of 9 Oct. 1961	68
Dec. of 25 Sept. 1962	67, 68
Dec. 69/494	67
Dec. of 16 Dec. 1969	11
Dec. of 12 May 1971	179
Dec. 73/55	179
Dec. 74/214	123
Dec. of 22 July 1974	12
Dec. 80/45	79
Dec. 80/47	70, 84, 150–151, 171, 172, *179–181*, 182, 200

Dec. 80/605 .... 151, 201
Dec. 80/1278 17
Dec. of 15 Jan. 1980 189–190
Dec. of 27 June 1980 180
Dec. 81/149 17
Dec. 82/205 151
Dec. 82/372 178
Dec. 82/577 177
Dec. 82/2871/ECSC 204
Dec. 82/2872/ECSC 204
Dec. 82/2873/ECSC 204

Dec. of 12 July 1982 11
Dec. 83/125 163
Dec. 83/215 163
Dec. 83/3081 204
Dec. 2177/84/ECSC 195
Dec. 85/304 151
Dec. 86/19 67
Dec. 86/456 67
Dec. 86/638/ECSC 26
Dec. 87/60 144

DIRECTIVES

Dir. 76/119 146
Dir. 77/62 192

Dir. 80/767 192
Dir. of 28 March 1983 191

IV. INTERNATIONAL AGREEMENTS

Association Agreement EEC–Cyprus (1972) 27
Association Agreement EEC–Malta (1970) 27
Association Agreement EEC–Turkey (1963) 27, 140
Benelux–Japan (1960/1963) 62, 68
Brussels Convention on Customs Nomenclature (1950) 24
Customs Cooperation Council Valuation Convention (1950) 29
EEC–Argentina (1971) 4
EEC–Brazil (1973) 4
EEC–China (1978/1985) 4, 25
EEC–Mexico (1975) 4
EEC–Morocco (1978) 27
EEC–Romania (1980) 25
EEC–Uruguay (1973) 4
EEC–Yugoslavia (1983) 25
France–Japan (1963) 62, 67, 68
Germany–Japan (1960) 67
Italy–Japan (1969) 67
Lomé III (1984) 27, *142–143*, 160
Long Term Arrangement for Cotton Products (1961) 122
Multifibre Arrangement (I, II and III) 22, 61, 68, 84, 121, *122–134*, 160, 209
Short Term Arrangement for Cotton Products (1961) 122
Spain–Japan (1966) 62
Tokyo Round Codes (1980):
 – Agreement regarding Bovine Meat 187, 202
 – Agreement on Civil Aircraft 187, 202
 – Agreement on Government Procurement 6, *192–194*, 202
 – Agreement on the Implementation of Art. VI GATT (Anti-Dumping Code) *197–200*, 202
 – Agreement on the Implementation of Art. VII GATT (Customs Valuation Code) 29, *200*, 202

Tokyo Round Codes (1980) – *cont.*
- Agreement on Import Licensing Procedures 44, 187, 202
- Agreement on the Interpretation and Application of Arts. VI, XVI and XXIII GATT (Subsidies and Countervailing Duties Code) 6, 101, 186, 187, *194–197*, 202
- Agreement on Technical Barriers to Trade (Standards Code) 6, 79, *187–191*, 202
- International Dairy Arrangement 187, 202
Treaty of Accession Portugal (1985) 77
United Kingdom–Japan (1962) 62, 67, 68

GATT ARTICLES

Article	Pages
Art. I	20, 21, 120
Art. II	20, 102
Art. III	20, 21, 91
Art. VI	20, 22, 98, 103, 197, 198
Art. VII	20, 22, 29, 30
Art. VIII	21
Art. IX	21
Art. X	21
Art. XI	19, 34, 35, 91–99
Art. XII	64
Art. XIII	20, 21, 93–98, 100
Art. XIV	20, 93, 189
Art. XV	20, 64
Art. XVII	20, 21
Art. XIX	19, 22, 34, 35, 41, 51, 60, 92, 93–94, 95, 98, 99, 100, 101, 102, 103, 124, 136, 145, 155, 186
Art. XX	21, 93
Art. XXI	21, 64, 93
Art. XXII	48, 93, 113, 202
Art. XXIII	22, 48, 92, 96, 97, 111–119, 202
Art. XXIV	22, 26, 28, 33, 35, 36, 61
Art. XXV	22, 26, 93, 96
Art. XXVIII	102, 103, 104
Art. XXVIII bis	19, 102
Art. XXXV	60–63

INDEX

ACP
- countries: 142
- EEC commercial cooperation subcommittee: 143
- facility (v. also Group I products): 135, 142

Actual value: 29

Agriculture
- bovine meat: 185, 187
- common agricultural policy: 8, 187, 205, 212, 213, 216
- criticism on CAP: 212, 213
- multilateral framework, absence of: 185, 209, 210, *215–216*

Aluminium: 80, 82
American Selling Price: 200
Anti-dumping duties: 13, 14, 15, 19, 20, 37, 58, 70, 71, 80, 98, 195
Anti-dumping regulation: 195, *197–200*
Antitrust and government action: *79–83*, 89, 96
- aluminium: 80, 82
- ballbearings: 80, 82
- mushrooms (canned): 79, 108
- sugar: 81
- tobacco: 81
- zinc: 81

Aramid fibres (Akzo complaint): 111
Association partners, trade with: 27, 140, 142–143, 146–149, 160, *177–178*
Autonomous measures: 4, 5, 7, 9, 25, 143–144, 146, 147, 160, 178
Autonomous textile régime
- State-trading countries: 143–144, 146, 147, 161, 163, 170, 178
- Taiwan: 144

Average growth rates: 135

Ballbearings: 80, 82
Basket exit mechanism: 136, 138, 144, 155
Bilateral tendency: 204–205
Bilateral textile agreements (MFA III): *130–139*, 146, 160, *171–177*, 205, 209–210

Bilateral textile agreements – *cont.*
- average growth rates: 135
- basket exit mechanism: 136, 138, 144, 155
- burden sharing (key): 139, 149, 167, 174
- consultations: 136, 137, 138
- cut-back clause: 131, 134, 139
- distribution among Member States (v. also: National subdivision of quotas): 137, 149–150
- extension of product coverage (paragraph 24): 130, 155
- fraud prevention (circumvention of restrictions): 131–132
- flexible agreement: 138, 155
- global ceilings: 135, 136–137, 166
- group I products (v. also ACP facility): 135, 142
- protection of trademarks and designs: 130, 131, 137, 139
- reciprocity in opening up of markets: 130, 131–132, 139
- reservations of China and India: 130
- textiles committee: 139, 144
- third extension protocol MFA: 130–134
- threshold level: 136
- transfer of unused quantities: 137

Bound products: 102
Bovine meat: 185
- arrangement regarding: 187
Boycott: 13
BRITE: 66
Burden sharing (key): 139, 149, 167, 174

Cars (Japanese): 74, *76–79*, 83, 85, 88, 205, 209
Certificates of origin: 31, 33
Certification systems: 187
Chernobyl: 10
Charges of equivalent effect: 24, 54
China, trade with: 34

CIF value: 30
Classification of goods: 23, 24, 25
Committee on customs valuation: 30, 33
Committee on origin: 33
Committees in Tokyo Round Codes: 202, 204, 205
Commodity agreements: 8
Common Agricultural Policy: 8, 187, 205, 212, 213, 216
Common Commercial Policy
– exclusive powers: 4, 7, 8, 52, 62, 64, *65–67*, *160–165*, 170, 182
– general: 3, 4, 5, 7, 8, *65–67*
– *per se* rules of: 6
Common Customs Tariff: 2, *23–34*, 103, 108, 147
Community interest: 38, *42*, 47
Community origin: 33
Community substitution in GATT: 63–64
Community trade-agreement with Japan, absence of: 67–68
Community VER's with Japan: 69–72
Compact-disc players: 102, 104
Confidential information: 40
Constructed value: 199
Consultations: 39, 136, 137, 138, 162, 186, 190, 193, 196, 201, 202, 203–204
Conventional duties: 25
Cooperation agreements: 12, 141
Council Quota Decision: 144
Counterfeit goods, trade in: 13, 209, 214
Countervailing duties: 13, 14, 15, 19, 20, 58, 71, *194–197*
Country-specific quotas: *93–96*, 107
Cuba, trade with: 34
Customs Cooperation Council: 25
Customs tariffs: 17, 18, 19, 26
– preferential: 26–28
– suspensions: 26
– temporary amendments: 26
Customs union: 22, 26, 35, 42, 165, 174
– substantially all the trade criterion: 26
Cut-back clause: 131, 134, 139

Dairy products: 185
– Int'l Dairy Arrangement: 187
Delegation of powers
– Council to Commission: 40
Dillon Round: 61

Dispute Settlement
– after the Tokyo Round: 201, *202–209*
– new procedures: 186, 209, 210
– US Senate Finance Committee Report on: 205
Distribution among Member States (*v.* also National subdivision of quotas and Burden sharing (key)): 137, 149–150
Division of powers EEC/Member States: *v.* Common Commercial Policy
Dominant purpose theory: 6, 7
Dumping: 37, 38, 41, 80, *197–200*
– imput or upstream dumping: 198
– social dumping: 199

East–West trade: 209
EFTA: 28
ESPRIT: 66
European Act: 15
European Court of first instance: 15
Examination procedure: 47, 50
Experimental list: 75
Export régime: *50–52*
Extension of product coverage (paragraph 24): 130, 155

Films, colour photograph: 85
Flexible agreement: 138, 155
FOB value: 30
Fraud prevention (circumvention of restrictions): 131–132
Free trade area: 27, 28, 189

GATT
– Community substitution in: 63, 64, 90
– direct effect of GATT rules: 106, 107, 109
– dispute settlement: 50, 92, 96, 101, 111, *112–119*, 186, 191, 193, 194
– and EEC law: 105–111, 192
– exceptions to GATT rules: 20, 92, 96, 99–100
– general: *18–23*, *90–93*
– Japan's accession to: 59–60
– and MFA: 124
– non-violation complaints: *115–117*, 118

GATT – *cont.*
 – nullification or impairment: 111, *114–119*, 190, 196, 204
 – panel: 113
 – study on trade in textiles: 129
Generalized System of Preferences: 5, 26, 33, 36, 138
Global ceilings: 135, 136–137, 166
Government procurement: 21, *192–194*, 209, 219
Group I products (*v.* also ACP facility): 135, 142

Hong Kong, trade with: 94–96
Hypothetical sales price: 30
Hijzen Statement: 67

Illicit commercial practices: 16, 38, *44–50*, 111, 115
Import régime
 – common: 4, 5, 7, 9, 70, 88, 107
 – national restrictions under the: 73–83
 – for textiles: 34, 177
Imput or upstream dumping: 198
Indicative ceilings: 140, 142
Informal textile arrangements: 140, 142, 147, 177
Injury: 20, 38, 40, 41, 196, 198–199, 204
 – *de minimis* rule: 198
 – material: 41, 47, 196, 198–199
 – substantial: 41
 – threat of: 47
Instruments of commercial policy: 17
Intellectual property rights: *v.*
 Protection of trademarks and designs
Intercompany sales and pricing: 30
Interim protective measures: 10, 43, 44, 74, 162
Intra-community surveillance: 150, *151–152*, 179, 180, 181
Investigation procedure: 39, 40, 44, 71, 159, 201
Investment and trade restrictions: 86–87, 210
 – Triumph Acclaim: 86
 – Zippers: 86–87

Japan, trade with: 9, 11, *57–63*, *64–65*, *67–79*, *83–90*, 98, *102–104*, *111–113*, *117–120*, 198, 205, 210, 212
 – Community VER's with: 69–72

Japan, trade with – *cont.*
 – technical standards or regulations: 191
Jenkins Bill: 129

Kennedy Round: 25, 197

Last manufacturing stage: 32
Last substantial process: 33
Leutweiler Report: 71, 72
Like product: 16, 21, 198
Litigation tendency: 205–209
Local government regulation: 188, 189
Lomé (III) partners, (textile) trade with: 27, *142–143*, 160, *177–178*
Low Developed Countries (LDC's): 124, 128, 129, 130, 133, 186, 209, 210, *212–214*

Market disruption: 123, 130, 132, 138, 144
Market sharing arrangement: 80
Marks of origin: 21
Measures with equivalent effect to q.r.'s: 37, 54, 75, 76, 78–79
 – Japanese cars: 78–79
 – Poitiers: 75–76
Mediterranean countries, trade with: 27, 140, 142, 146, 160, *177–178*
MFA III régime: *v.* Bilateral textile agreements
Minimum import price arrangement: 37
Most Favoured Nation (MFN) treatment: 18, 20, *21*, 23, 51, 120, 188, 189, 192
Multifibre Arrangement: 22, 61, 68, 84, 121, *122–134*, 160, 209
 – and Community safeguard measures: 153–154
 – and GATT safeguard measures: 124
 – and LDC's: 124, 128, 129, 130, 133
 – market disruption: 123, 130, 132, 138, 144
 – reasonable departures clause: 125, 126, 127, 129
 – Sub-Committee on Adjustment: 132–133, 134
 – Surge mechanism: *126–127*, 129, 131, 139, 155
 – textiles committee: 124, 125, 134
 – Textiles Surveillance Body: 124, 127, 131, 134

Multilateral Trade Negotiations: 68
Mushrooms (canned): 79, 108

National commercial policy: 170, 171, 173, 175
National market-repartitioning: 53
National measures
– permitted under the common import régime: *73–83*, 160
– specific authorization of: 9, 13, 35, 51, 65, 73, 74, 75, 77, 85, 161, 162, 163, 164, 170, 173, 179
National origin: 33
National subdivision of quotas (*v.* also Burden sharing (key) and Distribution among Member States): 160, *166–168*, 172, 176
National treatment: 20, 21, 91, 188, 189, 192
National triggering procedure: 10
Negative list: *73–74*, 77, 84, 85, 88, 93, 107, 163, 164
Newly Industrialised Countries (NIC's): 212, 213
New Trade Policy Instrument: 14, *44–50*, 201
– community industry: 46
– community interest: 47
– decision-making procedure: 50
– direct effectiveness of breaches: 49
– examination procedure: 47, 50
– full exercise of rights: 49, 201
– illicity: 48
– measures: 50
– private right of complaint: 39, *45–46*, 201
– proof of material injury: 47
– representation requirement: 46
– threat of injury: 47
Nomenclature: 23, 24
Non-discrimination: 20, 21, 51, 91, 93, 108, 109, 122
Non-tariff barriers: 18, 20, 25, 118, 185
Non-violation complaints: 115–117, 118
Normal price: 29, 198, 199
Notification: 186
Nullification or impairment: 22, 111, *114–119*, 190, 196, 204
– non-violation complaints: *115–117*, 118

Orderly marketing arrangements: *v.* Voluntary Export Restraint Arrangement
Origin of goods: *31–34*, 85–87
– certificates of origin: 31, 33
– last manufacturing stage: 32
– last substantial process: 33, 86
– petroleum products: 32
– tariff jump: 32, 86
– textiles: 33, 133
– Triumph Acclaim: 86
– Zippers: 86, 87
Outward Processing Traffic: 140, 142, *146–149*

Parallel import: 53
Petroleum products: 32, 52
Poitiers: 75–76
Preferential textile agreements: 140, 142–143, 146–149, 160, *177–178*
Preferential trade agreements: 33, 36
Private parties
– improvement of position of: 14–16, 110
– judicial review for import régimes: 181–183
Private restrictive business practices: 96
Private right of complaint: 39, *45–46*, 181–183, 201
Protective measures: 9, 10, 14, 15, 16, 42, 57, 159
– i.c. economic difficulties: *152–153*
– interim: 10, 43, 44, 74, 162
– national: 160, 162, 163, 179
– national subdivision of quotas: 160, *166–168*, 172, 176
– regional: 9, 160, 166, *168–169*, 172, 176, 177, 178
Protection of trademarks and designs: 130, 131, 137, 139, 209, 210, 214
Punta del Este, Ministerial GATT-meeting 1986: 12, 210

Quantitative restrictions: 13, 17, 18, 19, 20, *33–37*, 38, 39, 41, 51, 53, 54, 70, *73–79*, 83, 91, 92
– cars (Japanese): *76–79*, 83, 85
– country-specific quotas: 93–96
– experimental list: 75
– indirect imports: 83–87, 89
– interim safeguard measures: 74
Quartz watches: 41, 92, 94–95
Quotas: *v.* Quantitative restrictions

RACE: 66
Reasonable departures clause: 125, 126, 127, 129
Reciprocity in opening up of markets: 130, 131–132, 139
Regulatory Committee procedure: 30, 33
Reservations of China and India: 130
Roll-back agreement: 211
Rule of reason; dominant purpose theory: 6, 7

Safeguards Code, New: 68, 99, 186, 209, 210
Safeguard measures (XIX GATT, 115 EEC)
  – on exports: 51
  – on imports: 34, *37–44*, 62, 63, 92, 99, 186, 195, 200, 201
  – on textiles: 122, 140–141, 142, 145, *149–154*, 160, 168, *169–181*
  – interim: 74
  – and MFA: 124, 153–154, 177
Semiconductors: 103, 120, 210
Services: 4, 12, 191, 193, 209, 210, *219–220*
Siberian gas pipe-line: 13, 45, 196, 211
Specific authorization
  – agreements: 10, 11, 161
  – national measures: 9, 13, 35, 51, 65, 73, 74, 75, 77, 85, 161, 162, 163, 164, 170, 173, 179
State-trading countries, trade with: 9, 11, 21, 25, 34, 36, 37, 44, 48, 54, 120, 186
  – autonomous textile régime: 121, *143–144*, 147, 161, 163, 170, 178
  – common liberalization list: 36
  – and dumping: 199–200
Stoneware (Korean): 41, 42, 70
Subsidies: 37, 38, 41, 100–101, *194–197*, 209, 215–216, *216–218*
  – other than export subsidies: 196
Substantially all the trade criterion: 26
Sugar: 81
Surge mechanism: *126–127*, 129, 131, 139, 155
Surveillance: 13, 16, 39, 73, 88, 142, 147, 148, 150, *151–152*, 159, 163, 179, 180, 181, 201

Taiwan, autonomous textile régime with: 144

Tariffs: 19, *102–104*, 185
  – bindings: 18, 102, 104
  – concessions: *v.* bindings
  – jump: 32, 86
  – multilateral negotiations: 19, 102
  – schedule: 19, 102
Technical standards or regulations: 2, *187–192*, 209, *218–219*
  – Japanese: 191
Textiles: 33, 34, 61, 62, 98, 210
  – autonomous textile régime: 143–144, 146, 147, 160, *178*
  – bilateral textile agreements: *130–139*, 146, 160, *171–177*
  – preferential textile agreements: 140, 142–143, 146–149, 160, *177–178*
Textiles Committee: 124, 125, 134
textiles committee: 139, 144
Textile Surveillance Body: 124, 127, 131, 134
Third extension protocol (MFA III): 130–134
Threshold level: 136
Tobacco: 81
Tokyo Round: 22, 25, 29, *185–204*
Trade
  – with association partners: 27, 140, 142–143, 146–149, 160, *177–178*
  – with China and Cuba: 34
  – in counterfeit goods: 13, 209, 214
  – East–West: 209
  – with Hong Kong: 94–96
  – with Japan: 9, 11, *57–63*, *64–65*, *67–79*, *83–90*, 98, *102–104*, *111–113*, *117–120*, 205, 210, 212
  – with Lomé partners: *v.* association partners
  – with Mediterranean countries: *v.* association partners
  – and monetary policy: 214–215
  – with State-trading countries: 9, 11, 21, 25, 34, 36, 37, 44, 48, 54, 120, 161, 163, 170, 178, 186, 199, 200
  – with US: 45, 51, 145, 197, 204, 209, 210, *211–212*, 215, 217
Transfer of unused quantities: 137
Transaction value: 30
Triumph Acclaim: 86
Two-tier import adjustment policy: 13

Unfair trade restrictions: *v.* Illicit commercial practices
Upstream or imput dumping: 198
Uruguay Round: 120, 129, 156, *210–211*
US, trade with: 45, 51, 145, 197, 204, 209, 210, *211–212*, 215, 217
US Senate Finance Committee Report on trade dispute settlement: 205

Valuation of goods: *28–30*
    – actual value: 29
    – CIF value: 30
    – FOB value: 30
    – hypothetical sales price: 30
    – normal price: 29
    – transaction value: 30

Videorecorders: 69, 70, 71, 72, 75–76, 88, *102–104*
Voluntary Export Restraint Arrangement (VER): 22, 39, 51, 66–67, 83, 88
    – containment of: 100
    – status under EEC law: 69–70
    – status under GATT: 71, *96–102*, 113
    – and third countries: 97–99

Waiver: 21, 91

Zinc: 80
Zippers: 86–87